Great Themes from the Old Testament

Great Themes from the Old Testament

by Rev. Norbert Lohfink S.J.
translated by Rev. Ronald Walls

FRANCISCAN HERALD PRESS
1434 WEST 51st STREET • CHICAGO, 60609

T. & T. CLARK LTD.
36 GEORGE STREET, EDINBURGH

Great Themes from the Old Testament by Rev. Norbert Lohfink S. J., translated by Rev. Ronald Walls from the German *Unsere grossen Worter Das Alte Testament zu Themen dieser Jahre*, Freiburg: Herder, 1977. American edition published with original publisher's permission. Copyright © 1981 by Franciscan Herald Press. All rights reserved. No part of this book may be reproduced, stored in retrieval system, or transmitted, in any form or by any means, electronic, mechanical, photo-copying, recording or otherwise without written permission of Franciscan Herald Press, 1434 West 51st Street, Chicago, Illinois 60609.

Copyright © T. & T. Clark Ltd. 1982

IMPRIMI POTEST:
 Johannes G. Gerhartz S.J.

IMPRIMATUR:
 General Vicar Seidenather
 Diocese of Limburg
 April 14, 1977

Library of Congress Cataloging in Publication Data
Lohfink, Norbert.
 Great themes from the Old Testament.

 Translation of Unsere grossen Worter.
 1. Bible. O.T.—Criticism, interpretation,
etc.—Addresses, essays, lectures. 2. Christian
life—Catholic authors—Addresses, essays, lectures.
I. Title.
BS1174.2.L6313   221.6   80-10532
ISBN 0 8199-0801-0   0 567 09333 6

MADE IN THE UNITED STATES OF AMERICA
FIRST PRINTED. . . . 1982

Table of Contents

Preface ix

Theme 1 Unity *The Unity of Israel and Judah as Historical Reality and Theological Motif in the Old Testament* 1
The Facts of History 1—The Yahwistic Theology of Unity 5—Separation of the Kingdoms, with No Results 8—When All Seemed Lost 12—The Hour of Dreaming 14

Theme 2 Pluralism *Theology as the Answer to Plausibility Crises in Emergent Pluralistic Situations, Taking the Deuteronomic Law as the Basis for Discussion* 17
The Deuteronomic Law Contains Theological Systematization 20—Systematization Based on a Nongiven Starting Point 24—Earlier Attempts at Sociological Explanation of Deuteronomic Theology 28—Neo-Assyrian Cultural Pressure and Deuteronomic Theology 30—Conclusions 35

Theme 3 Sovereignty *The Sovereignty of God as the Abrogation of Human Sovereignty in Deuteronomic Theology* 39
The Deuteronomic Theology of Sovereignty 40—The God Who "Leads Out" 43—"Following God" 45—To Love God 49—The Preaching of Jesus 52

Theme 4 Distribution of the Functions of Power *The Law in Deuteronomy That Governed Ministries, a Constitution in Terms of Power Distribution, and Catholic Canon Law* 55
The Deuteronomic Laws Concerning Offices 58—A Coherent Constitutional Scheme 64—Dating the Chief Redaction of the Constitution

Table of Contents

67—Distribution of the Functions of Power as the Key Concept of the Constitution 68—The Torah and Free Charisms 72

Theme 5 Salvation History *The Theology of History, Exemplified in a Salvation-Historical Exhibition of Recent Decades* 77
The "Little Historical Credo" 79—Introduction to the Text of Deuteronomy 26:5-10 81—The Events of Which the Credo Speaks 83—Models Used in Interpretation 85—The Relationship between Man's Action and Yahweh's Action 90—Conclusions 92

Theme 6 Liberation *Old Testament Ideas and the Theology of Liberation* 95
Sin, Atonement, and Forgiveness in Liturgy 97—Distress and Complaint, Help and Thanksgiving in the Liturgy 98—Statements about Redemption from the Sion-Ideology in the Jerusalem Liturgy 103—Education and Its Theory of the Connection Between Actions and Reward 105—Redemption—Story Additions to the Narrative Books 106—The Once-For-All Exodus Act 108—The Yahwist and Curse and Blessing in National History 111—Eschatological Soteriology and World Structures 113

Theme 7 The People of God *The Old Testament and the Central Concept of the Council's Verbal Fireworks* 117
"The People of Yahweh," Not "the People of God" 119—"The Family of Yahweh," Not "the People of Yahweh" 121—"The Family of Yahweh": Used Only in Special Situations 124—The Family of Yahweh and Mankind in Poverty and Distress 129—"The People of God" Today 132

Theme 8 God *The Polytheistic and the Monotheistic Way of Speaking about God in the Old Testament* 135
Yahweh Is a Jealous God 136—The Common Interpretation of the Jealousy of Yahweh 138—Ancient Eastern Polytheism 139—Mono-

theism in Israel 142—The "Languages," Not Two Things 147—The Jealousy of Yahweh as the Affirmation of a Special Revelation 150—Conclusions 152

Theme 9 Projections *On the Enemies of the Sick in the Ancient East and in the Psalms* 155
Enemies of the Sick in the Ancient World 156—Enemies of the Sick in Israel 159—Faithless Friends 162—Conclusions 165

Theme 10 Growth *The Priestly Document and the Limits of Growth* 167
Christians and the Myth of Growth 168—The "Image of God" Is Not Necessarily Equivalent to "Domination" 170—Commandment or Blessing? 172—The Blessing of Fecundity: Only for the Birth of Nations 173—The Peoples Take Possession of Their Territories 176—Dominion over the Animal Kingdom 178—Open Questions 181

Theme 11 The Future *Biblical Witness to the Ideal of a Stable World* 183
The Atrahasis Epic 185—The Priestly Chronicle 188—The Priestly Document and Instability 196

Theme 12 Leisure *The Work Week and the Sabbath in the Old Testament, and Especially in the Priestly Chronicle* 203
The Status of Man and the Life of the Gods 204—Did Israel's Sabbath Win the Day? 207—Consecrating Leisure 209—The Distinguishing Feature of the Priestly Chronicle 211—The Cosmogonic Work and the Leisure of God 212—Egypt: Alienated Work 215—Work as Gathering Up and Discovery of the Sabbath 216—Perfection of the World through Technical Skill and Worship 218

Theme 13 Power *The Sin of All Mankind and the Sin of the Elect, according to the Priestly Document* 223
Sin in the Older Historical Writings 224—The Priestly Document and

Its Sources 226—The Sin of Mankind: Violence 229—The Sins of the Elect: Disparagement of God's Gift and Unbelief 231—Problems of Exegesis 234

Theme 14 Love *The Ethos of the New Testament: More Sublime than That of the Old?* 239
The Historical Changing of Ethical Norms 239—Generic Links in the Moral Teachings in the Old Testament 241—The Thesis of a New Ethic of Love 244—Love of Neighbor in the Old Testament 246—Love of Neighbor in the New Testament 248—The Supreme Ethical Norm in the Language of the Old Testament 252—Conclusions 253

Theme 15 Charisma *The Burden of the Prophets* 255

Preface

From 1966 until 1970 I lived abroad, in Italy. These years were certainly no less eventful in Rome, where I lectured at the Pontifical Biblical Institute, than they were in Germany. There, too, youth was in revolt. A new-style university, a New Society, and a New Church were being conceived. Every day one learned new words, even new languages. I, however, did not learn these new words in my own tongue. This may have been why, after returning to Germany, these words, and others that soon joined company with them, seemed to advance toward me like huge, strange animals. But often they were none other than well-known, simple words in my own language. Suddenly, however, they had acquired a new value in a new currency. New emotions latched onto them. Without realizing it, I began to make household pets of these animals.

This happened above all when I was invited to lecture. Often it was not until long after that I discovered I had again made friends with one of these splendid beasts. Instinctively, I have always tried to catch all our great words in the nets of the Old Testament. Many of these new words were captured almost of their own accord. Others resisted and had to be lured for a long time. Some escaped and are missing from this collection.

In recent years, bitter methodological battles have broken out in Old Testament exegesis. Specialization by individual scholars has made yet another upsurge. The impression we give the outsider is that preambles and problems of detail prevent our ever coming to the point. Indeed this danger is great. My desire, at least in this book, is to speak to the point, to speak of what concerns the Old Testament and us, to speak of the concern that is common to the Old Testament and to our own times. I would like to demonstrate that there is such a common concern, and that those whose ears are open to the great words of our time will profit by taking counsel from the Old Testament.

Preface

Whoever expects to find a program or completeness will be disappointed. Here are to be found only some of our words. From the standpoint of the Old Testament, these words will be scrutinized kindly but critically. Conversely, these words will be permitted to pose questions to the Old Testament, questions which often it cannot answer without manifesting aspects that formerly we had not noticed. No chapter claims to speak the last word on its subject. I will be satisfied if each chapter provokes reflection in the reader, each in his own style.

This book contains lectures that have been delivered previously—several many times over, in varying forms, and to very diverse audiences. It follows on my two collections of lectures, *The Triumphal Song at the Sea of Reeds* and *Scripture Exposition in Transformation,* of 1964 and 1967. Anyone who knows these books will observe a change in the author's viewpoint on many topics—but I still hold to the same hermeneutic starting point that is evident in these two volumes. All the lectures in this present book, including those already published, have been recast.

I have to thank (especially), for conversation or correspondence on detailed points, G. Braulik, F. Menrekes, B. Schüller, W. Steinmüller, and my brother Gerhard.

NORBERT LOHFINK, S. J.

Unity

The Unity of Israel and Judah as Historical Reality and Theological Motif in the Old Testament

Unity: one of our deepest longings. How we long for a unified Germany, a unified world, our Church! We dream of these things; but we are realistic, and proceed a step at a time. We experience, too, the power of hard facts. Divisions persist; with difficulty we learn to live with them. Even so, our dreams persist.

Ours is not the first generation to suffer from division. Over and over in the past, divisions have rent men apart. The Bible itself is marked by division. The New Testament is very largely first-aid dressing hastily applied to a gaping wound, the constantly bleeding wound caused by the separation of Christians from the Jewish community. And on reading the Old Testament, one is shattered when one discovers how soon the twelve tribes, who constituted Israel, split up to form a northern and a southern kingdom: Israel and Judah. No one was able to heal this schism. Let us examine how this came about.

The Facts of History

Toward the end of the second millenium B.C. within west Jordanian Palestine, which was slowly putting off Egyptian hegemony, new population groups became recognizable alongside the old city-states. They established themselves chiefly in the otherwise unpopulated mountains and hill country; but they conquered some of the cities of the plain as well. It may be that they were partly the aboriginal, but not liberated, peasants. Most of them, however, must have been nomads

Unity

turned farmers. They were organized in tribes, and the several tribes regarded themselves as related to each other. In accordance with nomadic traditional thinking, this sense of belonging together was expressed in terms of a common genealogy. The "fathers" of the twelve tribes were regarded as the twelve sons of a common patriarch, Jacob, who bore, as his second name, the name of this tribal confederacy: Israel. Reaching back to even earlier progenitors, a relationship was constructed to other groups: Moabites, Ammonites, and Edomites, who inhabited east Jordan at roughly the same time. But this link is more remote.

The twelve tribes who called themselves Israel had, above all else, this bond of unity: they worshiped the same God, Yahweh. Led by this God, several groups (now forming Israel) before their immigration into Palestine had broken out of Egyptian slave camps. Thereupon the whole of Israel had recognized this God, who had effected their freedom, as *their* God. He was identified with the creator God, El, who had been worshiped from of old. The history of these groups, whom Yahweh had delivered from Egypt, was recited by itinerant bards and teachers of children as the history of the whole of Israel. This is a typical nomadic method of expressing in words the unity of the tribes.

On the whole, that is about as far as the expression of unity went. People gathered in festival pilgrimage to the shrines of Yahweh, which were scattered across the land. People felt they were brothers. When enemies attacked, several tribes would band together, led by charismatic (rather than institutionally legitimized) savior figures.

The situation was altered by the immigration of another population group, the so-called Philistines. The Philistines and Israel contended for supremacy in west Jordan. At first, Israel was defeated. To free themselves from the Philistine occupying power, Israel finally developed a more strongly organized unity. This was accomplished through the erection of the monarchy. The first king was Saul, of the tribe of Benjamin. He succeeded in getting the tribes to act as one but did not achieve liberation; and after his death in battle, unity was still so inchoate that it was several years before all twelve tribes accepted the Judaean, David from Bethlehem, as king.

David liberated Israel from the Philistines, and more. He built a great kingdom, which embraced not only Israel but several other political powers. He developed Jerusalem as his capital, and to it he brought the ancient Ark of the Covenant, to be its central shrine. And now, for the first time (shortly after 1000 B.C.), we may speak in a genuine political-juridical sense of the unity of Israel. But before a hundred years had passed this unity was again shattered.

The first ruptures already showed in David's time. David had to put down the insurrection of his son Absalom, who looked for support to the very stock of David, to Judah. From that time onward, David seems to have developed Judah as a kind of heartland of the kingdom, in order to acquire a sure grip on it. Solomon, David's surviving son and successor, widened the gap between Judah and the other tribes. He effected a reform of administration among the northern tribes, and in that territory levied taxes and imposed forced labor in support of his vast building program. In 922, immediately after his death, the unity crisis came to a head.

The northern tribes wanted to recast the contract between themselves and the king. They made conditions for their recognition of Solomon's son, Rehoboam. Because Rehoboam refused to accept the conditions, they rejected him and chose their own king, Jeroboam I, and the schism began.

The kingdom of David had two successors. The northern kingdom, now called Israel, had—to begin with—Shechem and Tirzah, then a little later Samaria, as capital; and the southern kingdom, under Davidic rulers, had Jerusalem as capital. This latter kingdom called itself Judah, but it included part of the tribal territory of Benjamin. To counterbalance the sanctuary at Jerusalem, magnificently completed by Solomon, Jeroboam I developed two older Yahweh shrines as imperial sanctuaries: in the north the shrine of Dan and, on the southern frontier (that is, adjoining Judah), the shrine of Bethel. (At the heart of the

Jerusalem temple was kept the Ark of the Covenant.) In both of his chief temples Jeroboam, reviving another ancient form of the El/Yahweh cult, erected two bull images, intended to be cult symbols of Yahweh worship.

At first there was tension and border warfare between the two kingdoms, but soon a state of peaceful coexistence was reached; indeed, there were periods of friendly cooperation and dynastic intermarriage. Under several dynasties, the northern kingdom lasted almost 200 years. In 721 Samaria was destroyed by the Assyrian emperor, Sargon II. Bits of territory had already been torn from the kingdom; now the whole northern kingdom became an Assyrian province. For the most part, the population was deported to other parts of Assyria and replaced by non-Israelite peoples. This was the Assyrian practice; they sought in this way to destroy traditions and break ties that might be dangerous to the government. The deportees from the northern kingdom were to prove unable to maintain their identity indefinitely. They assimilated with their new environment.

The southern kingdom lasted longer—for most of the time as an Assyrian vassal state—until the sack of Jerusalem in 587. In the meantime, the Assyrian state had fallen. Jerusalem was razed by the neo-Babylonians, who likewise deported part of the population, in three waves. But they did not proceed as the Assyrians had done. They introduced no new people into the land, and the deportees from the southern kingdom stayed together in Babylon.

Thus, after the conquest of Babylon by the Persian king Cyrus (539), a return and a religious and semipolitical fresh start were possible within the framework of the all-embracing Presian empire. Meanwhile there had emerged in Samaria (in the north) a center that adhered to the ancient Israelite traditions. The tensions between north and south revived, and slowly the Jews and the Samaritans parted company. It is not clear, however, to what extent the postexilic tension between Jerusalem and Samaria was the direct continuation of the old antagonism, dating from the time of the two coexisting monarchies.

Our discussion is limited to the antipathy between Israel and Judah in the time of the kings, but it will not be sufficient merely to note facts. The whole point is the way in which these facts were experienced and interpreted.

The Yahwistic Theology of Unity

When first we take it in, we are confounded by the fact that this nation of twelve tribes was unable to maintain, for as long as a century in its millennia-long history, a visible, institutional unity of all the tribes, and that from the death of Solomon it lived in schism and from the fall of Samaria in fragmentation. We incline to project into this fact the emotions that are aroused in us by division in the world, in Christendom, in our own nations. Did the Israelites feel the same way? Were they, too, confounded to discover that division had come upon them, almost overnight? Did they then begin to dream of, to strive for, to long for realization of a new unity? And if they did, was this unity experienced as a postulate of faith; was it desired as an act of God for his people? That is to say, did the notion of the reunion of Israel and Judah exist as a theological and religious motif? Let us follow these questions down the centuries.

When the schism between Israel and Judah emerged, the problem of unity was no stranger to the elite in Israel. There is literary evidence that in Solomon's reign people reflected upon the problem of unity, and did so, moreover, from a religious perspective. However, in Solomon's time the problems of unity did not flare up as problems concerning the unity of Israel. This unity was effected automatically through the genealogical connection of the tribes, through the common worship of Yahweh, and in addition through the Davidic kingdom, with its many new and cohesive institutions. And so, for the reflective spirits at Solomon's court, the problem of unity immediately took on a larger dimension—a global dimension, if you will.

Unity

Evidence for this is to be found in the so-called Yahwistic chronicle. Modern biblical scholarship considers that the five Books of Moses, in their present form, appeared after the Babylonian Exile. At that time, they were compiled from various older documents and separate traditions. One of these sources was the book that, according to the few indications we possess, was produced at Solomon's court, which we call the Yahwistic chronicle. It can be extracted from the corpus of the five Books of Moses and almost totally reconstructed.

It began with the story of paradise and the fall in Genesis 2 and 3; told of Abraham, Isaac, and Jacob; and continued with the story of the patriarchs, the time in Egypt, the exodus from Egypt, and the wandering in the wilderness—down to the occupation by the Israelites of the land that had been promised to their forefathers. Obviously, the author belonged to the generation that had lived through the blossoming of Davidic power and the formation of an empire from many nations. The horizon of this generation had been widened. Men knew full well that, beyond the nations David welded into one kingdom, there were other nations, and that no one could bring them all into unity. Men may well have begun to sense the acute instability of David's kingdom and to realize that the seeds of decay were already within it.

The "Yahwist" had already raised this problem of division among the nations of the world, in the story of the Tower of Babel. We find this in Genesis 2, and it begins straight off with the telling caption:

> Throughout the earth men spoke the same language, with the same vocabulary. [v. 1]

Then it recounts how mankind lost the sign of its unity: a single language. Men built a city and, in the city, a tower that reached up to heaven. This was a symbol of empire and of mankind's self-exaltation against God. God's reaction is seen even before the building could be completed. What had been "a single people with a single language" (v. 6) was stricken with a confusion of tongues and scattered abroad over the face of the earth.

It is clear how the Yahwist wants this story to be interpreted. In reality, mankind should be one, but it is not one because of sin's obstructions. It is important to note how the Yahwist characterizes sin, revealing his skepticism of the very thing his generation had achieved. Sin, for him, is linked with the creation of or aspiration toward an empire founded upon power and prestige. Do we not discover in this an early suspicion that David's kingdom will go exactly the same way as the "city" of the ancient Babylonians? Is not that which is striven for, as at least a partial unification of mankind, instead—because of the sin which runs through it—the beginning of greater disunity?

This kind of reflection by the Yahwist is continued in another Genesis story, in respect of another problem affecting the Davidic empire. Even within its heartland, the Davidic empire embraced others than Israelites. Thus the problem of unity was posed specifically in the problem of, the possibility of, intermarriage between Israelites and other inhabitants, who were now cocitizens in the empire. Formerly, all mixed marriages with non-Israelites had been forbidden by the law of Yahweh (Ex 34:16). Now, however, the presuppositions behind this law seem to have altered. The Yahwist deals with the problem thus presented (so it seems) in the context of the Jacob tales, particularly that in Genesis 34 of the bloodbath of Shechem. The point of this tale is that the Canaanite prince of Shechem wants to marry his son to Dinah, a daughter of Jacob, so that (this is stressed several times) the Canaanites and the Israelites may become "one people" (vv. 16, 22). We cannot at present go into the details of this many-sided story, but the moral of the tale, at least in the Yahwist version, seems to be this: No good can come from such a thing; it has to end in catastrophe.

According to the Yahwist, therefore, the different peoples will have to live separated from each other. Not even the non-Israelite cocitizens of David's kingdom may be allowed inside the barrier. Once divisions emerge through sin, fresh unity, which is consonant with the mind of God, can be effected only if one respects the separations and differences that exist. The Yahwist indeed had something to say about how this might be possible. His view is that unity proceeds not from the unfolding of human power but from God, through the spreading abroad of his blessing.

In precise terms, he thinks the promise made to Abraham and his posterity will become a blessing for all the races of the earth (Gn 12:1-3). In the stories of the fathers he tells how this blessing can leap across from one group of men to another: through Abraham's intercession for others (Gn 18), through Isaac's peace treaties with other groups (Gn 26), through Joseph's assistance for starving nations (Gn 41). This sounds like a modest achievement but it is manifestly more, and more permanent, than the establishment by power and domination of a unity that is to be disrupted only once more.

We may now draw our first conclusions. The externally grandiose and expanding power of David and Solomon—apparently generating unity—prompted a sensitive theologian at the royal court to reflect on the problem of schism and unity. There ought to be, he thought, unity among all mankind. But once that unity has been broken, it is dangerous for mere men to try to reconstitute it. The blessing of Yahweh can come to men only on the presupposition of their plurality. God has his own, freely sovereign way of disseminating this blessing.

Separation of the Kingdoms, with No Results

While he was thinking these believing yet skeptical thoughts on the theme of unity, the Yahwist made a supposition about which he entertained not the slightest doubt: Israel itself, this community of twelve tribes, chosen by Yahweh from among all nations, constituted a blessed and forever-enduring unity. In actuality, not only did the empire of David soon break up, so badly that most of the non-Israelite peoples, who had been forced into it, broke away, but Israel itself broke into two parts that were never again to unite. How was all this felt and theologically expressed?

All I say in what follows is said with reservation. It was quite possible that people experienced sorrows and feelings that are not evidenced in the biblical documents that have come down to us. The information we have concerning these centuries is, indeed, full of gaps. But we do know certain things, and from what we know and understand we have to assert that it was not until the time of the prophet Hosea in the northern kingdom and Isaiah in the southern—in the eighth century, that is, and not in the tenth, when the schism occurred—that the motif of hope for the restoration of unity between the two kingdoms is discernible with any certainty. This was just before the collapse of the northern kingdom, no earlier.

Let us start with these two prophets. The hope of each for reunion is distinguished from that of the other by nuances that betray their northern and southern origins.

Hosea—the one and only biblical prophet who came from the north, the last great and stirring voice from the ten Israelite tribes that declined so early—had to proclaim to the people Yahweh's rejection of the northern tribes as the people of Yahweh. He gave his own son the symbolic name "Not My People" (Hos 1:9); but he assessed the period only after rejection, punishment, and judgment. There had been a possibility that God would turn graciously even toward the northern tribes. And so the collector and editor of Hosea's sayings in chapter 2 was able to add another saying, immediately after the description "Not My People," that proclaimed abrogation of the rejection. It runs thus:

> And the number of the sons of Israel will
> be like the sands on the seashore,
> which cannot be measured or counted.
> In the place where they were told,
> "You are no people of mine," they will
> be called, "The sons of the living God."
> The sons of Israel and of Judah will be
> one again and choose themselves one
> single leader,
> and they will spread far beyond their country;
> so great will be the day of Jezreel.
> To your brother say, "People of Mine,"
> to your sister, "Beloved." [Hos 1:2]

Unity

It is typical of Hosea that he points back beyond the period of the monarchy to the preceding, more loosely organized period of the judges. The children of Judah and the children of Israel will come together as at a gathering of the clans, such as took place in those days ("the day of Jezreel"). They will not set a king over themselves, but—avoiding a specific title—"a common chief."

With Isaiah it is different—the Judaean from Jerusalem, with his celebrated oracle of the birth of the Davidic savior-king: "A child is born for us, a son given to us" (Is 8:23-9:6). The occasion of this oracle, as the beginning shows, was the annexation of the northern territory of Galilee by the Assyrians, a few years before the fall of Samaria. The land that has known such humiliation is promised a new brightness in the future. And this happens in the announcement of the wonderfully powerful heir to the throne of David, of whom it is said:

> Wide is his dominion
> in a peace that has no end,
> for the throne of David
> and for his royal power. [Is 9:6]

This son of David will again restore to its former glory the old kingdom of David, and at the same time the newly lost territories of the north will be assimilated into the new kingdom of David. Whereas Hosea saw the future unity of Israel and Judah on the model of the period of the judges, the Judaean Isaiah saw it as the restoration of the grandeur of David, in peace and justice.

The difference is important. In the context within which we are working, one thing is supremely important: before the decline of the northern kingdom it was these two prophets, and no one else, who gave any thought to the idea of reunion. Both lived at the end of the schism that had already lasted 200 years, before becoming ever worse. Both saw catastrophe coming upon the northern kingdom. And it was no doubt this very fact that had first aroused thoughts about reunion in them. Before their time, the idea did not exist. Clearly, before their time, no one had longed for a reunion of what had been divided.

If the account of the oracle of God through the prophet Ahijah of Shiloh to Jeroboam (1 Kgs 11:29-30) contains an ancient tradition and is not a later construction of the tenth century, designed to explain the process of the schism in the kingdom, then the prophets themselves took a positive hand in effecting the schism. According to this account, the prophet Ahijah, while Solomon was still alive, took him who was later to become the first king of the northern kingdom into the field, tore his outer garment into twelve pieces, and gave Jeroboam ten of them, saying:

> Take ten strips for yourself, for thus
> Yahweh speaks, the God of Israel,
> "I am going to tear the kingdom from
> Solomon' hand and give ten tribes to you."
> [1 Kgs 11:31]

Even if this narrative should have no basis in history, we have sufficient, reliable historical evidence, at least from the moment of the schism until shortly before the end of the northern kingdom, to allow us to assert: The guild of prophets was critical of individual northern kings; they had even overthrown dynasties and created new ones. but they never described the existence of the northern kingdom and the political division of Israel itself as an injustice in the eyes of God. Even the erection of new national shrines at Dan and Bethel, and worship of Yahweh in association with the image of a bull in these shrines, do not seem at first to have disturbed the prophets. The story of the man of God from Judah, who came to Bethel and threatened Jeroboam with the destruction of the shrine (1 Kgs 13), seemed to have been attached later to Jeroboam I, and to have originated shortly before the fall of the northern kingdom. Thus the only conclusion we can draw is that, for two centuries, the prophets (at least) did not feel the division of the kingdom was a religious problem. And the prophets were the conscience of Israel.

Perhaps we can throw light on the subject by asking the relevance of such things as the Davidic empire and the division of the kingdom for

Unity

the man in the street. It may be that they made scarcely any impact upon the real life of the average man. Always, the fundamental institutions, even during the time of the great kingdom, were the extended family and the local community. In them, too, were anchored the religious life and the numerous shrines throughout the country, which were visited without regard to state boundaries. Thus we learn incidentally, from two texts in Amos, that the inhabitants of the northern kingdom liked to make pilgrimages to the shrine at Beersheba (Am 5:5, 8:14); and Beersheba was in the south of Judah. The prophet Amos himself is a sign of close religious ties, despite political separation; he came from Judah, and lived there, but as far as we can tell he appeared as a prophet only in the northern kingdom. At all events, when he denounced the northern king, he was expelled. In such a case in Jerusalem, whose subject he was, he might not have been expelled, but arrested and punished.

Let us sum up again. It would appear that the political division touched only peripherally those areas in which the ordinary life and the religious life of the people operated. Thus, until shortly before the fall of the northern kingdom, it was accepted almost without comment. Only when the existence of the northern kingdom was threatened did the prophets display a change in attitude. For the first time, Hosea and Isaiah formulated a promise of salvation, prophesying the coming reunion of Israel and Judah. In this, Hosea follows the model presented by the period of judges, Isaiah that of the time of David.

When All Seemed Lost

After the northern kingdom ceased to be, one would expect that all foundation would have been destroyed in Judah for any notion of reunion of the two kingdoms—a notion that had scarcely existed before—and that this notion would never be reencountered. But the exact opposite happened. Now begins—if at first slowly—the real history of the political-religious idea of the unity of Israel and Judah. Let us follow its course.

The prophet Jeremiah began his activity about a century after the collapse of the northern kingdom. As the seventh century passed, the fall of Judah was only a few decades away. In spite of the considerable lapse of time, Jeremiah was moved by the fate of the Israelite population of the north, deported a century before to far-distant lands. Twice—in chapter 3 and chapters 30-31—in glowing terms he promises them a return home. For our context, it is important to note how he conceived the situation after the homecoming. Cities would be rebuilt, life would flourish again, the soil would be blessed, and from among the people themselves will come a ruler who, like a priest or prophet, will have access to Yahweh (Jer 30:20).

He is called quite simply "a ruler." Nowhere in the authentic Jeremiac sections of this chapter is there mention of either a king or a new David. Thus the question of the relationship of the returned Israel to Judah remains open. Only one comment is made:

> Yes, a day will come when the watchmen
> shout on the mountains of Ephraim,
> "Up, let us go to Zion,
> to Yahweh our God!" [Jer 31:6]

Zion is the temple hill in Jerusalem. It was precisely in Jeremiah's early years that, in Judah and in former northern territories, all Yahweh shrines were closed in the thoroughgoing cult reform under Josiah, so that the temple in Jerusalem remained the one, great sanctuary. To this, according to Jeremiah, the returning people of the northern kingdom would turn their steps. All the more astonishing is the fact that nothing is said about the unified, self-reviving empire of David. For Jeremiah, the concept of two separated political entities still seems dominant—and does not present problems.

Josiah, however—the king just mentioned as instigator of the centralization of the cult—quite obviously saw things in a different light. He was able to carry out his reform of the cult because at that time the Assyrian empire was breaking up. Hence, for a few years he was able to occupy the territory that formerly belonged to the northern kingdom. He

Unity

probably saw himself as the reviver of the Davidic empire. He was seen in this role by the editor of the first redaction of the so-called Deuteronomic chronicle, which covers the historical books of the Old Testament from Joshua to 2 Kings. This ambitious work, in its first version, tells what happened between David's and Josiah's time:

Because of Solomon's sins, Yahweh ordained the splitting away of the ten northern tribes. But because of the promise to David, Yahweh did not interrupt the rule of David's dynasty over Judah. The northern kingdom, then, straightway, fell into dreadful sins, notably the erection of bull images at Dan and Bethel. These images were interpreted by the Deuteronomic author as symbols of strange gods. Because sin had gone beyond all measure, Yahweh destroyed the northern kingdom. Since, by contrast, King Josiah had persevered faithfully and piously in all things—like his ancestor David—Yahweh permitted the old territories of David's empire to fall again under Josiah's rule. He was able to carry out his cult reform everywhere, so that, territorially and liturgically, the unity of David's kingdom was restored.

In this view of the first Deuteronomic redaction, the schism in the Davidic kingdom was a transitory punishment by Yahweh, provoked by irreligious disobedience and speedily reversed under Josiah, the new David. But this was all illusion. Josiah was killed by the invading Egyptian pharaoh, Nebo; Judah's conquests were again taken from her; and two decades later Jerusalem itself was destroyed and the Judaeans were deported. The Deuteronomic school had to rewrite its chronicle.

The Hour of Dreaming

From this moment on even the schism between Israel and Judah was at last but a memory. Neither entity existed any longer. Both populations had been torn from their lands and settled somewhere or other in a foreign country. And yet, now was the very hour when the idea of the unity of Israel and Judah began to emerge. The more hopeless the situation, the more eagerly did men reach toward the future—the more radiant the picture painted for them by the prophets of a new, twelve-tribe people to come.

Representative of this is Ezekiel and his school. They announced the return home and the union of Israel and Judah. The new constitution of the complete twelve-tribe nation, ruled over by a new and greater David, was explicitly described. Through an action symbol, Ezekiel presents us with this new unity:

> The word of Yahweh was addressed to me as follows: "Son of man, take a stick and write on it, 'Judah and those Israelites loyal to him.' Take another stick and write on it, 'Joseph, the wood of Ephraim, and all the House of Israel loyal to him.'
>
> "Join one to the other to make a single piece of wood, a single stick in your hand. And when the members of your nation say, 'Tell us what you mean,' say, 'The Lord Yahweh says this: 'I am going to take the sons of Israel [for Ezekiel this means all twelve tribes] from the nations where they have gone. I shall gather them together from everywhere and bring them home into one nation in my own land and on the mountains of Israel, and one king is to be king of them all; they will no longer form two nations, nor be two separate kingdoms. . . . My servant David will reign over them, one shepherd for all. . . I shall make a covenant of peace with them, an eternal covenant with them. . . . I shall settle my sanctuary among them for ever. I shall make my home above them; I will be their God, they shall be my people.' " [Ez 37:15-27]

This detailed text, deliberately chosen for quotation, must be taken as representative of many others. Its various motifs are taken up with great frequency in later Old Testament texts and in many glosses added to older texts; so there is no point in multiplying quotations. The vital thing to recognize is that the unity of Israel and Judah became a genuine theological motif only after the population of Israel had been scattered and that of Judah no longer lived normally in its own country.

Unity

In the very nature of things, the motif could not at that time generate any program of action. It was a code, used to express something quite different. In future, one would wait for Yahweh's helping and wondrous action. No one knew what form this would take; no one possessed the means of expressing it in words. And so men looked back to a brief, transitory, but most glorious hour in their past history. One of the things they found in that hour was the unity of Israel and Judah. A phenomenon so great as this very elusive benefit must surely return when—soon—Yahweh begins to act. In this manner, unity, originally in the form of the unity of Israel and Judah, became a utopian-eschatological code or sign.

From this period it was there to stay. We can trace its course through the centuries down to our own time. John the Evangelist has Jesus pray that his disciples may be one (Jn 17:11). The Letter to the Ephesians rejoices that the gospel has broken down the wall that separated Israel from the pagans (2:14). And we suffer once again because of the disunited face of Christendom. Always and everywhere, we seek fundamentally one Israel in Israel and Judah. And we seek it even there, where the code sign works in secularized form. Also, the one world that we desire is a form of the one Israel, as is the unity of our own particular nations. The utopian code-sign unity began to exist at that time; now it forms a part of us all.

Perhaps it helps to know just how unique its beginnings were. As long as men could strive for unity between Israel and Judah only through political action, no one thought about it. When all seemed lost, people began to dream of unity. Are we to learn from this that unity is not all that important, that one ought not let oneself become too fascinated by this late dream of a defeated and frightened nation? Or should we learn the lesson that we must not hesitate in accepting the dream of a new David after all hope seems lost?

It is for us to make the decision. At all events, we must not mindlessly mouth the word "unity," but know that in every forum where it is offered today we have to decide critically, for or against it. It is an ancient code sign; but its very beginnings make us ponder.

Pluralism

Theology as the Answer to Plausibility Crises in Emergent Pluralistic Situations, Taking the Deuteronomic Law as the Basis for Discussion

Looking back to the sixties and the early seventies, we are sorely tempted to liken Catholic theology to Sleeping Beauty. Had not this tender creature, called *Theologia,* fallen (as it were) into a hundred-year sleep behind thick hedges, until a prince came and kissed her awake? The prince was the Second Vatican Council.

To change the metaphor: For at least a decade, theology in the Catholic world has been booming. Seldom in history has so much theological newsprint been sold. Seldom have there been so many theological conferences. Seldom have theologians been given such a hearing outside their own circles. Seldom—so some at least assert—have they caused so much mischief.

Everywhere, theologians have been seen as connected with the crisis which was striking the Church. According to some, they are to blame for it. According to others, they are the only ones who can help. According to yet another group, they are neither to blame nor can they help, for they themselves are caught up in a gigantic crisis.

However that may be, theology has been booming—although, meanwhile, "outsiders" do not, perhaps, feel the crisis quite so acutely. To them, theological output may seem to be subsiding. Why all this back-and-forth thought? Why theology at the very time a crisis peaks? Must there be a connection? What exactly is theology? Is there, perhaps, in the nature of things, an affinity between theology and crisis?

These questions lead into the theme of the following discussion; their answers are to be sought with the help of some aspects of modern sociology, culture, and knowledge. The phrase "sociology of knowledge" makes us think not so much of Karl Marx of the last century and Max Scheler or Karl Mannheim of the twenties of this century as of the more modern trend, which tries to link philosophical-phenomenological theory with a broad basis of positive sociological and ethnological facts. The leading names associated with this trend are Peter Berger and Thomas Luckmann. The best introduction to their theory is their joint work, *Die Gesellschaftliche Konstruktion der Wirklichkeit* (Frankfurt a.M., 1969). It might be well to take a closer look at some fundamental ideas of this sociology of knowledge.

Every society has its system of action patterns and institutions. These patterns would not exist, however, were there not, at the time, appropriate knowledge, for they exist only in the expectations of individual members of the community. At a higher level are theories concerning whole areas of institutionalized actions, and above that is what one might describe as a symbolic world of ideas and an ultimate world view. This embraces all reality. It legitimizes reality and interprets it as a whole. It is the matrix of each intelligibility. In terms of this, even the smallest relational pattern finds its ultimate legitimation. It is able to exercise its authority quite unreflectively from the background of consciousness. But it can also be formulated in a highly reflective, theoretical, and systematic manner, and be "operated" by theoreticians.

A community's symbolic world of ideas is constantly threatened. It has to be interiorized afresh by each succeeding generation. Not all young people, however, interiorize the world of their fathers according to the same standards; hence every society has means at its disposal of assisting the process of socialization—so-called sanctions.

The threat to the world of ideas becomes even greater than within the framework of normal socialization when whole groups of inhabitants of a particular symbolic world of ideas support a deviant version. In the Church, one speaks of heresy. This threatens the whole body, for it demonstrates the possibility of an alternative. In the scarcely founded early Church, theology emerged as the theoretical-systematic formulation of the symbolic world of ideas in reaction to the first heresies. Thus at that time theology was a protective action, assisting the accepted world of ideas in the face of heretical alternatives.

But the threat to an accepted world of ideas can be even greater. It may be that the alternative is not a laboriously born variant from the womb of the same world but a full-grown bastard, from a thoroughly equipped world of alien ideas, resplendent in its assurance. The climax of threat is reached when such a competing world of ideas proves its superiority by the most convincing proofs: power and success.

Such situations produce what cultural or social anthropology calls "cultural shock." The individual who goes abroad to an unknown but (because he is isolated) superior culture is liable to experience cultural shock. But cultural shock can also strike a whole nation—when, for example, it loses a war and becomes politically, economically, and culturally dependent upon the conquering nation. Or when superior colonizers and their theorizers (they might be missionaries) overrun a culture that is peacefully going its own way.

Men's eyes are suddenly opened. Have they been sleeping for centuries? But no prince has kissed them; rather, the world has become strange. They see now what they did not know formerly: people can act, think, and pray differently than used to seem right. One can do it—and no thunderbolt falls from heaven. New things are possible; indeed, something new is here. And the new vessel sends far-reaching waves in its wake. The plausibility of one's former world vanishes. Everything begins to slip. The first "marginal" persons in the old world of ideas—school children and students, women, perhaps, or slaves or workmen—prepare to desert. Others flee to hastily dug shelters, huddled together in terror and panic. Suddenly the world has become pluralistic. In it, everyone feels homeless. How can a world thus threatened with ruin be propped up and stabilized?

My theses is this: The cultural shock situation, far more than the emergence of heresy, is the hour of the theorist—in the case of a religious community, the hour of theology.

Obviously, I can address myself to this thesis only in the manner that is appropriate for an Old Testament scholar. That is, I can choose and analyze an example from my field that is shrouded in the twilight of the past. I choose for this purpose the Deuteronomic literature, limiting myself, within this field, to the Deuteronomic law. Do contemporary parallels exist? How, today, might we learn something from this example? These are questions that an Old Testament scholar can scarcely answer on his own. Nevertheless, exotic examples can have an advantage. Their very remoteness prevents their producing too much emotional stimulus and thus our examination falls more easily into an intelligible pattern.

The Deuteronomic Law Contains Theological Systematization

By "deuteronomic law" we denote essentially that text to the observance of which, in 621 B.C., King Josiah of Judah bound himself and the inhabitants of Jerusalem by oath. The text had been discovered not long before this, when the temple was being repaired. Before proceeding further, they had consulted a prophetess, Huldah (2 Kgs 22). Today we find this text in chapters 5–28 of the Book of Deuteronomy. These chapters, however, contain considerable expansions that date from after Josiah's time.

The Deuteronomic law incorporated material that was ultimately of northern provenance, but it may have recovered its distractive form, as Josiah discovered it, in Jerusalem. Many things point to its composition in several stages. The first version can be placed in Hezekiah's reign—that is, about 700 B.C. It is linked with Hezekiah's attempt at a first centralization of the cult in Jerusalem and his revolt against Assyrian rule. And the law must have undergone more revision under Josiah himself.

Concerning the group of editors, there seem to me many objections to the theory, supported by G. von Rad and his school, that the work goes back to the country Levites. Moshe Weinfeld, in his book *Deuteronomy and the Deuteronomic School* (Oxford, 1971), is probably nearer the mark. He suggests a traditionally established group of the Judaean intelligentsia who, over many generations, maintained important positions of influence at the court. The Shaphan family seems to have been at the center of this group. They were mostly the so-called scribes; but it seems to me—in contrast to Weinfeld—that priests, too, belonged to it. They composed this law from ancient materials, probably in connection with their plans for independence and restoration—and at first, to be sure, underground. With Josiah came the possibility of introducing it as the official code. From the start, the text was adapted to public reading. Something appears in this Deuteronomic law in one sense for the first time in Israel—which one must describe as theology. Let us try to grasp this phenomenon in two steps.

The ancient, broad, in many ways disparate traditions of Israel were systematized. This is seen most clearly in the "little historical credo." In Deuteronomy 26 it is prescribed as a prayer for offering the first fruits: "My father was a wandering Aramaean. He went down into Egypt... few in numbers; but there he became a nation, great, mighty, and strong." And so it goes, until the concluding offertory gesture: "Here then I bring the first fruits of the produce of the soil that you, Yahweh, have given me" (Dt 26:5-10).

G. von Rad considers this credo extremely ancient, at least in its basic form. He dates the text to the time of the judges. From the aspect of "form history," the content provides the basic skeleton of the Hexateuch, but this ingenious hypothesis has been refuted. True, the credo developed from an older layer, possibly dating from the time of the judges, but this earlier layer was not a credo but a straightforward offertory prayer. What in the present text appears as a credo is Deuteronomic. The credo in Deuteronomy is not the root of the Hexateuch but its retrospective, systematic summing up.

The details of the present text seem to have emerged thus. The Deuteronomic author made use of an ancient short offertory prayer: "My father was a wandering Aramaean—but look; now I am bringing the first fruits of the produce of the soil which you, Yahweh, have given me!" This prayer presented the circumstances of the first fruits after the

Pluralism

transition of a nomadic family to the settled possession of land. Every Israelite could make it refer to the ancestor of his own family; at the heart of this prayer, the primeval history of Israel was not interpolated. A historical reminiscence, put into the mouth of Moses by the Elohist, was taken as a framework: "Our ancestors went down into Egypt, and there we stayed for a long time. But the Egyptians treated us badly, as they did our ancestors. We cried to Yahweh. He listened to us and sent an angel to bring us out of Egypt" (Nm 20:15ff).

All that is omitted is mention of the angel; for the rest, the text is expanded and lengthened, down to taking possession of the land. The expansion was affected through the use of key expressions from the stories of the patriarchs in Genesis and from the exodus stories in the Book of Exodus. In this way a text has been composed which proceeded in three solemn stanzas and undoubtedly sounded well in public recitation.

> My father was a wandering Aramaean.
> He went down into Egypt
> to find refuge there, few in numbers;
> but there he became a nation, great,
> mighty, and strong.
>
> The Egyptians ill treated us;
> they gave us no peace
> and inflicted harsh slavery on us.
>
> But we called on Yahweh, the God of our fathers.
> Yahweh heard our voice
> and saw our misery, our toil and our oppression.
>
> Yahweh brought us out of Egypt with mighty
> hand and outstretched arm, with great
> terror and signs and wonders.
> He brought us here
> and gave us this land, a land where milk
> and honey flow.

> Here, then, I bring the first fruits of the
> produce of the soil that you, Yahweh,
> have given me.

This text begins with the patriarchs and finishes at the moment it is recited by the pious Israelite. All of his nation's history is embraced within it; it forms a single idea. The cry rose out of misery, was heard by God, and God intervened; he saved them by leading them out of one land and into another; and the present harvest is thus the immediate result of the gift of the land. The baroque plenitude of the Pentateuch stories is reduced to the simplest system: history is presented so that it is transparent to all men.

Nonetheless, this credo occurs at the very start of the systematizing thinking of the Deuteronomic authors. Their brief formulae could be even more compressed—when, for example, they coined a stereotyped subordinate clause which, on the slightest excuse, could be attached to the catchword "land": "the land which he swore to your fathers Abraham, Isaac, and Jacob that he would give to you" (6:10). "That he would give you" is the formula for the promise of the land, as it is found many times in the patriarch stories of Genesis. "Which he swore" points back to the oath which, according to Genesis 15:18, Yahweh made to Abraham. "Your fathers Abraham, Isaac, and Jacob" is shorthand for the entire line of ancestors, whose fates are recounted in Genesis. "The land" is that in which Israel was living. And so a mighty arc is drawn, joining promise with fulfillment. All the nation's history can be enfolded within it. Once again, history has become transparent.

The same thing can be demonstrated by many other examples; and the object is not just cognitive but normative systematization. All norms of behavior are referred back to the few basic norms, which are listed in the Decalogue, and even these are reduced to the First Command: To worship Yahweh alone as God—the chief command. There is, indeed, a wealth of different formulations of this command: To serve Yahweh, To love him, To fear him, To follow behind him, To walk in his ways, To cling to him, To turn neither to right nor left, etc.

We assert, therefore, the most thorough systematization, in both the cognitive and the normative sphere. The credo even has the effect of creating its own language.

Systematization Based on a Nongiven Starting Point

So far we have dealt with the systematization of traditions of Israel in the light of what was already rooted in these traditions. If the historical credo of Deuteronomy 26 describes the whole history of Israel (to some extent) as a one-time liturgy of lamentation (distress, complaint; being heard, help), then, for the sake of systematization, a category was used, which had already been introduced into the exodus stories by the Yahwist, in order to interpret for the reader the flight from Egypt as the act of God. Thus, in the historical credo, the tradition settles into the system in terms of its own substance. But the total phenomenon of the systematization in Deuteronomy is grasped only when one recognizes that in a second stage new motifs, not so obviously present in the tradition, are also at work. I am thinking above all of what is usually called the "covenant."

In this connection, it would be better to use the less loaded and more prosaic word "contract." And there is even more that ought to be excluded, that is normally associated with the "theology of the covenant" in the Deuteronomic writings, for the narratives of the making of the covenant and its renewal at Horeb in Deuteronomy 5 and 9 probably do not belong in the law book of either Hezekiah or Josiah. Such expressions as "to transgress the $b^e rit$" or "to abandon the $b^e rit$," denoting transgression of the First Commandment, may likewise belong to material that appeared only after the time of Josiah. The so-called "covenant formula" (that is, the scheme of the contract, which we know best from the vassal contracts of the Hittite archives) cannot be traced back to the genuine Deuteronomic law. It first appears in layers of the Deuteronomic literature that originated in the time of the Babylonian Exile.

To that extent, we are not concerned with many things that we commonly associate with the catchword "covenant." Nor are we concerned simply with what L. Perlitt set out in *Theology of the Covenant in the Old Testament* (Neukirchen-Vluyn, 1969), for he made too little distinction betweeen the several layers of the Deuteronomic-Deuteronomistic literature. In what follows, our interest will be confined to one thing: the overall stylizing of the book of the law as the text of the contract and, specifically, as the text of a contract between Yahweh and Israel. This must have already been a characteristic of the Deuteronomy of Josiah. Everything depends upon a few verses, but they are central: Deuteronomy 26:17-19. In a certain measure, they are the link that joins the actual law of Deuteronomy 5-26 with the attached blessing and curse texts of Deuteronomy 28.

Deuteronomy 4:45 may have been the title of the law of Josiah. This places the origin of the law not in the historically and precisely determined Moab situation (shortly before the crossing of the Jordan and Moses' death, as became necessary later to suit the framework of the Deuteronomic historical treatise but in the early days of Israel: "These are the laws (*huqqim*) and customs (*mispatim*) that Moses proclaimed to the sons of Israel when they came out of Egypt." The same terminology provides the summing up at the end of the law: "Yahweh your God today commands you to observe these laws (*huqqim*) and ordinances (*mispatim*); you must keep and observe them with all your heart and with all your soul" (26:16). Chapter 28, the blessing-curse text, obviously refers to the laws, but here a different terminology is used of the law—why, we do not know. Now the text speaks of the *miswot*, the "commandment." In the original Deuteronomic law, only the three verses (26:17-19) were found between the two groups of texts. In these, however, the law was described by yet a third expression, which combines the two terminologies: *huqqaw, umiswotaw, umispataw*—"laws, commandment, ordinances." This declares these three verses to be the real linking point in the Deuteronomic law.

In fact, they supply an interpretation of the whole law as a contract concluded between Yahweh and Israel. In the process, the complicated juridical mechanism of a bilateral contract is expressed in words, and each party, in making the contract, has to make his own declaration and accept the declaration of the other party through an oath. Each declaration accepts one's own obligation and that of the other party. In translation, which somewhat clarifies the rather dense Hebraic infinitive constructions, the text reads like this:

> Today you have accepted Yahweh's declaration.
> He has declared to you:
> He will be your God,
> and you are to walk in his ways, and pay
> heed to his laws, his commandments, his ordinances.
>
> And today, Yahweh has accepted your declaration.
> You have declared to him:
> You wish to be his people, his personal possession,
> as he has promised you;
> You will heed all of his laws;
> he will exalt you above all nations he
>   has created—for praise and renown
>   and honor;
> and you shall become a people holy to
>   Yahweh, your God—as he has promised.
>   [Dt 26:17-19]

Here is reflected all the complexity of the juridical construction of an ancient Oriental international treaty. But here too is proclaimed a comprehensive system in which everything finds its place: Yahweh's deeds and promises in past times, Israel's faithfulness or unfaithfulness in the specific present, Yahweh's blessing or curse in the future.

When the Deuteronomic law was found in the temple, and was promulgated as the law of the state, this entire concept was transposed into the liturgy. Josiah took his oath upon the newly found book and the people concurred in the oath (2 Kgs 11:17). As a result, from the "text of instruction" (*sefer hattorah*) emerged a "text of contract" (*sefer habbᵉrit*). And there are indications which permit the conclusion that, even earlier in Jerusalem, in connection with the enthronement ceremonies, a kind of sealing of a contract between Yahwah, king, and people had taken place through which, from time to time, the "people of Yahweh" came anew into being (2 Kgs 11:17). At an early date the Decalogue, likewise, seems to have been designated $b^e rit$, but this, perhaps, had nothing to do with the idea of a divine contract, but merely affirmed that one accepted the obligation to keep the law on one's oath. But now, in our text, "contract" has become a central category, and concluding the contract an important liturgical event. The category "contract" provides a most comprehensive shape for a new theology. How normative this shape was to become is demonstrated by the whole Deuteronomic and Deuteronomistic corpus of literature which soon followed, with its ever more emphatic development of "covenant theology." At the end of the long process of evolution—which was now beginning—"covenant" came to be the synonym for "faith" or "religion."

However, these beginnings, which we have observed in the original Deuteronomic law, were not taken as a matter of course, as the following fact demonstrates. In the traditional royal liturgy of Jerusalem, concepts such as the "election" of the Davidic dynasty and the adoption of the king as "Yahweh's son" undoubtedly played a much greater part than the contract between Yahweh, king, and people. In the Deuteronomic corpus, these concepts, too, are integrated in the theological synthesis, in a modified form, which puts more stress upon the people. Israel—no longer just the king—is mentioned as the people of Yahweh, and hence Israel is Yahweh's son. These affirmations, however, do not hold the key position in the overall system that the contract category enjoys because of Deuteronomy 26:17-19.

And so we may say that the theology we find in the original Deuteronomy is not only a systematization of the earlier, less systematic conditions of Israel, is not only the gathering together and interpretation of all details from the viewpoint of this new system, but is a systematization that proceeds from a new starting point, which was, indeed, originally alien to the systematized material, or certainly existed only on the edge of consciousness.

Pluralism

Earlier Attempts at Sociological Explanation of Deuteronomic Theology

The phenomenon described in step one has been evident, at least in a vague way, for a long time. If you like, it was seen as early as de Wette, who in 1805 (on this theory) took Deuteronomy from Moses and bestowed it upon Josiah—making it, that is, at least 700 years more modern. But having placed Deuteronomy more or less in the correct historical perspective, how do we explain the phenomenon?

Wellhausen and his school saw Deuteronomy as the conscious propaganda instrument of the party that wanted to spread the "ethical monotheism" of the great prophets (upon which they themselves piteously foundered) more effectively among the nation. Even Isaiah had had the idea of founding a party, but he achieved very little. Later, however, those who were more gifted took up the idea. In the end, the priests realized that in this way they could enhance their power, which originally had been questioned by the prophets. In this way Deuteronomy won the day, and with it—even if wearing the clown's dress of legalism—ethical monotheism.

Thus theology is seen as the means of establishing a new world of ideas within a state society. In this case, however, a few things contradict this theory, chiefly this: We cannot prove that the connection, which is here assumed, existed between the great prophets and Deuteronomy.

Even less probable, however, is another view, which is rarely made explicit but which one can detect, even today, behind the statements of some Old Testament scholars. They maintain that development of such a theology should be regarded simply as a product of our natural evolution of old traditions. Just as a tender lettuce plant grows with the rain and the sun until, one day, full-hearted lettuce appears, so the law that was preached at the covenant festival slowly grew to the height of theological reflection. However, quite apart from the fact that the hypothesis that there *was* a covenant cult in Israel's early period finds progressively less support, this view places history on the level of biology. The evolutionary concept of a gradual raising and refining of reflection, however, if given a certain slant, can be brought within the categories of sociological thought. As soon as a society has reached a certain level of differentiation, specialists in law and theory appear. Once they become established as groups, by the ethos of their vocation they have to maintain continuous activity, even in times when there is not much call for them. Hence they elaborate the field of their activity and reach, naturally, toward ever more sublime heights of reflection. In this sense, an evolutionary theory of Deuteronomic theology might be acceptable; but the peculiar circumstances of the introduction of the Deuteronomic law, as well as its central content—that is, centralization of the cult in the face of all tradition—contradict the theory of continuous development through secret dialogues in an ivory tower. There must have been problems. Concrete actions must have been taken. People must have reflected on what they had been doing.

It is considerations of this sort that other modern authors have in mind when they take account of a serious religious crisis in Israel, which men tried to cope with by having recourse to their ancient traditions. To present the traditions in up-to-date, appealing, and comfortably fitting garb, they had to be thought through systematically and thus transformed into theology. This theory provides the basis for several modern views of the emergence of Deuteronomy. The best example is G. von Rad, who regards Deuteronomy as a kind of textbook for the restoration propaganda and activity of the Judaean country Levites. The theology which these Levites worked out was an instrument they used to ward off a far-reaching crisis into which the Yahweh faith had fallen. So runs his argument in the chapter "Crisis Resulting from the Creation of the States" in *The Theology of the Old Testament*.

All this sounds plausible—provided we ignore the fact that—of all people—the country Levites, about whom we know absolutely nothing, are regarded as the motivators of the restoration movement. Problems begin for this theory when we ask, What caused the crisis? and how von Rad would specify it. Then one discovers that, in the last analysis, it has to do with the erection of the state and introduction of the monarchy.

And so von Rad considers that this crisis had been simmering over a period of four centuries. People had tried to settle the issue in several stages, first by the Davidic and Solomonic court—by new religious institutions (a sacral monarchy, the temple upon Sion) and the collection of traditions (for example, those in the Yahwist historical writings). Then came the prophets, with their denunciations of the social decadence the monarchy brought with it. And finally came the country Levites with their preaching, which is supposed to have found an echo in Deuteronomy. Von Rad explicitly considers the possibility that even the rise and hegemony of Assyria might be set within this framework. In this, however, he sees at most an intensification of the crisis. He denies any original connection between the independence movement under Josiah and the Deuteronomic movement, which, according to him, thrived in the rural areas. Only secondarily did Josiah use Deuteronomy as an aid in his policy of consolidation of power and expansion of dominion.

In the description of the crisis, which is supposed to have been resolved by Deuteronomy, is (in my view) the weakness of von Rad's explanatory thesis. One can scarcely imagine a crisis lasting 400 years. Moreover, there is a great deal in Deuteronomy which links it specially to the Assyrian hegemony, and, moreover, it was in the neo-Assyrian period that Deuteronomy became really effective. For details, we may refer simply to the collation of material provided by M. Weinfeld. Might not the crisis, therefore, which Deuteronomy was designed to obviate have been the cultural shock which must have struck Judah when it fell under the dominion of Assyria?

Neo-Assyrian Cultural Pressure and Deuteronomic Theology

This would explain at least one fact upon which we have stumbled. The last and most comprehensive systematization, which characterized the Deuteronomic theology—the notion of a contract between Yahweh and Israel—did not emerge from the ancient traditions. How was it that the contract category came to be the most all-embracing entity? If we consider it unprovable that there had always been a "covenant cult" at the center of Israel's worship since the so-called amphictyonic epoch— and it *is* unprovable—then the theory that there had been a four century-long crisis, caused by the creation of the state, and which Deuteronomy sought to rectify, does not explain the prominence in Deuteronomy of the contract category. But this becomes explicable, indeed it becomes a hinge of the entire phenomenon, if one relates Deuteronomy to a more specific crisis, which emerged for the Yahwist world of ideas with the extension into Judah of Assyrian sovereignty. To demonstrate this, I present an overall picture of the circumstances as I see them.

Judah came under Assyrian rule when Ahaz of Jerusalem made submission to Tiglath-Pilezer III at the time of the Syro-Ephraimite war of 733. Very soon, Assyrian rule came to mean not just the payment of tribute but a massive cultural injection into all areas of life, rather than any compulsion toward a cult of the state.

Following the destruction of the temple in Jerusalem, Ahaz remodeled its central structures. He built a new altar, modeled on one in Damascus; and this was done, indeed, "on account of the king of Assyria" (2 Kgs 16.18). Immediately, that is, one of the most central objectivications of the Yahweh faith was manipulated in favor of an alien religious world of ideas. The imported altar model was Aramaic, not Assyrian—for there were no burnt offerings in Assyria. The point is that people immediately started to change the cult, and did so, moreover, in deference to the new overlords—though we cannot say precisely what this deference involved.

Hezekiah's rebellion, between 705 and 701, was the first reaction against Assyrian rule. It failed. Jerusalem was not conquered by the Assyrians, it is true, but Hezekiah again became a vassal, and he had to make amends. Manasseh then followed a consistent policy of subjection. Not until the second half of the seventh century, when Assyria had passed the zenith of its power and the decay of its sovereignty was detected throughout the vast empire, was Josiah able, step by step, to gain *de facto* independence, and even begin to contemplate restoration of the old Davidic kingdom, comprising the north as well. Altogether, we have to reckon with more than a century of massive Assyrian influence. National independence movements emerged only after the first third of this period had passed, that is, under Hezekiah, and then, at the end of the period, under Josiah.

We will not be far off the mark if we see Judah's sudden encounter with the totally new, totally superior Assyrian culture, which was backed up by force, as a cultural shock, which had to be overcome. Assyrian culture was more attractive; and it had the assurance that characterizes the conqueror and the colonizer. With corresponding severity, the plausibility of the traditional Yahwist world of ideas was shattered.

No more exact formulation of the problem that faced the Judaean mentality can be given than that in the demand at the siege of Jerusalem (701) by the chief cupbearer of the Assyrian king to the simple people of Jerusalem:

> Do not listen to Hezekiah, who is deluding you when he says: "Yahweh will save us." Has any God of any nation saved his country from the power of the king of Assyria? Where are the gods of Hamath and Hopad? Where are the gods of Sepharvaim and Hera and Ivvah? Where are the gods of the land of Samaria? Did they save Samaria from me? Tell me which, of all the gods of any country, have saved their countries from my hands, for Yahweh to be able to save Jerusalem?

We have to look coldly at what really was happening in such a situation. Were we to imagine that a new culture that appeared superior would have an easy victory, we would underestimate the toughness of institutions, traditions, and ideas. What happens at first is no more than a gradual decay of old certainties, an ominous advent of insecurity. And perhaps not so much the victory of other cultures as emergence of possibilities that had long been immanent in the old, but suppressed. Now these possibilities emerge from their caverns and assume public status. The rival culture, however, soon encounters the most complicated and, in each case, most varied processes of accommodation and resistance. Today, the countries of the Third World are (unfortunately) an object lesson of all this.

Battles between two cultures are waged at all levels—not by any means only at the ideological (if one may use this word without any value connotation))—and the final outcome is usually determined by power. Because, in the end, Hezekiah did not have sufficient power, things became worse after the rebellion than before. Because Josiah *did* have power—more precisely, because in Josiah's time Assyria lacked power—the ideology of the liberation and independence movement was victorious. And this was reflected in the Deuteronomic law. But only the final thrust lies with power.

Conversely, Josiah would probably not have become a national liberator, for a brief moment in history, had not the conceptual mechanism been constructed and popularized which allowed the man in the street in Jerusalem and Judah to abandon the spacious and pleasant ambience of Assyrian ideas, in which he had been quite at home for several generations, and return to the more restricted dwelling of his ancestors. But his family home had been renovated; it had been made so attractive that no one need miss the Assyrian amenities. This is the proper context of the theology we have noted in the Deuteronomic law.

When ancient traditions become systematized, they are thereby increased in value. Once again, they suddenly become pliable. Their concise formulae are comprehensible. The linking of all particular elements to the systematic central thought gives fresh cogency to the whole. In a word, theology as system makes a threatened world of ideas once again attractive. In the case of Deuteronomy, there was no longer any need to be ashamed of the Yahwist world of ideas—as no doubt had formerly been the case—vis-à-vis the superior Assyrian culture. Above all, there was no need for shame if the indigenous culture were dressed in as magnificent rhetorical garb as the Assyrian. In Assyria, in these centuries, an almost baroque rhetoric had become the fashion, and I find Deuteronomic rhetoric most easily explained as an accommodation to this modish verbosity.

In "accommodation," however, we come upon another important catchword. As systematization, theology signifies enhancement of one's tradition; but as systematization with the aid of a rival world of ideas, it signifies, at the same time, integration of the rival, whose threat is thus removed. This happened when the contract category was made the most all-embracing principle of the theological system of Deuteronomy, for the neo-Assyrian empire was held together by a conflation of oaths and contracts of every sort. Making contracts was in vogue. Federation mania had reached such a pitch that, on some occasion or other (possibly after a revolt), Esarhaddon, the superior of Manasseh of Judah, had a covenant drawn up—by the priests of Astarte, no less—between the god Ashur; himself, the king; and the people of Assyria. (Whose ears were not ringing?) As Judah was bound to Assyria by a vassal contract and as this contract undoubtedly had to be read out regularly with great pomp, taking a covenant oath might well have seemed more distinctive of the victor's culture in the eyes of an inhabitant of Jerusalem than it seemed to the average Assyrian, living in Assyria.

At all events, at that time the Judaeans regarded government through contract as characteristic of a higher culture. To be hedged about by contracts—that was an inviolable privilege of the man in the street. On the other hand, should one be successful in integrating the making of contracts into one's own culture, and of providing a rationale from one's own world of ideas, one would be able to give this practice a new, fashionable value. And that is what was done. A brief rite (probably already in the coronation liturgy) was the peg upon which to hang the new concept. The whole Deuteronomic law was conceived as a contract between Yahweh and Israel. And to make this quite clear, Josiah performed the great ceremony of taking the oath to the law in the temple, as we read in 2 Kings 23.

The extent to which this practice was taken to heart is evidenced by the great success of the covenant concept in the later strata of Deuteronomist literature. An even greater proof is the tremendous effort which priestly theology soon had to make to obviate misunderstandings which were bound to corrupt any notion of man's relationship with God that is based on the analogy of a contract.

For the rest, the introduction of the contract into the relationship between God and Israel could be interpreted as a direct legitimation of the independence movement. For the contract with Yahweh could count as abrogation of the previously valid contract with the Assyrian emperor. The Assyrian contract had legitimized Assyria's sovereignty; the contract with Yahweh, accordingly, legitimized independence.

In this way, the various elements and aspects of our discussion fit together. Because the threat to the Yahwist world of ideas came from the superior and power-buttressed Assyrian culture, theology became necessary—this particular theology. It had to be a theology that was neither sheer repetition of tradition nor yet pure innovation. It had to continue tradition and, at the same time, make it attractive (once more) through systematization that rendered harmless the most dangerous features of the rival culture, by integrating them into its own world of ideas. It did this by developing the system itself from elements in the rival culture.

Conclusions

Let us return to our opening questions. Since the Council, we have seen symptoms of crisis within the Catholic Church. Many of the hurriedly called in or self-appointed physicians diagnosed cultural shock, a plausibility crisis, caused by pluralism.

The Western world has long been pluralist, but Sleeping Beauty could sleep on because a dense hedge had grown up around her tower. Until the Council, Catholics may have been so screened off as a society that they experienced the world as the "holy world" and not as pluralistic. In the mission fields, too, the big battalions were on the side of the missionaries. It was the *other* man's world of ideas that experienced crisis. And so it was perhaps a series of effects of the Council that first—intentionally or unintentionally, rightly or wrongly—opened the eyes of many people. For the first time they saw that other people were living in other worlds of ideas, and were quite happy to do so. This led to a sense of insecurity.

The prince, nevertheless, had bestowed his kiss. Theology—no less—rubbed her eyes. It was only natural that theology quickly drew herself to her full height, began singing on every street corner, and attracted an ever growing following. Crisis in the world of ideas and the hour of theology belong together.

However, nothing is gained by the mere fact that theology is awake, for it cannot be taken for granted that theologians, working at high pressure, will put the "right theology" on the market.

We have to take utmost care to understand the term "right theology" in the right way, and here we may find our ancient example from pre-exilic Judah helpful. A theologian is not up to much if he produces merely "true" theology. Were that so, theologians could have remained content with the old book of the covenant and the Yahwist, and need never have written Deuteronomy. Besides being true, a theologian's theology must fulfill its function within the crisis. Everything depends upon this. It is "right" only when it knows how to make the traditional world of ideas attractive again.

Deuteronomy shows us paths that lead in this direction. Through systematization, it made the confusing complexity of the traditional institutions and their attached theories clear and comprehensible once again. In doing so, it was not afraid to take, as the centerpiece of its own system, basic elements from the rival world of ideas. But now they were there, and no one was any longer obliged to abandon his tradition in order to possess what counted most in his own day.

All of this may seem like a slow approach to praising a new intellectual and sociological Machiavellianism in theology. It cannot delight either traditionalists or ecclesiastical system changers. Will it please the Church authorities? Their convictions will certainly be strengthened by our affirmation that authority must be strong. At the same time, they must bear in mind that authority alone is of no use. They will have to go along with theology; and they must ally themselves with the "right" theology.

We have explained what "right" means in this context. It must be faithful to tradition, and unwilling to lose anything from its store. But this is only the first of two essential characteristics. The second is that it must be able to think and formulate in a new way.

Sovereignty

The Sovereignty of God as the Abrogation of Human Sovereignty in Deuteronomic Theology

"The rule of men by men"—this is one of the negative slogans we hear all about us. In sharp contrast in Christian groups, who model themselves upon the gospel, and for whom the words "kingdom of God" still ring too loud, with a note that was out of date even a thousand years ago, we hear the positively intended phrase "the sovereignty, or rule, of God." But in the resonance of this cry we cannot pretend to hear exclusively positive overtones. Why does God have to *rule?* Can it not be said, at least of God, that he has no desire for domination?

This is one of our many problems of language. It is the problem of emotionally charged phrases. Often such problems are solved only by choosing other words which say the same thing, but without disagreeable overtones. Frequently, however, this does not work, because a word occupies positions that are too central in texts that are too important. Then one can try, perhaps, to gain detachment by annotation and reflection. The following considerations may be helpful along these lines.

The phrase "the kingdom of God," as used in the time of the gospels, was powerfully evocative of a host of meaningful images. It was a key that opened a door for the Israelite to all he hoped for; it epitomized the longings of centuries. Although it acquired its strongest coloration in Jesus' times from apocalyptic literature, older theologies survived in the phrase; and we recognize this if we heed the sayings that Jesus links with this phrase. He calls men to imitate him; his God is Father; his commandment is love. This points above all to the Deuteronomic theol-

Sovereignty

ogy. We shall now discuss what this theology has to say about the sovereignty of God.

The Deuteronomic Theology of Sovereignty

The so-called Deuteronomic literature reflects the dominant school of religious thought in Jerusalem at the time the monarchy was declining and the Babylonian Exile was beginning—that is, in the seventh and sixth centuries B.C. This was a time of severe crisis in Israel. To outward appearances, everything was falling to pieces. The only things one might hope to save were those one could grasp and appropriate interiorly. An effort to do this was made preeminently by the Deuteronomic theologians and writers—at first, no doubt, in the temple and at the royal court; then, after the destruction of Jerusalem by Nebuchadrezzar, in exile in the Babylonian heartland. Jeremiah was in close touch with these men. His disciples, who composed his book, were certainly members of this school. The school becomes palpable for us in the grand syntheses of their thought, which they left us in the fifth Book of Moses, Deuteronomy, and in many interpretive and elaborative texts, which they interpolated in other books of the Old Testament by way of revision or editing.

Deuteronomic theology was the first attempt at a great synthesis of all previous religious traditions, stretching back over a millenium of the nation's history. Every later development in Israel and in postexilic Judaism had to come to terms with this synthesis, either accepting or rejecting it. The importance of Deuteronomic thought is also seen in the way the New Testament takes for granted a Deuteronomic starting point and develops along the same lines. The Pauline dialectic of law and grace, Paul's doctrine of the righteousness of God, and the very concepts he uses have their roots in Deuteronomic theology; and as we have indicated, Jesus' slogans about following and loving take up Deuteronomic motifs.

There is one passage, above all others, in which sovereignty, as presented by the Deuteronomic theology, becomes the theme: in the historical books, where the introduction of the monarchy is recorded. Historically, this occurred under Samuel and Saul, shortly before 1000 B.C., and the Deuteronomic commentary is contained in what purport to be long speeches of actors in the drama, interpolated into the older chronicle of 1 Samuel 8 and 12. From a distance of 500 years, Deuteronomic theology is able to systematize the events in such a way as to see the period before the introduction of the monarchy as the period of God's reign over Israel, which later was abrogated by human sovereignty. The consequences of human rule are described with great precision.

> These will be the rights of the king who is to reign over you. He will take your sons and assign them to his chariotry and cavalry, and they will run in front of his chariot. He will use them as leaders of a thousand and leaders of fifty; he will make them plough his ploughland and harvest his harvest and make his weapons of war and the gear for his chariots. He will also take your daughters as perfumers, cooks, and bakers. He will take the best of your fields, of your vineyards and olive groves and give them to his officials. He will tithe your crops and vineyards to provide for his eunuchs and his officials. He will take the best of your manservants and maidservants, of your cattle and your donkeys, and make them work for him. He will tithe your flocks, and you yourselves will become his slaves. When that day comes, you will cry out on account of the king you have chosen for yourselves. [1 Sm 8:11-18]

Exploitation, military service, armaments, expropriation, taxation, enslavement—these are the key words.

The rule of God that had gone before can be described as a history of liberation:

Sovereignty

> When Jacob and his sons came to Egypt the Egyptians oppressed them, and your ancestors cried to Yahweh who sent Moses and Aaron; they brought your ancestors out of Egypt and gave them a settled home here. Then they forgot Yahweh their God and he sold them into the power of Sisera, general of the army of Hazor, as also into the power of the Philistines and the king of Moab who fought against them. They cried to Yahweh "We have sinned, for we have deserted Yahweh; we have served the Baals and the Astartes. Rescue us now from the power of our enemies and we will serve you." Then Yahweh sent Jerubbaal, Barak, Jephthah, and Samuel. He rescued you from the power of the enemies surrounding you, and you lived in security. [1 Sm 12:8-11]

Here, too, there are black patches, but the explanation is straightforward: it was always when Israel forsook its God that darkness fell. When the people repented, a fresh liberation was granted them and they lived again in security. The archetype of God's assumption of sovereignty was their liberation from Egyptian oppression and being led into "this land."

The Deuteronomic theologians regarded the demand for a human ruler as a renunciation of submission to the rule of God. As they were unable to blot out past history, and could not totally deny that God's presence had been known in the time of monarchy, they devised a formula that could reconcile God's rule and man's rule:

> Yahweh has set a king over you. If you reverence and serve Yahweh and obey his voice and do not rebel against his order, and if both you and the king who rules over you follow Yahweh your God, all will be well. But if you do not obey the voice of Yahweh, if you rebel against his order, his hand will be against you and against your king.
> [1 Sm 12:13-15]

In spite of the king—along *with* the king, indeed—they could continue under the rule of God, if they obeyed his law and listened to his prophets. That is what is meant by "following" God. By this we are to understand that God's law and his prophets would prevent a form of human sovereignty from emerging, for which the handwriting on the wall appeared from the very start. The theologians who wrote thus already knew that the experiment had misfired—they were living as deportees in Babylon. They drafted a constitution for the time for which, perhaps, they still hoped—after the return from exile, when a system of distributed functions would limit the power of the king and the prophets would be given a juridically guaranteed freedom of action. This was interpolated into the Deuteronomic law at Deuteronomy 16:18-18:22.

For the most part, it is important that in this theology the rule of God and the rule of men are seen as sharply opposed. Fundamentally it succeeds, it is true, in working out a formula that reconciles the two; but in fact this unstable compromise never stood up to the tests of history. Human sovereignty prevailed, in a form that no longer submitted to the rule of God, which is so utterly different in kind. Dire consequences followed.

What, then, according to Deuteronomic theology, are the distinguishing features of the rule of God? This question leads us to the Book of Deuteronomy and close to the gospels, where Jesus calls men to forsake all, follow him, and love one another.

The God Who "Leads Out"

One would like to say "the God who frees," but "freedom" is not one of the key words of Deuteronomy. With all its modern overtones, the word "freedom" did not exist in those days. It is true that a slave could be freed, but all that happened was that he escaped from one kind of slavery into a slightly more agreeable kind. His status was still

Sovereignty

precisely determined by norms; he was a "freed slave." All that we make the word "freedom" express in these days was approached from different angles and embodied in different words.

The Deuteronomic authors thought in concrete terms. Without having been taught by Karl Marx, they knew exactly how much economics matters. For them, freedom, in terms of the economic structure, was the unimpeded, equal possession of land, giving to each in equal fashion, as well as food and happiness, and all this was destroyed neither by enemy hordes nor natural catastrophes. If we want to know how Yahweh gave his people freedom, we have to ask how he led his people into the land "flowing with milk and honey," the land he had already promised, under oath, to the patriarchs "Abraham, Isaac, and Jacob." These are recurrent formulae in the Deuteronomic language. To live in this "beautiful land" and to be ruled by no human lord, but only by one's own God—that was their concept of freedom. Israel gained this freedom only by an act of liberation, for it was living under alien rule. Being ruled alienates men, and rulers are alien to the ruled. And to make sure that this is plain, the Deuteronomic liberation myth fastens onto an actual alien rule in an actual foreign land, onto life in Egypt, the "house of slavery," as it is called in the first sentence of a central text in the Decalogue.

Yahweh had "led out" Israel from the Egyptian "house of slavery"—one of the numerous formulae of Deuteronomic language. It is expounded in the profession of faith which, according to Deuteronomy 26:1-11, the Israelite farmer declared before Yahweh each year at the harvest thanksgiving festival. The Israelites, too, knew freedom—the freedom of the nomads of the desert. They were subject to no one, but sought their food in a condition of want. Famine had taken them to Egypt, where there was food, but no freedom in which to enjoy it. And so they became slaves by degrees. At first they lived in Egypt as "guest citizens" (*gerim*); they were not full citizens but they had many rights nonetheless (we might liken them to our immigrant workers). Generations passed and they became numerous—proletarians; and so they suffered the fate of the proletariat: their rights were curtailed; they were made to forced labor. "The Egyptians ill treated us; they gave us no peace and inflicted harsh slavery on us" (26:6). This was the situation from which Yahweh, their God, freed them.

"Yahweh led us out" (26:8); this meant, in banal terms, that their God helped them get out of Egypt. But "to lead out" is also a juridical term. A slave who is given his freedom is said to be "led out." In the world of that time, a slave could gain his freedom in two ways: by payment of a redemption price or by force. Israel's liberation came about in the second way, by force, as expressed in the formula "Yahweh led us out of Egypt with a mighty hand and uplifted arm." This profession of faith comes very close to a theology of revolution. Obviously, the violent freeing of a slave is just only if his enslavement had been unjust, which is why it was so strongly stressed that the Israelites were, at first, guest citizens in Egypt. The rights that this status brought had been unreasonably taken from them by the rulers, and God, who freed them by force, gave them back their ancient rights. And when this God, Yahweh, has once given freedom to an enslaved group of men, he gives them complete freedom.

In one great sweep he led them "out of Egypt" and "on into this holy place"—that is, Jerusalem and the whole land—and "gives over to them this whole land." It is a land of almost mythical well-being, as the old sacred phrase put it: "a land flowing with milk and honey." In this land they were subject to none but Yahweh. This statement can also be expressed in Deuteronomic language: They are to "follow" none but Yahweh.

"Following God"

We must be sure we understand the meaning of this expression. Very often it means, quite literally, to follow behind another. However, we must at once ask who, in the society of that time, followed whom. The answer is: the superior, the lord, the leader, went on ahead; the lesser ones, the vassals—those who were led—followed behind. Hundreds of works of art from every region of the ancient East provide evidence of this. In many contexts, the statement that someone "followed behind" someone else can have a wide range of meaning. Whoever "followed" a prince was his vassal or official; whoever "followed" a general was an officer or soldier in his army. Were it affirmed that someone "followed" a particular god, that meant not merely that the person was accustomed to go in procession behind the statue of this god but that he regarded this divinity as his own, personal god, whom he "served" in a special way (this word also is much used in Deuteronomy). These meanings of "to follow someone" occur not just in Hebrew, the language of the Israelites, but in many other Oriental languages as well—for example, in Accadian, the language of Mesopotamian law (written in cuneiform characters). To "follow" a god implied being the servant and worshiper of this god.

The interesting thing is that the Deuteronomic theologians use the concept "following" frequently, but mostly in prohibitory or deprecatory texts. They forbid Israel to follow gods other than Yahweh—or disapprovingly, they report how Israel *had* followed baals and other gods. Their prohibition of following other gods is another formulation of the First Commandment of the Decalogue: "You shall have no other gods beside me."

Expressed positively, this meant that Israel should follow the God Yahweh alone. And this is how it is put in several passages—for example, in Deuteronomy 13:

> If a prophet . . . arises and offers to do a sign or a wonder for you . . . and if he then says to you, "Come, then let us follow other gods," and even if the sign or wonder comes about, you are not to listen to the words of that prophet. Yahweh your God you shall follow, him you shall fear, his commandments you shall keep, his voice you shall obey, him you shall serve, to him you shall cling. [Deuteronomy 13:2-5]

We may have been struck by the wealth of synonyms with which the highly rhetorical Deuteronomic language expresses the same thing over and over again, which is: No one dare exercise the lordship over Israel but Yahweh. For Israel, to follow Yahweh means to have him alone as Lord.

Israel had been freed from one rule, that of Pharaoh. By this liberation, however, Israel not only entered into freedom (that is, into a land flowing with milk and honey) but automatically submitted to another rule—of him who had liberated them, solely to become their lord. It is not easy to grasp this fact, and here is the difficulty that even a man of the stature of Ernst Bloch has with the Bible. How few has Bloch made see how explosive, how pregnant for the future, how laden with the pathos of freedom is the biblical message of the exodus from Egypt. (But he has discovered that other expressions in the Bible, about the God who claims sovereignty over those he has liberated. Bloch writes, using a hyphen: the message of the "Lord-God." In this he sees the great falsification, the fraud of authority: generations of hungry priests, the obscuring of the revolutionary light.)

If, in the language of those days, to "follow someone" meant to recognize him as one's lord, Bloch's problem has to be taken seriously. This is the same problem that formed the starting point of our discussion, and now we find it turning up again at the heart of the Old Testament. To get the problem into perfect focus, let us look at a variant of the profession of faith of Deuteronomy 26 that we find in Deuteronomy 6, where these words are addressed to the Israelite head of the family:

> In times to come, when your son asks you, "What is the meaning of the decrees and laws and customs that Yahweh our God has laid down for you?

(Obviously the question of a young man who sees the world of his ancestors constrained within a net of forms of authority, both gross and

Sovereignty

subtle, and yet they appeal to the name of God, and the young man wonders why such forms exist)

> you shall tell your son, "Once we were Pharaoh's slaves in Egypt, and Yahweh brought us out of Egypt by his mighty hand... to lead us into the land he swore to our fathers he would give to us. And Yahweh commanded us to observe all these laws."

If this answer of the head of the family is supposed to contain a logically clear solution of the youth's problem about the sense and non-sense of the many laws, then again we are thrown back for interpretation upon juridical categories. The logic behind this is the change of master. Whoever buys a slave out of his slavery or delivers him by force is, in the eyes of the law, the lord of this slave. If the slave is a friend or relation, this means a return to home and family, and is equivalent to freedom. But if the slave is just anyone, his deliverer becomes the new lord and master.

It is precisely this legal logic that the father is supposed to present to his son, if the son does not understand why there are so many laws and precepts in Israel and why they are still traced back to Israel's God. The father would explain: Without him, we would have remained under the laws of Pharaoh, and been exploited by him; for such an existence as that he has freed us, and so we are legally under his rule. This rule of Yahweh is, nonetheless, not slavery, nor exploitation, but the gift of a good life; for the text goes on to say that the father must tell his son:

> "Yahweh commanded us to observe all those laws and to fear Yahweh our God, so as to be happy for ever and to live, as he has granted us to do until now." [Dt 6:20-24]

It is not until the last sentence that we are taken a step further and find a hint of a solution to Bloch's problem. God's sovereignty is indeed sovereignty. But as the sovereignty of *God*, it is the abrogation of human sovereignty. It never oppresses, but liberates. It does not crush to death, it gives life. One of the ways in which Deuteronomic theology expresses this idea is by saying: To follow Yahweh is to love him.

To Love God

The passage in Deuteronomy 13 about following Yahweh was quoted above in abbreviated form. One of the "missing" sentences contains the motif of love precisely in connection with the idea of following. Let us therefore quote it again, more fully:

> If a prophet arises among you and offers a sign or a wonder for you, and if the sign or wonder comes about; and if he then says to you, "Come, then, let us follow other gods... and serve them," you are not to listen to the words of that prophet. Yahweh your God is testing you to know if you love Yahweh your God with all your heart and all your soul. Yahweh you God you shall follow, him you shall fear, his commandments you shall keep, his voice you shall obey, him shall you serve, to him shall you cling. [Dt 13:2-5]

The long list of synonymous terms is introduced by the words "love Yahweh... with all your heart and all your soul." The Deuteronomic theologians took for granted the laws, commandments, and legal utterances of their people. This heritage was many centuries old. This whole ordered system, moreover, was always traced back to Yahweh as the lawgiver. Even had they wanted, these theologians could not have called these ordinances in question. Quite plainly, however, they had no desire to do so.

It is true that they did not shrink from modifying the law whenever they saw that something was not right, in spite of the tradition of divine origin. On the whole, they gave an essentially more human form to the old ordinances, but this was a side issue; their chief concern was to draw

Sovereignty

men's attention from the various details of the law that stood in Yahweh's name and direct it to something that affected Israel over and above observance of particular laws—to that which made sense of all the rest. The correct fundamental relationship of Israel to its God, Yahweh, was mutual love. In the sermonlike introductions to the Deuteronomic law, sayings about the love of Yahweh for Israel and Israel's love for Yahweh stand out as so many climaxes.

At this point reference must be made to something that complicates the issue even more. The very word "love," as used in the ancient Eastern ideology of sovereignty, had long been commandeered and abused. Subjugated princes had to make contracts and ceremonial obeisance to their overlords, promising not just friendship but love. They had to bond themselves to love their sovereign "like a father"; they had to love him "with their whole heart." Such phrases are found in diplomatic correspondence from the second millennium B.C., and even then they had become empty formulae. All this must be said so that we do not make it seem as though Israel was the first to join sovereignty with love.

Israel restored love to its original status, and therein we find the contribution of the Deuteronomic theologians. The first climax in the Deuteronomic introductory sermons runs thus:

> Listen, Israel: Yahweh is our God alone. You shall love Yahweh your God with all your heart, with all your soul, with all your strength. [Dt 6:4f]

Yahweh is one Yahweh—that is, unique. This is the language of love, not law. In the Song of Songs, Solomon sings: "There are sixty queens, and eighty concubines and countless maidens. But my dove is unique" (Sg 6:8f.).

Moreover, Israel's love for Yahweh, which transcends all legalism and transforms Yahweh's sovereignty into something totally different from what human sovereignty can ever be, provides the answer. First, it was Yahweh who loved Israel; then love went back and forth. This relationship stands out most clearly in a passage in the seventh chapter of Deuteronomy, again from the introductory sermons:

> For you are a people consecrated to Yahweh your God; it is you that Yahweh our God has chosen to be his very own people out of all the peoples on the earth.
> If Yahweh set his heart on you and chose you, it was not because you outnumbered other peoples: you were the least of all peoples. It was for love of you and to keep the oath he swore to your fathers that Yahweh brought you out with his mighty hand and redeemed you from the house of slavery, from the power of Pharaoh, king of Egypt.
> Know, then, that Yahweh your God is God indeed, the faithful God who is true to his covenant and his graciousness for a thousand generations toward those who love him and keep his commandments. [Dt 7:6-9]

This closes the circle of love, and reciprocal love; but it is extended yet again. Yahweh loved Israel when its people were still strangers, guest citizens, in Egypt; and this relationship invited Israel to extend its love as wide as the love of Yahweh himself.

> It is he who loves the stranger and gives him food and clothing. Love the stranger then, for you were strangers in the land of Egypt. [Dt 10:18]

The catchword "love of neighbor" is not found in the Deuteronomic vocabulary. It has a place in the law of holiness, which belongs to another tradition. In its laws, Deuteronomy describes in concrete terms how one ought to treat one's *compatriot,* which is the primary meaning of "neighbor." That this does not exclude the standard of love from the area ruled by these laws is proved by the saying concerning love of the stranger. Treatment of one's compatriot, too, clearly falls within that love, whose prototype is the love that bonds Israel with its God, and is the real form in which God exercises his "lordship."

Sovereignty

Hence, as most typical of God's sovereignty in the Deuteronomic sense, one may take as concrete representations those sacrificial meals that the Deuteronomic law describes at the conclusion of the cultic regulations concerning festivals and sacrifices at the central shrine, always using these or similar words:

> There you will eat in the presence of Yahweh your God and be thankful for all that your hands have presented, you and your households blessed by Yahweh your God.
> [Dt 12:7]

> There you shall rejoice in the presence of Yahweh your God, you and your sons and daughters, your serving men and women, and the Levite who lives in your towns.
> [Dt 12:12]

> Then you are to feast on all the good things Yahweh has given you, you and your household, and with you the Levite and the stranger who lives among you.
> [Dt 26:11]

In the joy of feasting, when all social distinctions are annulled, and God himself is one of the party and "president" of the feast, liberation from Egyptian slavery reaches its goal, and the sovereignty of God, which consists in love, is demonstrated. The fact that there was a king in Israel is lost sight of in this context, and in another passage—1 Samuel 8 and 12—the Deuteronomic theologians affirm that it would be better if there were no king, and Yahweh alone were king.

The Preaching of Jesus

Five hundred years later, Jesus proclaimed that the kingdom of God is at hand. The saying baffles us because we still conceive of "kingdom" or "sovereignty" in a negative way. When Jesus announced the kingdom of God, he did not mean exactly the same thing as the Deuteronomic theologians, for meanwhile the word had lived a long history. In particular, apocalyptic thought had endowed it with new dimensions and color.

Nonetheless there is an amazing consonance. Jesus leads those who believe in him out of their former bondage. Clearly, they have to abandon everything that formerly enslaved and dominated them. He calls them to follow him. And he speaks to them of love—the love of God, love for God and for one's neighbor. In one of his parables he has a father prepare a joyous feast for his returning son. Following in Jesus' steps, later communities were so at odds with the world's rulers that they were persecuted for centuries.

It is not every kind of sovereignty that we have to fear, but only that of men. The rule of God, as Jesus offers it, is the exact opposite of man's rule.

Distribution of the Functions of Power

The Laws in Deuteronomy That Governed Ministries, a Constitution in Terms of Power Distribution, and Catholic Canon Law

In 1748 Charles Baron de Montesquieu published a book titled *De l'Esprit de Loi*. This was the first time anyone had systematically worked out a theory of organizational distribution of the functions of the power of the state. Since then, distribution of functions of power has been accepted as one of the basic principles of most democratic constitutions. The decisive thing about this theory is the separation and counterbalancing of the various functions of the state, all of which must be regulated by a fundamental law. The number of separated functions and their precise demarcations may vary, but the classic trinity is the legislature, the executive, the judiciary. Montesquieu, who got his ideas from observation of what obtained in England at that time, illustrated these ideas with examples from classical antiquity. As far as I can see, he failed to notice that he might also have cited an example from the Bible.

The Church of Jesus Christ is not a state. Good arguments can be adduced that it should be, in reality, a *communio* of congregations, supervised in such a way that they are able to live according to the principle of unanimity. Even such congregations must have something resembling law, but whether such an issue as distribution of functions of power need be raised is open to question. The charisms of the early Christian congregations were something different.

There are also arguments, however, for an organized structure in the nature of a "greater Church," and, *de facto*, such "greater churches" exist. They are seen, preeminently, in the ecclesial entities of today. Even in a departmentalized society, they manifest many similarities with the state, and we cannot ignore the fact that their laws show tendencies to assimilate to state parallels. The Roman Catholic Church, in particular, according to a statement of the canon lawyer Klaus Mörsdorf, "has developed fully the concept of the unity of power." The origins of this concept are various. It can hardly be disputed, however, that in the course of this development great pressure was exerted in the direction of assimilation to state models, particularly in ages when the concept of the absolutist state was dominant. Today the demand is constantly made, especially by American canonists, with perhaps only partial success, that Catholic canon law be reformed in accord with the principle of the distribution of functions of power. There are real prospects of introduction of an independent executive jurisdiction, though not in the highest instances.

Obviously, we face the question: Are not tendencies to assimilate to state models again at work, rather than the effort to find genuinely ecclesial constitutional forms? If imitation of the state model of distribution of power functions is too external, can the written word of God (for example) and the full emergence of charisms be assured the place they ought to have in the Church of Christ? And so the further question arises: Might we not be able to find, in the Bible itself, possibilities for the distribution of power functions that are proper to the Church, and need not be imitated? They would have, it is true, an element of historical relativity, but they would provide the right starting point for our discussions.

Most Catholic canon lawyers still see unrestricted discussion of a thoroughgoing distribution of functions of power within the Church as fraught with theological problems. Their theology pushes them, rather, in the direction of centralization of power, which, is linked with the traditional Catholic rationale of the structure of the Church. This theology posits a legislative act of the historical Jesus, by which he conferred powers upon the Church he founded. Through this posited act, the monarchical papacy and the unified authority of the Church were established once and for all, and no one has the right to alter any of it—at least not at the highest level, although at lower levels some compromises may be allowed. Moreover, in the theory of ecclesial authority an important part is played by the concept of the representation of the *one* Christ, who combined in himself all the offices of the Old Testament dispensation of salvation (one is accustomed to speak of the offices of teacher, priest, and pastor, associated respectively with prophet, priest, and king). Finally, it may be that vestiges of the neo-Platonist idea of emanation still operate underground. If, in the last analysis, the Church is ruled by God, then God's will must necessarily flow down from above, step by step, as it were; hence at least at the apex of the human order there must be a single channel, directed by God himself, and only at lower levels could the streams of God's will begin to branch into subsidiary channels. Where things otherwise, the divine guidance of the Church would not be assured, according to this conceptual model.

Today, however, the theory of the formal institution of the monarchical papacy by the historical Jesus is exegetically untenable. Furthermore, in the New Testament the fulfillment of all the Old Testament offices in Jesus was intended to be a Christological affirmation, and Jesus was thereby designated the all-embracing, unsurpassable, eschatological mediator of the new covenant. From this affirmation, should this mediator be succeeded by something in the form of a Church—and such a development is indeed necessary—nothing can be deduced concerning the differentiation of offices within the Church. One can share in the power of Christ, in the latter or in the former respect. On the latent notion of emanation, one may say conclusively that we are not under any obligation to neo-Platonism. Is the intellectual problem really altered if, instead of saying God guides only one free being infallibly (the pope) and all others only through him, we say that he guides many free beings infallibly?

We are not committed, therefore, to a theology that insists upon unification of the functions of power. We are on a better theological tack if we proceed from the idea of a Church that is instituted not in juridical detail but in its essence, and is irrevocably bound by the word of God, and possesses the assurance that it will preserve that word unfalsified throughout the ages. But this Church will have the right—the duty, indeed—to form its official structure to suit the circumstances of history. Part of this historical accommodation will consist in refraining from capriciously tampering with structures that are in place and functioning. But one does not have to justify this sort of well-founded conservatism in law by reference to the historical Jesus; it is simply human common sense. And on the very same plane belongs accommodation to those forms of law that each epoch finds best and most suited to it. It is precisely in this context that we must place the current question about greater distribution of the functions of power—a very proper question.

If one wishes to discover typically ecclesial possibilities of such distribution, it is useful (to say the least) to keep one's eyes open to such models as may be found in Holy Scripture. And because we are concerned with a Church that has in many aspects accommodated to the state, it may be wise to look at the Old Testament, for in those days Church and state had not yet become differentiated. Obviously, we will not find a model there that can be simply transposed; but we may perhaps learn to what things we must always pay heed concerning the distribution of the functions of power, as this would operate within the community of the faithful.

With this in mind, we shall present and discuss the laws concerning offices in Deuteronomy. They may well form a draft of a constitution that is based upon the distribution of functions of power, although scholars have not hitherto really observed this fact.

The Deuteronomic Laws concerning Offices

The first part of the Deuteronomic law book (Dt 12:2-16:17) is devoted to the regulation of the cult. It deals with the central sanctuary of Israel, the exclusiveness of the cult of Yahweh in Israel, clean and unclean foods, and the obligations attached to various holy seasons.

A new theme is introduced abruptly at Deuteronomy 16:18: judges and officials. Here begins the law concerning offices, and this interests us in the following details. A kind of ideal for judges is set out (16:19f.); then, following an introductory section (16:21f-17:1), containing a few apodictically formulated cultic precepts, comes the casuistically conceived description of a model process, with its inbuilt rule of the two witnesses (17:2-7). All of this is attached, by association, to the prescription for setting up local courts in 16:18. The main thread is picked up again in 17:8 and developed: as well as local courts, there is to be a central court of justice (17:8-13). At the end of this law, the death penalty is decreed for nonacceptance of the verdict of this central court (17:12f).

> [16:18] You are to appoint judges and scribes in each of the towns that Yahweh is giving you, for all your tribes; these must administer an impartial judgment to the people. You must not pervert the law; you must be impartial; you must take no bribes, for a bribe blinds wise men's eyes and jeopardizes the cause of the just. Strict justice must be your ideal, so that you may live in rightful possession of the land that Yahweh your God is giving you.
>
> You must not plant a sacred pole of any wood whatsoever beside the altar that you put up for Yahweh your God; nor must you set up a standing stone, a thing Yahweh your God would abhor. To Yahweh your God you must sacrifice nothing from herd or flock that has any blemish or defect whatsoever, for Yahweh your God holds this detestable.
>
> If there is anyone, man or woman, among you in any of the towns Yahweh your God is giving you, who does what is displeasing to Yahweh your God by violating his covenant, who goes and serves other gods and worships them, or the sun or the moon or any of heaven's array—a thing I have forbidden—and this person is denounced to you; if after careful inquiry it is found true and confirmed that this hateful thing has been done in Israel, you must take the man or woman guilty of this evil deed outside your city gates, and

there you must stone that man or woman to death. A man may be put to death only on the word of two witnesses or three; and no man may be put to death on the word of one witness alone. The witnesses shall be the first to raise their hands against him in putting him to death, then all the people shall follow. You must banish this evil from your midst.

If a case comes before you which is too difficult for you, a case of murder, legal rights or assault, or any dispute at all in your towns, you must make your way to the place Yahweh your God chooses, and approach the Levitical priests and the judge then in office. They will hold an inquiry and give a decision for you. You must abide by the decision they pronounce for you in that place which Yahweh chooses, and you must take care to carry out all their instructions. You must abide by the verdict they give you and by the decision they declare to you, swerving neither right nor left of the sentence they have pronounced for you. If any presumes to disobey either the priest who is there in the service of Yahweh your God, or the judge, that man must die. You must banish this evil from Israel. And all the people shall hear of it and be afraid and not act presumptuously a second time. [17:13]

The central court of justice of Deuteronomy was not, as one often reads, a court of appeal, which could reverse the verdict of a court of first instance. Rather, it was supposed to uphold—not overthrow—the judgments made by normal means in the local courts over particular cases. It was superior to the local courts because it had a sacral character. Thus the law concerning the central court of justice provides for the presence, alongside the "judge" (17:9, 12), of the "Levitical priest" (17:9), that is, "the priest who is there in the service of Yahweh your God" (17:12).

Because formerly the king had been the highest judge, the "system of justice" theme is followed by the theme of kingship (Dt 17:14–20). The Deuteronomic law concerning kings is based upon the presupposition that Israel, having completed occupation of the land, will want to install a king (17:14). First it determines the qualifications of kingship: the king must be chosen by Yahweh and he must be an Israelite (17:15). There follows a kind of picture of the ideal king (17:16-17). This leads to the prescription that the king possess a copy of the Deuteronomic law, must have it always by him, and read from it daily (17:18-20).

> [17:14] When you reach the land that Yahweh your God gives you, and take possession of it and live there, if you say to yourself, "I will appoint a king over me like all the surrounding nations," it must be a king of Yahweh's choosing whom you appoint over you; it must be one from among your brothers that is appointed king over you; you are not to give yourself a foreign king who is no brother of yours.
> Ensure that he does not increase the number of his horses, or make the people go back to Egypt to increase his cavalry, for Yahweh said to you, "You must never go back that way again." Nor must he increase the number of his wives, for that could lead his heart astray. Nor must he increase his gold and silver excessively. When he is seated on his royal throne he must write a copy of this Law on a scroll for his own use at the dictation of the Levitical priests. It must never leave him and he must read it every day of his life and learn to fear Yahweh his God by keeping all the words of this Law and observing these laws. So his heart will not look down on his brothers and he will swerve neither right nor left from these commandments. If he does this, he will have long days on his throne, he and his sons, in Israel. [17:20]

By an association of ideas, the theme of kingship is followed by the theme of the ministers of the cult (Dt 18:1-8). The priests had already been mentioned in the law concerning the central court, and in the law concerning the king. Their chief function is the offering of sacrifice, from which they derive their livelihood. The law concerning the priesthood starts off with the principle that priests may not own heritable land, but must live from the parts of the sacrifices that belong to Yahweh (18:1f). All Levites from the rural towns, who had lost their livelihood as a result of the centralization of worship, are guaranteed the right of participating in the service of the central sanctuary and of sharing correspondingly in the portion of the sacrifices (18:6-8).

> [18:1] The Levitical priests, that is to say the whole of the tribe of Levi, shall have no share or inheritance with Israel: they shall live on the foods offered to Yahweh and on his dues. This tribe is to have no inheritance among their brothers; Yahweh will be their inheritance as he promised them.
> These are the priests' dues from the people, from those who offer an ox or a sheep in sacrifice; the priest is to be given the shoulder, the cheeks, and the stomach. You must give him the first fruits of your corn, your wine, your oil, as well as the first of your sheep's shearing. For Yahweh your God has chosen him out of all your tribes to stand before Yahweh your God, to do the duties of the sacred ministry, and to bless in Yahweh's name him and his sons for all time.
> If the Levite living in one of your towns anywhere in Israel decides to come to the place Yahweh chooses, he shall minister there in the name of Yahweh his God like all his fellow Levites who stand ministering there in the presence of Yahweh, and shall eat equal shares with them, no count being taken of the claims he has on the Levitical families for the goods he has sold. [18:8]

A kind of transition is then made to the law concerning prophets, which we find in Deuteronomy 18:9-22. At times in the ancient East, activities in the sanctuaries included such things as rites of child sacrifice and various forms of soothsaying and sorcery; all of this is forbidden (18:9-12). The positive intention of these practices was the desire to find, in specific life situations, individual contact with the deity. For

Israel, too, this motive was recognized and a means was provided, but one that was not under the control of the priesthood. The prophets take their place beside the priests (18:13-15). Then follows the etiology of these men, who are inspired afresh from time to time by Yahweh for the sake of his people. The office of the prophet is seen as having been instituted at Horeb, in association with the giving of the law (18:16-18). Within the framework of this etiology is recorded Yahweh's promise and his commandment. The promise: Those who do not obey the words of the prophets, Yahweh himself will judge (18:19). (It is different in disobedience to the verdict of the central court, when Yahweh does not take part in punishment but delegates its execution to Israel.) The commandment: Prophets who are not commissioned by Yahweh, or prophets who speak in the name of other gods, are to be punished by death (18:20). There follows a criterion which enables one to recognize a prophet who has no genuine commission from Yahweh: the nonoccurrence of what he foretold (18:20-22).

> [18:9] When you come into the land Yahweh your God gives you, you must not fall into the habit of imitating the detestable practices of the natives. There must never be anyone among you who makes his son or daughter pass through fire, who practices divination, who is soothsayer, augur or sorcerer, who uses charms, consults ghosts or spirits, or calls up the dead. For the man who does these things is detestable to Yahweh your God: it is because of these detestable practices that Yahweh your God is driving these nations before you.
>
> You must be entirely faithful to Yahweh your God. For these nations whom you are dispossessing may listen to soothsayers and diviners, but this is not the gift that Yahweh your God gives to you; Yahweh your God will raise up for you a prophet like myself, from among yourselves, from your own brothers; to him you must listen. This is what you yourselves asked of Yahweh your God at Horeb on the day of the Assembly. "Do not let me hear again," you said,

> "the voice of Yahweh my God, nor look any longer on this great fire, or I shall die"; and Yahweh said to me, "All they have spoken is well said. I will raise up a prophet like yourself for them from their own brothers; I will put my words into his mouth and he shall tell them all I command him. The man who does not listen to my words that he speaks in my name shall be held answerable to me for it. But the prophet who presumes to say in my name a thing I have not commanded him to say, or who speaks in the name of other gods, that prophet shall die."
>
> You may say in your heart, "How are we to know what word was not spoken by Yahweh?" When a prophet speaks in the name of Yahweh and the thing does not happen and the word is not fulfilled, then it has not been spoken by Yahweh. The prophet has spoken with presumption. You have nothing to fear from him. [18:22]

The next section of the law treats the cities of refuge, and the law concerning offices is thus completed. It comprises the law concerning the judicial system, the king, the priests, and the prophets, The persons or classes of persons who are dealt with are judge, official, priest, king, prophet.

A Coherent Constitutional Scheme

Recent biblical scholarship agrees on the thesis that all the laws concerning offices are not of the same antiquity and that all intrinsically manifest several strata, so that at least part of the text, as we now have it, was not originally formulated with the intention of forming a component of a set of laws concerning the various offices in Israel. But for the most part the matter is left there, and one refrains from asking further whether the four laws about offices belonged together at least from a certain stage in their development onward, and from that point were intended to be read as a single system of pronouncements. This problem for the history of redaction is posed in what follows.

Obviously, it is possible that when the laws were gathered together, the dominant idea was that this was a kind of museum of ancient unrelated, individual laws. But it is equally possible that they had come to be understood as a self-consistent piece of legislation. That the latter possibility is more probable can be shown, and serves as a preliminary to the explication of the date of the decisive comprehensive redaction of this group of laws.

If anyone had regarded the whole Deuteronomic law as a unity, that person would have been the editor, or—for the law undoubtedly has many strata—the last reviser of the law concerning the king. He demands that the king possess a copy of "this *torah.*" Nowhere else within Deuteronomy 12-26 is this *corpus* itself designated comprehensively as *torah*. On the contrary, the term *torah* recurs in the sections of the Book of Deuteronomy which are placed around the older middle section (Dt 5-28) and which belong to the total redaction of the book. It always denotes the whole middle section—paraenesis, laws, blessing, and curse, all of these. Wherever the word *torah* appears, it is this section that is designated a unity, and the laws concerning offices stand at the center of this unity.

The techniques that were used in the ancient East to arrange material in a comprehensive collection of laws have nothing in common with modern principles of presentation of laws. Linking often occurs from sheer association of ideas. In the process, it may happen that in the middle of the treatment of theme A, a new theme, B, emerges. In such a case, theme A suffers temporary interruption; theme B is first dealt with, then theme A is continued. If the sequence A, B, A2 occurs, one may count on it that, in the eyes of the author of the sequence, the laws that are grouped under B are so closely related that they can be driven, like a wedge, into the equally well related laws of group A. The Deuteronomic laws concerning offices, which start with the laws concerning the judicial system, provide just such an example. In contrast to

Distribution of the Functions of Power

the laws which follow, they are more concerned with a collection of things—the judicial system—than a group of persons. However, three different groups of persons appear within them: judges, officials, and priests. Clearly, this leads to thoughts about the different groups of persons, and thus we arrive at the themes "king," "priest," "prophet." And at 19:1, with the law concerning cities of refuge, we are back at our original material, the judicial system, for the "cities of refuge" theme leads to the special procedure in cases of manslaughter or murder. After a short paragraph on the shifting of boundaries (19:14), the list of laws on the judicial system continues with a paragraph on the principle of the two witnesses (19:15) and one paragraph on the punishment for perjury under oath in court (19:16-21).

The sequence A, B, A2 is clearly evident. The laws concerning the constitution of the courts in Deuteronomy 16:18-17:13 have two aspects. In themselves, they form the beginnings of a series of laws concerning Israel's judicial system; these continue in 19:1. At the same time, however, they treat of persons and offices in Israel, thus stimulating the treatment of a series of laws about offices. And so we have to regard them as the first in that series. From the point of view of a legal system, therefore, all the laws concerning offices belong together.

It might be objected—if it is a question of the systematic treatment of all the important offices in Israel—that a matter of such great importance as the supreme military command is never mentioned. On close examination, however, this objection turns into confirmation. In the view of Deuteronomy, a distinction must be made between the mercenary troops, who are directly subject to the king, and the conscript army of the whole people. The mercenary force is given only passing mention in the law concerning the king, when it is decreed that the king must not acquire too many horses (17:16), for the number of horses indicates the size of the royal charioteer force. The leadership of the army is regulated by Deuteronomy in the law on calling up the army (Dt 20:1-9). At the calling up, two groups of persons take part: the priest and the scribes. "Priest" (in the singular) most probably indicates the figure known to us from 17:12, who delivers the battle sermon. The scribes, a group of officials known to us from 16:18, form the troops. When these units have been formed, they place officers over them (20:9).

According to the theory of Deuteronomy, there is no permanent officer corps for the conscript army. This corps is reconstituted for each war, as is the host. In contrast, those who have to live permanently in relation to the army are treated in the laws concerning offices, although in that context their sporadic operations on the occasion of the calling up of the army are not mentioned. We cannot expect to find, on Deuteronomic presuppositions, explicit law concerning a supreme military hierarchy.

The list of laws concerning the most important offices in Israel is complete, and so we have good reason to assume that the chief redaction of this section of the Deuteronomic law was intended to be a comprehensive piece of legislation concerning the principal functions of power in Israel.

Dating the Chief Redaction of the Constitution

To date the chief redaction of the section, one must look for the most recent strata that stretch through several laws. We may ignore more recent glosses and additions in only one law, because there cannot be any design behind them that comprehends the entire group of laws. In what follows below, a few reasons will be indicated for thinking we must set this redaction in the period at the beginning of the exile—that is, late in the first half of the sixth century B.C.

The Torah, which is stressed in the law concerning the king, is written on a roll (*sefer*) and kept safe by the "Levitical priests." This connects it with the Deuteronomic Chronicle, which belongs to the beginning of the exilic period. According to the law concerning priests, every rural Levite had the right to offer sacrifice in Jerusalem. According to 2 Kings 23:9, this right was not granted to the rural Levites by the reform of Josiah (621 B.C.). It is commonly concluded from this fact that the Jerusalem priesthood engineered this omission in executing the

Deuteronomic law in its own vital interest. It is more likely, however, that this passage was not yet in the law at this time, and now expresses a further-reaching claim of the one-time rural Levites. On the other hand, the passage must be dated before the end of the exilic period, for by then the great compromise between the Zadokites and the Levites was beginning to take shape, and Deuteronomy knows nothing of this.

The rule at the end of the law concerning prophets, and distinguishing between authentic and false prophets of Yahweh, may well be ancient, but it turns attention forcibly to the problems that exercised Jeremiah and his school.

If, on the basis of such observations, one accepts the beginning of the exile as the time when the decisive redaction of the group of laws concerning offices was made, and if one links this redaction with the Deuteronomic revision of the historical traditions of Israel, the draft of a constitution which developed as a result is not the description of an existent reality but a utopian theory. Much that is in the draft may have been adumbrated during the time of the monarchy in Judah. But the laws concerning offices are also the result of a critical encounter with the constitutional arrangement in the time of the monarchy. Much in the draft may have asserted itself after the exile, when Deuteronomy again became accepted as law; but at least one element had forever been severed from the total system: after the exile, there was never a restoration of monarchy. As the lack of one element affects all other elements in a system, the constitutional theory in Deuteronomy was never concretely realized. It remained a utopian theory.

Distribution of the Functions of Power as the Key Concept of the Constitution

What, then, was the essential principle of this theory? My thesis is that something like the notion of the distribution of functions of power was its guiding force. We will demonstrate this thesis step by step.

Certainly we find no official structure in Deuteronomy in which all functions are gathered up and held in a single hand. The model of the nomadic community, in which the sheik is everything—leader, teacher, priest, lawgiver, judge—already lay far in the past, and the princely absolutism of early modern times (or papal centralization of power) was hidden in the future. We are dealing, rather, with a system in which various functions are distributed among various groups of people. The fact that these functions included those that no longer fall within the competence of the modern state, such as the sacrificial cult and the creation of contact with the deity, should pose no problem for the historically minded observer—especially if transference to the Church of the secular notion of the distribution of functions of power is a matter for debate.

Of as little account, too, should be the fact that the separate functions are in part distributed to others, and combined, in a way that is not customary today. Even today, however, the distribution of functions need not automatically be understood in the civil-juridical sense. It might well be that in a system wherein functions are distributed, a specific authority is regarded as supreme, allowing all the rest to flow from it by delegation, and as always capable of redefining or totally recalling them to itself. But neither is this the case with the Deuteronomic draft constitution.

In the conditions that prevailed in the ancient East, that sort of supreme authority was associated solely with the king. We think, for example, of the rule of the pharaohs in Egypt. In the Deuteronomic laws concerning offices, however, the monarchy is in the middle of the list, not at its head. Nor is it said anywhere that the king defines functions or installs officials. According to Deuteronomy 16:18, Israel itself provides its judges and officials, and its king as well (17:15). The priests and the judge at the central court are simply there—there is no indication whence they came. Presumably the text has in mind hereditary office. The prophet is called from time to time by Yahweh himself (18:15). And we inquire about the functions of the king, only one function is named: he must read the Torah daily and live exactly according to its prescriptions (17:18–20). Thus he never had the right to alter its regulations on the distribution of functions among the various offices, in order, for example, to enlarge his power at the expense of others.

This leads to the last requirement, if we are to speak about a distribution of functions in the modern civil-juridical sense. The functions must be distributed among *different* authorities—that is, no one authority is simply a delegation from a superior authority—and delegation of the separate, distributed powers must be made in accord with an antecedent constitutional law that exists for these powers. Precisely such a law is found in the laws concerning offices in Deuteronomy.

There is no need for astonishment, however, if we do not find that this law exists separately, as a kind of fundamental law, but see it embedded in a codex which claims to contain all of Israel's laws. This fact is connected with another: after Deuteronomy, Israel had no continuously active legislature. Deuteronomy takes no account of the necessity of creating new laws and altering old ones. Israel had received the laws at Sinai—once and for all; hence they are valid for all time, and are never to be changed (Dt 13:1). Yahweh was the legislator.

On such presuppositions, obviously, it is not necessary to distinguish between constitutional and other law. The laws concerning offices, which form only one part of the Deuteronomic book of laws, can nonetheless be regarded as genuine constitutional law. Even the last condition is fulfilled: we are able to speak of a genuine distribution of the functions of power.

However, when we speak about this distribution it is important to take account of more than the formally juristic viewpoint. When in modern times systems of the distribution of functions of power have been introduced, it was, as a rule, against a very concrete background. There had formerly been abuse of power, concentrated in a single hand. As a rule, also, people were striving toward a concrete political goal: a balance of powers.

In a well-functioning state, no one group or individual should be allowed to become too powerful, and a balance of powers automatically engenders mutual control of powers. Montesquieu describes all this in great detail, and the fathers of the American Constitution were imbued with this spirit. Historically, we see the reaction against princely absolutism, but it is important to ascertain whether the same thing was happening in the draft constitution of Deuteronomy.

There, too, a balance of powers was being brought about. In practice, the formerly much wider powers of the king and the priests were circumscribed in favor of the judges and the prophets. In earlier times the king had also been supreme judge. Thus the law concerning the king by association of ideas follows the law concerning judges. But this is a purely historical association. In the laws concerning offices, the king no longer is the supreme judge; and nothing is gained by allowing older circumstances to color our interpretation of these laws—as sometimes happens in exegesis.

In earlier days the priests had served the oracle, thereby creating individual contact with the deity. Because of this, the law concerning prophets became associated with the law concerning priests, which it now followed. This, too, is a purely historical association. In this law concerning offices there is no mention of priestly oracles, and individual contact with the deity is clearly the concern of the prophets.

Another prominent function of the king was the conduct of battles. For this purpose, the kings of Israel and Judah had their standing armies. All that remains of this in our legislation is the remark in 17:16, that the king shall not possess too many horses. Warfare, as we saw, was thought of in terms of the people's army; and in the passage in Deuteronomy devoted to this the king is not mentioned.

Small space is given in 17:17 to the harem and the property of the king. It delimits another function the king possessed, which we must not underestimate. He was a symbol. By a large harem and ceremonial display of splendor, he was a sign of the prosperity of the state.

In reality, only two things are left for the king: administration (so obvious as to require no mention) and the exemplary reading of the Torah. The king is now no more than administrator and model Israelite.

Where the monarchy was weakened, the judges became stronger.

Now the legal system is seen as an autonomous authority, no longer under the king and his governors in the garrison cities. The central court, however, is in the hands not only of judges but priests as well. The priests have three functions: exercising sacral-judicial power, offering sacrifice, and custody of the Torah. According to Deuteronomy 31:9-13, the last function includes the office of teaching the Torah to the rising generation.

The function of making contact with the deity is taken away from the priests; this now belongs exclusively to the prophets. The prophets are designated the successors of Moses, for their origin lies where Moses received the Torah, on Mt. Siani. This makes them the born interpreters of the Torah (the law), which is unchangeable, but times change; thus Yahweh sends the prophets to tell men what the ancient law means in new situations. In a certain sense, the prophets replaced the legislature. Certainly they are not representatives of the people, but representatives of God. They are regarded as charismatic personalities, not as cultic officials; hence they are hard to manipulate. They embody a counterbalance to all other authorities.

On the whole, therefore, we may put it like this: An earlier and greater concentration of power in monarchy and priesthood is scaled down and an attempt is made to create a balance of power between four different authorities: the judiciary, the king, the temple priesthood, and free charismatics. We may describe the distribution of functions of power as the guiding principle of this constitution for offices, although there is no sign of any historical continuity leading to our modern forms of such distribution of functions, and there are many differences in detail from modern systems.

The Torah and Free Charisms

The Deuteronomic draft constitution may well prove important for discussion of possible distributions of functions of power in the Church's system of ministries in virtue of the fact that it places this constitution firmly in the context of the word of God. However, its full significance appears when we become aware of the danger of following secular tendencies in the present battle for distributing functions in the Church, and when we pose the question whether there might not be special forms of distributing functions that are proper to the essence of the Church, in contrast to the state. Deuteronomy is well aware that it is not just *any* law book but the law book of the historically chosen people of Yahweh. Its system of the distribution of functions, too, is conceived in these terms. Two elements in particular emerge from this: in the Deuteronomic draft constitution, the Torah always has pride of place, and at a strategically important point there is a legally secured place for the eruption of free charism that eludes legal definition. In virtue of the fact that all offices are subordinate to the Torah, God rules in Israel through the revelation he had given in the course of Israel's earlier history, for this revelation is present in the Torah as scripture. Inasmuch as the prophets have a legally assured sphere of influence, God reserves for himself the possibility of exercising his sovereignty over this people in ever new ways, as occasions arise.

What does this mean in detail? First, the law concerning kings subordinates the king completely to the Torah. According to 17:18-20, he must possess a copy of the Torah and keep it always by him, reading from it daily, so that he learns to fear Yahweh and to observe all the words of the Torah. Like every other Israelite (17:20), he is thus totally subject to the Torah.

A second incidental statement concerning the Torah is contained in the law about the king. Because the original Torah is in the custody of the Levitical priests (17:15; cf. 31:9), it follows, from Deuteronomy 31:10-13, that custody of the Torah implies the obligation to teach it and hand it on to the rising generations in Israel. The ministry of priests is thus tied to the Torah—not exactly as is the ministry of the king, it is true, but insofar as it commands them to guide the people.

The judicial system in Israel also is related to the Torah. Deuteronomy 17:11 presupposes that the verdict given by the central court is identical with the Torah, although what exactly is meant by this may be somewhat obscure. Here we have an older text, dealing with inquiry directed to God, that has been applied to the Torah, and this could not have been brought about without internal tensions. We can at least expound the text by saying that the expanded version indicates that when judgment is pronounced, the spirit of the Torah ought to break through. This applies also to the local court. The word *Torah* is not used in this context, but the model process that is described concerns trespass of the First Commandment of the Decalogue, which is the very heart of the Torah.

The prophets likewise are bound to the Torah—but are perhaps less subordinate than parallel to it. In 18:16 is an etiology of the prophetic office, which is connected with Deuteronomy 5:23-31, where we learn how Moses was installed as mediator of the Torah. At that time Yahweh had foretold that Israel would never in future lack a prophet, and in the law concerning the prophets, Moses is twice described as the first of the prophets (18:16f.). The parallel between prophet and Torah is not so strongly stressed as to make us expect that Yahweh will expand the Torah with new laws, through the operation of the prophets. Rather, the prophets seem to be thought of as a means of concretizing and actualizing the will of God, as set out in general terms in the Torah. At all events, in another part of the Deuteronomistic historical writing (2 Kgs 17:13) they are even described as mediators of the law. Even though we do not cite this text in our interpretation of the Deuteronomic law concerning prophets, in the Deuteronomic draft constitution the prophets—those free and unpredictable charismatics—in all their dignity and significance are directly compared with the Torah.

The emergence of prophets is provided for. Paradoxical though it may sound, the sphere of operation that was juridically provided for them is one of the offices in the distributively structured constitutional system. But more is involved than with the other offices, for the prophets, like the Torah, have precedence over the other offices. From another point of view, less is involved, because as free charismatics they are not a legally definable entity in the strict sense. And so, conversely, their role is not canceled by the fact that with the other definable entities there is a real distribution of functions of power.

Through the priority of the written Torah and the legally provided sphere of operation for the free action of God through his charismatics, the Deuteronomic law concerning offices hints at what must be heeded when we undertake a specifically ecclesial distribution of functions of power—if we do not wish to fall into the trap of following purely civil models, as happened in former times when unification of powers was sought. Having recognized this danger, however, the fundamental problems, which we find exercizing many Catholic canonists, must be cleared up. It must at least be felt possible to admit a distributed system of offices right up to the highest level, should, in a particular period, the faithful feel the need of it and it is commended by reason.

In the end, however, we are left with the question we touched on by way of introduction: Is the assimilation of the Church to state models not, on the whole, much more questionable than is commonly supposed, and is the Church, in the New Testament sense, not best understood in terms of "congregation," and ought not its legal system reflect that understanding?

Salvation History

*The Theology of History, Exemplified in a
Salvation-Historical Exhibition of Recent Decades*

In recent decades, few theological catchwords have been successful as "salvation history." Just how influential it has become is shown by the fact that the greatest systematic compendium produced by Catholic theology for generations, the *Mysterium Salutis,* describes itself in its subtitle as an "outline of salvation-historical dogmatics." It is hard pressed to make good this promise, but it makes a brave effort. And the postconciliar liturgical reformers in the Catholic Church, too, have labored manfully in the cause of salvation history, even if they often concentrated on the word "history" and understood it in the sense of "chronicle." However deeply we may be in debt to these reformers for the "continuous readings" from the Old Testament, the selection of pericopes, and the way they have been sorted out, as well as the augmentation of Deuteronomic historical texts by additional information culled from Old Testament books of quite another provenance, give the impression that their chief end is to impart instruction to the daily Mass goer in the history of Israel. The same holds true of the revised calendar of saints. The reduction in the number of obligatory feasts was a praiseworthy objective, but the decision to suppress the feast of every saint whose life (or even existence) could not be documented was founded upon an attitude which others might well describe as historicist, although its exponents would no doubt call it salvation-historical. Christian people as a body have reacted with annoyance. Is the Christian body indeed so ill informed about salvation history?

One of the roots of this boom in salvation history is the view that all the other religions of the world stand outside time, or try to escape from the reality of history through cultically produced cycles of time, whereas the distinctive feature of the Jewish-Christian religion—the proof of its truth in fundamental theology, no less—consists in its taking time seriously and proclaiming the real action of God in the real, directed course of history. This view is often linked to a picture of history that is always evolving toward what is better, and thus the plausibility of the view is guaranteed to men of our times. It is precisely the Old Testament scholars who have taken upon themselves the task of vindicating this view. The difference between the religion of Israel and the religions of the surrounding world of the ancient East was summed up in the formula: history-religion *versus* nature-religion. The novelty with which Israel shed light in the world around her was said to have been because the deity could not become known through the cultic mediation of nature but through the contingent events of history.

This view cannot be maintained any longer—at least not in the black-and-white form in which it is usually represented. Its principal refutation is B. Albrektson's *History of the Gods* (Lund, 1967), which shows that ancient Eastern people—outside Israel and before Israel—were convinced that gods intervened in history and manifested themselves in unique constellations of events. Indeed, the concept of a divine plan for history was more highly developed in Mesopotamia than in the Old Testament.

Just how hard it is to reduce the Old Testament to the formula "salvation history" is demonstrated by the fate of that great master of this viewpoint, the teacher of a whole generation, Gerhard von Rad. With great vision he wrote his two-volume work, *Theology of the Old Testament,* which is unsurpassed and will be difficult ever to supersede. In this work, at every turn, salvation-historical theology is presented in the more sublime form of a tradition-historical theology. Even so, von Rad could not come to terms with one massive block of the Old Testament books: the whole of the Wisdom literature. He fitted it into the scheme as "Israel's response" to Yahweh's revelation in history, which does not do justice to these books. Von Rad sensed this himself, and in the last years of his life, after publication of his *Theology,* grappled with the problem. The result was a new book, *Wisdom in Israel,* published in 1970, one year before his death. It acknowledges and describes the distinctive quality of the Israelite concept of Wisdom, and does not attempt to relate it to some kind of salvation history.

But even within the parts of the Old Testament that are designated "salvation-historical," revisions, or at least qualifications, have meanwhile become necessary, affecting, moreover, key texts of the schemes of a salvation history. We shall demonstrate this with the example of the so-called "little historical credo" of Israel. We shall use, moreover, the chief documentation for this credo—what has become the "exhibition piece" of salvation history during recent decades.

The "Little Historical Credo"

The "little historical credo" was the name that used to be given to the basic content of a series of Old Testament texts, which provided, *seriatim,* a brief sketch of salvific events involving Yahweh and Israel. The most outstanding example—as it were, the fundamental text for salvation history—is Deuteronomy 26:5-9. Here, in the form of a profession of faith, the history of Israel from the time of the patriarchs to the occupation of Canaan is recounted. Since the publication of von Rad's *Das formgeschichtliche problem des Hexateuch* in 1938, Old Testament scholars have accepted the idea that, soon after the occupation of Canaan by Israel, such credo texts existed as liturgical texts. Then, at the time of first literary collection of folk traditions from Israel's past, the "little historical credo" served as a guide for the arrangement of the diverse story material, in which all that had to be prefixed was the "primeval tradition" and all that had to be woven in was the "Sinai tradition." The person who did this was the so-called Yahwist—or according to some, his precursor. Thus, in outline, the Hexateuch is ultimately based upon Israel's oldest liturgy. Because this liturgy was oriented toward salvation history, later, with a breadth and detail far beyond anything found in its contemporary neighbors, Israel recounted the past as salvation history. By a happy providence, the original nucleus of the Hexateuch has been preserved within the framework of a Deuteronomic law.

For a long time, doubts about this were voiced only in respect of a side issue: whether the Sinai tradition had originally been linked with the other traditions or had been handed on separately from them. This problem arose from the fact that in the key text of Deuteronomy 26:5-9 and its closer parallels in Deuteronomy 6:20-25 and Joshua 24, there is no mention of the happenings at Sinai.

Thus, since the beginning of the sixties, the textual basis of the main thesis has been disputed. Studies by L. Rost, W. Richter, C. M. Carmichael, and myself, carried out quite independently and in part following different approaches, all reached the conclusion that no such brief catalogue of salvific-historical events existed before the Deuteronomic literature. The "proof texts" for the "little historical credo" are all Deuteronomic at the earliest, and therefore credo stands not at the beginning but at the end of a development. It is the verbally stereotyped simplification and summarization of the substance of the Hexateuch. The Hexateuch does not follow from an antecedent, older, liturgical credo; the credo presupposes the former, or at least the old sources of the Pentateuch. The chief text in Deuteronomy 26:5-9, at least in its salvation-history record, is the work of the Deuteronomic hand. In this, it follows the model provided by Numbers 20:15f., which is not yet a credo.

Such a redating of texts that were thought to be early and normative in the reconstruction of origins is of considerable importance, for it is no longer so certain that the collection of Israel's ancient narrative traditions, which are to be found in the early sources of the Pentateuch, were undertaken under the guiding concept of "salvation history." Many things still support that view, but one has to put the further question: Are late compendia, such as Deuteronomy 26:5-9, unequivocal evidence of the salvation-history concept? The compendium may have been composed precisely to express a particular view—

theology, no less—of history, so that one would still be obliged to inquire whether it can be understood as "salvation history" in our modern sense.

We shall try, therefore, to bring out more clearly the theology that slumbers within Deuteronomy 26:5-9.

Introduction to the Text of Deuteronomy 26:5-10

The historical narrative in this text forms only the first and largest part of an offertory prayer. Verse 10 is then added, the formal expression of offering, and is in fact the more decisive part. The whole offertory prayer is within the context of a ritual law about giving the first fruits of the earth to the sanctuary (Dt 26:1-11). The Israelite had to say this prayer as he offered his gifts.

The law has been rewritten and expanded several times. In the older ritual, we may suppose that there was only the following offertory text, comprising the beginning and the end of our present offertory prayer:

> My father was a wandering Aramaean—but see, here I bring the first fruits of the land that you, Yahweh, have given me.

This prayer has more the flavor of a local than a wide Israelite horizon. It is constructed on the contrast between landless ancestors and the landowning present generation. Any idea of progressive history in articulated stages is absent. In the Deuteronomic period, interpolation of the intervening verses gave rise to the credo, which then ran as follows:

> My father was a wandering Aramaean.
>
> He went down into Egypt,
> lived there as a stranger, few in numbers,
> but there he became a nation, great, mighty, and numerous.

6. The Egyptians ill treated us,
   they took away our rights
   and inflicted harsh slavery on us.

7. We called on Yahweh, the God of our fathers,
   and he heard our voice
   and saw our loss of rights,
      our slave labor
      and our oppression.

8. Yahweh brought us out of Egypt
      with mighty hand and outstretched arm,
      with great terror,
      and with signs and wonders.

9. He brought us here
   and gave us this land,
   a land where milk and honey flow.

10. And see, here I bring the first fruits
    of the land that you, Yahweh, have given me.

The first sentence of the old offertory prayer has a hard three-rhythm beat (Hebrew: *'arammi', obed, 'abi*). This, obviously, inspired the author of the expansion, who created three groups of sentences; and even the individual sentences internally manifest the triad scheme (we have tried to demonstrate this in the verses above). We have here an example not of strophes but of units of statement of various length. The text is not poetry but strongly rhetorical literary speech.

From the composition thus presented, we may deduce the following to have been the arrangement of the actual profession:

I.	26:5	The Aramaic ancestor
II.	5	Journey to Egypt and becoming a nation
III.	6	Oppression in Egypt
IV.	7	Lamenting and being heart in Egypt

V.   8f.   Yahweh's redemptive act (exodus, entry, gifts of the land)

This is not an arrangement according to the uniform alignment of the individual acts of God. It was not consonant with the form of the text that the available facts of history be regarded as guiding elements in the construction.

Other facts concerning the form of the text also deserve attention. In groups I and II, the early history of Israel is recounted in the third person, that is, with the detachment of distance. From group III onward, the narrator identifies himself with the people; he uses "we" and "us." Moreover, in groups I–III the horizon is at first mundane; Yahweh is not mentioned; but the cry of complaint at the beginning of group IV bursts through this horizon. From now on, Yahweh is the grammatical subject of the statement. All of these facts are not without significance for our interpretation of the text.

The Events of Which the Credo Speaks

Before we inquire into the theology of history contained in such a text, we ought to ascertain what historical facts are being interpreted. In doing so, the question arises: What, in those days, were regarded as historical facts? Whether modern historical criticism would also recognize them as facts is beside the point.

At first sight, it seems as though this credo lists, without connection, a few events from Israel's early history; but these events are important. This is frequently said to typify this credo text; whether the same applies to other texts remains to be seen. In Deuteronomy 26:5-9, at all events, we find a totally different intention—on the supposition, that is, that the text is of late origin. The intention of the credo is to embrace in very few words all the historical events, as they are portrayed in the old Pentateuch sources and in the historical books up to 2 Samuel.

To carry out this intention, the Deuteronomic editor employed a subtle technique of allusion, using stereotyped Deuteronomic clichés that embody whole complexes of narrative.

The starting point of the Aramaean ancestor, already presented to the Deuteronomic editor, suggested familiarity with the story of the patriarch Jacob. However, the editor would like to think of Jacob as a symbol of all the patriarchs from Abraham onward, and so he uses formulae which are found in Genesis in the Abraham, and not in the Jacob, sagas. The linking of the phrases "went down into Egypt" and "lived there as a stranger" is found only in the Abraham sagas of the Yahwist (Gn 12:10). The expansion of the phrase "a great nation," typical of the promises to the patriarchs of a prolific posterity, into the double phrase "a great and mighty nation" likewise occurs only in the Abraham sagas of the Yahwist (Gn 18:18). If, further back, the credo speaks of Yahweh as "the God of our fathers," this could only be understood, in the Deuteronomic period and milieu, as "the God of our *three* fathers: Abraham, Isaac, and Jacob."

In the affirmation about the deliverance from Egypt, we find examples of clichés which stereotype whole complexes of events. The "mighty hand" of Yahweh is an allusion to the so-called "Egyptian plaques" of Exodus 3:19, 6:1. The "outstretched arm" adds a reference to the events at the Sea of Reeds, with its allusion to the Song of Moses in Exodus 15. The word "sign" is used by the Yahwist of some of the Egyptian plagues, and by the Elohist of the signs through which Moses had previously proved himself to the Israelites (Ex 8:19, 1:1f, and 4:8f, 17, 28, 30). "Wonders" occurs only in Exodus 3:21, and refers to the plagues. In Deuteronomic language, the double expression "signs and wonders," when it occurs in this context, means all the events recounted in the old sources of the Book of Exodus that occurred while the people were still in Egypt (cf. Dt 6:22, 29:2, 34:11). On the whole, the statement about the deliverance from Egypt makes it sufficiently plain that not only the event itself is meant, but a whole chain of events, the report of which can be read in greater detail elsewhere.

The sentence "He brought us here" may well reach into the time of David and Solomon. "Here" or "this place" is always to be understood in Deuteronomy as the place where the present speaker is (cf. Dt

1:31, 9:8, 11:5, 29:6)—and in the ritual law, according to Deuteronomy 26:2, the central sanctuary, which means Jerusalem and its temple. In the Deuteronomic period, Jerusalem and its temple are often referred to elsewhere as "this place," as we see especially from the Book of Jeremiah. But David was the first to conquer Jerusalem, and Solomon the first to build the temple there; and the being brought to "this place" was concluded only in their time.

This short sentence encapsulates the history of many centuries. For the rest, this connotation of the sentence does not exclude the conquest of the whole land. Whoever reached the center enjoyed everything that went before. And here we have another sublime allusion. In one or two ancient statements about Yahweh's promise of the land to Moses, the promised land of Canaan is introduced by this same word, *maqom* or "place" (Ex 3:8, 23:20; Nm 10:29). But the explicit expansion of outlook from the central sanctuary, to cover the whole land, first occurs in the last sentence of the credo: "He gave us this land, a land flowing with milk and honey." Here, at all events, in the first half of the sentence, we find the formula of the promise of the land, as in Genesis, and in the second half the characteristic formula of that promise, as in Exodus.

The credo of Deuteronomy 26:5-9 has in mind, therefore, just a few selected events from salvation history, but alludes to all that can be historically recollected from the nation's beginning to its zenith under David and Solomon.

Models Used in Interpretation

The author of the credo does not apply new models of interpretation to the course of history that are peculiar to himself. Rather, he harks back to the interpretive categories already provided in the great historical works and—dependent upon them—those that are found in Deuteronomic theology. However, he confines himself to a few models, taking care to maintain purity of execution.

The first model is the sequence of action: promise and fulfillment of the promise. This sequence belongs to normal and ever recurring human experience. Frequently, it becomes formally institutionalized, to some extent in forms of law. The Yahwist used this model to systematize in a single historical line the gifts of Yahweh to the patriarchs and his gifts to the group engaged in the exodus and the conquest of the land. According to him, the patriarchs had received the promise that they would become a nation and the promise was fulfilled in Egypt (cf. Ex 1). Canaan was promised to the patriarchs, and the exodus generation enjoyed its fulfillment. The schema "promise-fulfillment," making Yahweh's action in history intelligible, then assumed an important place in the Deuteronomic interpretation of history. By means of this interpretive model, God can be recognized as the one whose faithfulness rules the historical scene.

The credo of Deuteronomy 26:5-9 picks up the typical vocabulary of the promise of nationhood and the promise of the land (vv. 5 and 10), and to this extent, by allusion, it recalls the use of our promise-fulfillment model in the interpretation of other events. But we must note that it does not point explicitly to a promise of Yahweh—or an oath (to use the Deuteronomic variant) to the patriarchs. How easy that would have been, and how easy it is to find ready-made formulae in Deuteronomic language, is shown by the other affirmation in the rite, according to Deuteronomy 26:3: "Today I declare to Yahweh my God that I have come to the land Yahweh swore to our fathers he would give us." This is nothing but a series of Deuteronomic, stereotyped concepts, and one cannot avoid suspecting that this sentence emerged from a final revision of the text, whose editor failed to find this theologumenon, so important in Deuteronomy, in the credo. The absence of this theologumenon might be traced back to the constraint placed upon the Deuteronomic enlarger by the fixed beginning and ending of his text. But quite simply, he could have attached a Deuteronomic retrospective reference to the promise of nationhood to the patriarchs to his own statement about becoming a nation, and a similar reference to the promise of the land to the patriarchs to his own verse 9. In Deuteronomy 26:7 he also spoke about Yahweh, the God "of our fathers." Clearly, he was interested in not allowing verbal prominence to the model promise-fulfillment. In his view, presumably, this would have obscured the categories that really mattered.

A second model, with the help of which at least Deuteronomic theology and (in an elementary way) that the old source-documents interpret the course of history, is that of "enslavement" and "liberation from slavery." This has to do with legal processes which normally concerned individuals. A man could become a slave either licitly (through committing an offense) or illicitly (by abduction). Liberation could be effected by payment of a redemption price or by force (which in the case of illicit enslavement could be licit). In Israel, a specified relative, the redeemer (*go'el*), was responsible for the liberation of a member of his family who had become enslaved. The Israelites had been liberated from real slavery in Egypt; so to this extent we are not dealing with a model for the interpretation of history but with the historical event itself. A model is there, however, to the extent that we think not of an individual but a whole people. Moreover, the role of the liberating relative is played not by man but by God. D. Daube, in particular, has written in several publications about the various aspects of this model. It makes it possible for us to conceive of God's rule in history not so much as faithfulness to his own program as faithfulness to persons and groups.

In the credo, the model is prepared by the assertion that the patriarchs lived in Egypt as strangers. This indicates a certain legal status, similar to that of modern foreign workers—more restricted than the status of indigenous citizens but much wider than that of foreigners or slaves, who had no legal rights at all. The assertion sums up the content of Genesis 47:1-50. And then, in a crescendo comprising three statements, Deuteronomy 26:6 defines the Egyptians' violation of rights through which they enslaved the Israelites. Deuteronomy 26:8 proclaims the liberation from slavery by Yahweh. In legal language, the phrase "to bring out" is the technical term for "to free a slave." The liberation was effected not by paying a redemption price but by threat of the use of force, which was legitimate because the enslavement of the people by Egypt had been illegitimate. Here we see clearly how the separate

Salvation History

elements in the statement interweave and, together, make the model into a pure form. But one thing is lacking: the Israelites are not designated the kindred of Yahweh, nor he their *go'el*. This may be connected with the fact that, for the final Deuteronomic editor, the enslavement-liberation model was not first in rank. He used it only insofar as it could be linked with the model he regarded as most important, which begins only with the relationship inaugurated between Israel and Yahweh.

This model involves the connection between distress and help. A man or a group is in distress; their resources are insufficient to overcome the distress; they cry for help. Another man or group hears their cry for help and sees their distress, and hurries to their rescue. This sequence of interactions is frequently experienced by men, and in no set institutionalized form. It embodies a primitive human situation. It is the model of the religious situation when men cry to God for help and experience God's intervention. This experience can develop spontaneously at the individual level, but in religion it is usually found in an institutionalized form, that is, with cultic expression. In Israel, it may be said to have reached its perfect form in what can be called the "lamentation liturgy" of the people. In time of collective oppression, a common lamentation is instituted so that the people may experience corporate liberation. To this category belong several types of Old Testament texts, e.g., the lamentation songs of the people and the prophets' promises of salvation, in which we can distinguish four phases:

1. The Common distress
2. The common lament addressed to Yahweh
3. The transcending experience: Yahweh hears the cry, sees the distress
4. The saving intervention of Yahweh in the sphere of history

The Yahwist had already applied this model to interpret the exodus tradition; the Elohist used it in Numbers 20:14f in a short credo-like statement, which may well have been taken as the literary pattern for Deuteronomy 26:6-8. In terms of this model, Yahweh is seen as the God who spontaneously responds to a concrete situation. And in the lamentation liturgies and the Yahwist, at all events, the motif of Israel's belonging to Yahweh through kindred is employed. On the level of primitive human experience, the model can easily be linked with that of enslavement-liberation. Forced slavery becomes precisely the situation of distress and oppression, which provokes the cry for help.

That the model "distress-help" in the credo of Deuteronomy 26:5-9 represents the chief principle for the interpretation of history becomes clear from the very fact that organization is determined by this model in triads of statements. Groups I and II are preparatory in tone, as shown by the objectivity of their formulation in the third person. Statement group III describes the situation, of distress in Egypt; group IV tells first of the lament of the Israelites and then Yahweh's hearing their cry and seeing their distress; group V speaks of Yahweh's salvific intervention. Because the structure of the text is so closely bound up with the "phase structure" of the model, we have to conclude that not only Deuteronomy 26:8 (concerning the bringing or leading out from Egypt) but also the two statements in Deuteronomy 26:9 (concerning the movement to Jerusalem and taking possession of the land of Canaan) must be understood as a description of the salvific intervention of Yahweh. This lends weight to our concluding considerations.

The dominant words of Deuteronomy 26:7 recall the phrasing of the liturgical lament. "Cry," "hear," "see," "misery," "toil," "oppression"—all of these terms are found in the songs of lamentation and in related texts. In part, they had already been introduced into the ancient sources of the Pentateuch in the context of the exodus, but the author of Deuteronomy 26:5-9 makes more systematic use of the vocabulary of the lamentation festivals. Deuteronomy 26:6 was designed as a preparation for verse 7.

The reason why the Israelites turned to Yahweh in their hour of distress is indicated: he is "the God of our fathers." This in turn leads to the question: Why does Yahweh appear for the first time only at this point in the credo? Even if the opening statement—containing no mention of Yahweh—was already there, why did the Deuteronomic enlarger of the text not represent the creation of the nation as the work of Yahweh?

The Relationship between Man's Action and Yahweh's Action

The history of mankind is a confused happening, suffused by many causal sequences and never totally transparent to us. Whenever it is assumed that divine direction and divine purpose lie behind history, the question must arise: How can divine action in history be combined with the obscure complexity of the mundane historical process? This question must have been raised very early in Israel, for even in Solomon's time the authors of the story of the succession to David's throne and the Joseph saga in Genesis had developed very subtle narrative methods in order, on one hand, not to diminish the earthly reality of the chain of events and, on the other, to allow the whole of history to be seen as secretly directed by Yahweh. Gerhard von Rad has demonstrated this in several studies. It is therefore not impossible that, some centuries later, the author of the credo text in Deuteronomy 26:5-9 was conditioned by similar motives when he formulated his text in such a way that a whole constellation of forms and affirmations emerged, with which there is nothing comparable in any other credo text in the Old Testament.

Let us again specify the elements in this constellation:

1. The text does not speak of a few clearly definable events, but has in mind the whole span of Israelite history up to the time of David.

2. The intervention of Yahweh in history is developed in terms of a single model, and other, traditional models are either avoided or reduced. This single model is help in distress as response to cultic lamentation.

3. Within the framework of this model, however, all of history from Moses to David is regarded as Yahweh's salvific intervention in response to Israel's cry for help in Egypt.

4. The text of the whole prayer is so structured as to make even the harvests of later times—the specific occasion of the prayer—appear as the redemptive approach of Yahweh in response to the lament by the Israelites in Egypt.

Various older, roughly contemporaneous historical summaries speak in a sheerly profane manner of earthly agents of the historical process and introduce reference to Yahweh's intervention only when they come to the exodus. To this class belong principally the summaries, most of which are ascribed to the Elohist (Gn 15:13-16, Nm 20:15f, Mi 6:4f). Without a qualm, the much-cited text of Joshua 24:2-13 allows Yahweh and the most varied assortment of earthly actors to operate cheek by jowl, so that Yahweh appears almost like one of the historical factors. A cyclical alternation between human and divine action marks the Deuteronomic survey in 1 Samuel 12:8-12: Israel cries out in distress; Yahweh sends a savior and help is given through this savior; then Israel sins again and in punishment Yahweh sends fresh distress; Israel cries out again; and the cycle starts all over again. Other texts describe all the events they record as the action of Yahweh, departing from this principle (if at all) only when sins must be mentioned. Behind the structure of our credo text in Deuteronomy 26:5-9 seems to lie an independent cogitation on the relationship between Yahweh's action in history and the mundane course of history. This may be summed up as follows.

1. The history of the people of Israel may be made up of many separate events and their linkage: Yahweh's action upon Isreal is a single action. Thus he is not detectable at this or that juncture in history, as if he were not to be found in others. Rather, he is to be discovered nowhere and yet everywhere, for his action embraces all ages.

2. The action of Yahweh is by no means purely historical. Its effects are to be seen in the fecundity of nature. For this very reason, it does not end with David but makes possible ever recurring harvest thanksgiving festivals, at which the "little historical credo" is recited.

3. Yahweh's relationship to Israel, which is realized in history, is best expressed by the experiential model of the savior in time of distress.

4. We may ask whether the period from Moses to David, whose chief events the credo must mention to give verbal expression to its affirmations about history, may not have a special status, which is

comparable with the primeval age of the mythical religions and philosophical systems. This would be to affirm that Yahweh's action in other periods of history could never be more than repetitions of, and participation in, this primordial action of Yahweh on behalf of Israel.

Conclusions

All of this shows that the "little historical credo" of Deuteronomy 26:5-9 is quite other than a brief summary of the Hexateuch. It is like a consciously composed key for interpretation of the Hexateuch, the following historical books, and all possible future events in the history of Israel. Are we, then, to describe the interpretation as "salvation-historical"?

That depends very much on our definition of "salvation history." Most current definitions do not correspond to this interpretation—certainly not one that distinguishes Israel's "religion of history" from cultically shaped "nature religions." This credo allows human and divine historical actions to merge, without disruption, in the fecundity of the fields, and links itself precisely through the liturgical *Sitz im Leben* of which it makes use—the harvest thanksgiving festival—with the cycle of the natural year.

It does indeed lack all concept of evolution, ascent, and progress. A greater future never comes into view. Is that a mistake? We are tempted to think so, and we can cite other texts from the Old Testament which turn Israel's eyes to a future that will bring new and greater things, such as Yahweh had never performed in the past. But they stand, nonetheless, alongside texts such as this, which until recently has been accounted an exhibition piece of the salvation-historical thinking of Israel—in a sense, moreover, that seems very plausible to the man of today. And even if on closer examination of the whole of the Old Testament—of the whole Bible, indeed—these things are proved to be more important and more comprehensive, they must be seen relative to the text we are at present considering. This text must also be read when the others are declaimed.

Old Testament exegesis may have to learn to spell again. It will have to look again at other texts, hitherto naively claimed as heralds of "salvation history," in order to question them more closely about their theology of history. Only then may it again look for a synthesis and offer itself as a purveyor to systematic theology.

Liberation

Old Testament Ideas and the Theology of Liberation

From Latin America, in particular, waves of a "theology of liberation" beat upon our shores. The phrase allies itself with another that has been on all lips for a long time now, "emancipation." And other old words also appear suddenly with new meanings: "redemption" and "salvation," for example, as used nowadays by "depth psychologists."

Christianity is regarded as a religion of redemption. Even if only as a tract beside others, a doctrine of redemption, called "soteriology," is always found in systematic theologies. But what is written there seems far removed from all that the new words conjure up. Man is to be redeemed from sin, and his redemption will become manifest after death, in the hereafter.

This soteriology is derived ultimately from the New Testament; the Old Testament plays a more modest part in it. This also holds true of particular scholarly studies, which, on the basis of this soteriology, have probed the Old Testament. These studies have confined their interest to specific, set themes. They ask, for example, if Israel was conscious of original sin, from which one must be redeemed by Christ. They ask, further, whether and in what degree Israel had the expectation of a coming savior—a "messianic hope," as it is called—or whether Israel was awaiting a spiritual, universal, otherworldly, and final redemption. Besides this, there has been examination of the prehistory of New Testament soteriological terminology, especially the use of the Hebrew words *padah* and *go'el,* from which the word "redeemer" is derived.

Suddenly, people became aware that this type of very basic study ignored central topics of the faith of Israel. This awareness dawned when Ernst Bloch, in Christian lectures, began to thunder about the God

Liberation

of the exodus, who symbolized a thoroughly this-worldly hope, and when the theologians of revolution and liberation invoked the Old Testament in support of their new soteriology. And it was impossible to say to them: The foundation upon which you build does not exist.

It *did* exist. Israel *did* believe in a this-worldly salvation. The Decalogue, a central text of the Old Testament, begins thus: "I am Yahweh, your God, who led you out of Egypt, out of the house of bondage." And we must take note that *hosi'*, the Hebrew equivalent of "to lead out," was a legal term, meaning to free a slave—that is, *emancipatio,* in the original sense of that word. When later, in the Babylonian Exile, that prophetic literature, deutero-Isaiah, composed for the whole cosmos, for all peoples together with their gods, a mighty oratorio of world history, this had a single and thoroughly concrete theme: Keep hoping, for your serfdom is coming to an end! Babylon will fall! You will become free, and be able to return home!

This is central Old Testament preaching of redemption. It proclaims liberation from foreign rule and forced labor. It looks for salvation on this earth; for the healing of bodies, not souls; for the salvation of the nation and society, and not merely the individual. The theology of liberation asserts that none of this has been automatically pushed aside by the New Testament and replaced by a spiritualized, otherworldly hope. In my opinion, this assertion is justified. It must base its assertion upon the New Testament; but at the same time it has compelled us to take a fresh and more comprehensive and serious look at Old Testament soteriology.

The manner in which "philosophers of the future" and theologians of liberation employ the Old Testament can be explained only on the assumption that world revolution is at our very door, and putting it into effect leaves no time for closer examination. When Ernst Bloch arranges the texts of the Old Testament, according to their tenor, into two categories, associating one with the evil Lord God of the priests and the other with the God of Exodus, who ushers in the future, he is creating his own canon within the canon. Because the liberation theologians seldom get beyond global generalizations, they usually overlook the fact that in the Old Testament it is Yahweh, not men, who brings about the alteration of the world. When Hellmut Gollwitzer combines the Exodus saying with Genesis 1:28, in order to expunge from the system the embarrassment of such a *solus* Jehovah, all literary-historical differentiation is jettisoned and one is left with a theology of conclusions. It is not only traditional soteriology that leaves much to be desired in its approach to the Old Testament!

Let us, then, attempt to examine more closely what the Old Testament contains in the way of soteriology. In the most recent strata of the Old Testament is evidence of an expectation of resurrection and of what we call "apocalypticism." Let us set these aside. There remains, however, that whole, well-differentiated area of religious behavior and belief which we call "Israel," in the classical sense, which demands further review. With this, let us extend our thinking beyond the institutional basis of experience and try, in a second part, to discern important literary sketches of soteriology.

What we possess today are texts that speak about salvation. But the texts, principally the psalms, give us glimpses of recurring situations and circumstances in which Israel originally expressed experiences of salvation. These moorings (so to speak) for the experience of salvation disclose themselves only at two removes from the texts, but they should be sketched in briefly before their significance in the texts is described.

Sin, Atonement, and Forgiveness in Liturgy

This institutional context is still the best known; hence it suffices to examine it briefly.

From the time of the exile onward, the sense of sin and the cult of atonement greatly increased, and in the end were joined to ideas which originally had nothing at all to do with them, for example, the idea of "covenant." On the whole, however, we are dealing with concepts that were extant in Israel in every epoch.

Moreover, we may not count on finding a universal and all-embracing concept of sin, such as we have. We find, rather, several juxtaposed and variously designated types of action which throw men or society out of order. As diverse as the names they were given were the personal and ritual techniques that were employed to restore order before God and society. Ritual "purity tabu," which likewise had to be removed ritually, was part of this, just as much as genuine moral failure, for which one had to seek forgiveness through penance, prayer, and sacrifice. Only he who was *saddiq,* whom one found to be "righteous" at the entrance of the sanctuary, could take part in the liturgy. When sin had been expiated and forgiven; when it had been carried away, removed, and thrown out; when no memory of it was left, because God had healed a man of his sin; when the Israelite once again took part in the praise of God within the circle of the congregation, he must have had that experience with which today's psychologists would probably associate the words "redemption" and "salvation."

Oppressive sin had been recognized and named by the sinner himself and by the representative of the community. It had been objectified in a rite—in a thing, indeed, such as a sacrificial animal—and thus detached from the sinner. The man had left something behind him and was once again accepted by his fellow men, even by God. The man was *himself* again.

This applied to the individual. But it also applied to the whole of Israel when it concerned the recognition of national guilt and its national expiation.

Distress and Complaint, Help and Thanksgiving in the Liturgy

This is the most important institutional group of experiences in all of Israel's experience of salvation, and it provides the key to the most important of the broad soteriological schemes in the Old Testament. This area of thought corresponds to the supplication, pilgrimages, making of vows, votive offerings following an answer to prayer, and other similar acts in traditional Christian practice.

The custom of complaint and thanksgiving comes alive to us chiefly in the prayers of supplication and thanksgiving which we find both within and apart from the Psalter, and also in isolated allusions in the narrative and prophetic writings. When reviewing this material, one has to distinguish between the supplication and thanksgiving of the individual in his private and domestic concerns and the supplication and thanksgiving of the community in public affairs. A special form is found in the supplication and thanksgiving of the king, in several psalms.

The characteristic feature of this kind of experience is best discussed with reference to the first half of Psalm 18, a song of thanksgiving by an individual. This text may also have been the formula of a royal thanksgiving liturgy. In the introduction to Psalm 18 the word "save" appears and the definitive motif of the psalm is announced thus:

1. I love you, Yahweh, my strength.
2. Yahweh is my rock and my bastion,
    my deliverer is my God.
   I take shelter in him, my rock,
    my shield, my horn of salvation,
   my stronghold and my refuge.
3. On Yahweh I call
    and am saved from my enemies.

Then follows, in thanksgiving, an account of an act of deliverance from distress. We must note, too, the strict sequence of events, for we will meet it over and over again in similar circumstances: distress; man cries for help; Yahweh hears the cry; Yahweh intervenes, saving and healing. Over and above this, we must take note of the mythologically colored imagery. Distress is seen as the power of death, the underworld, engulfing waters; Yahweh's intervention is seen as the coming down of a thunderstorm from on high, as engagement in a kind of battle with chaos, with the evil waters that are under the earth. This Canaanite

Liberation

mythological imagery of the battle of Baal with chaos expressed what rational theology calls "the conservation," as distinct from "the creation," of the world. Man in distress sees the cosmos dissolving in chaos about him. When help comes, order returns to the cosmos: the Lord of the world has joined in the battle:

4. [Distress] The waves of death encircled me,
   the torrents of Belial burst on me;

5. the cords of Sheol girded me,
   the snares of death were before me.

6. [Cry] In my distress I called to Yahweh
   and to my God I cried;

   [He hears] from his Temple he heard my voice,
   my cry came to his ears.

7. [Mythical interlude] Then the earth quivered and quaked,
   the foundations of the mountains trembled
   [they quivered because he was angry];

8. from his nostrils smoke ascended,
   and from his mouth a fire that consumed
   [live embers were kindled in it].

9. He bent the heavens and came down,
   a dark cloud under his feet;

10. he mounted a cherub and flew,
    and soared on the wings of the wind.

11. Darkness he made a veil to surround him,
    his tent a watery darkness, dense cloud;

12. before him a flash enkindled
    hail and fiery embers.

13. Yahweh thundered from heaven,
    the Most High made his voice heard;

14. he let his arrows fly and scattered them,
    launched the lightnings and routed them.

15. The bed of the seas was revealed,
    the foundations of the world were laid bare,
    at your muttered threat, Yahweh,
    at the blast of your nostrils' breath.

16. [Salvation] He sends from on high and takes me,
    he draws me from deep waters,

The long poetical narrative does not really make clear the nature of the distress. The only hint is found at the end of the prefatory verse—the caption "my enemies."

And now we come to a summary of the description of saving acts, which is a little more concrete:

17. He delivers me from my powerful enemy,
    from a foe too strong for me.

18. They assailed me on my day of disaster,
    but Yahweh was my support;

19. he freed me, set me at large,
    he rescued me, since he loves me.

A large number of terms having to do with redemption and salvation are found in this summary. It is from this language of the complaint and thanksgiving ritual that the soteriologies of salvation history derive their concepts.

A word more about "enemies." Psalm 18 is obviously dealing with deliverance from real enemies, but behind them lurks *the* enemy, viz. death, which is identified with empty but all-engulfing chaos. In other psalms, notably in songs of complaint of the sick, human enemies likewise play an important part, although deliverance from distress in battle is not the issue. Much has been written on who these enemies really were and why they played such a prominent part in Israel's lamentation. Most stimulating of all, perhaps, is Othmar Keel's *Feinde und Gottesleugner* (Stuttgart, 1969), which shows that these prayers are far from factual descriptions; they are, rather, objectified projections of the fear of the man at prayer. In the prayers of the Mesopotamian world, terrifying descriptions of sorcerers and demons were fabricated as images of the enemy. The Egyptians, in their prayers, expressed terror at the prospect of vengeance and malice emanating from the still-active dead in another world. The believer in Yahweh was denied all such superstition; thus he knew of only one ultimate enemy: nothingness, in the shape of death, and its incarnation in hostile men.

If this hypothesis is correct, we may ask whether even Psalm 18 could be used only as a prayer of thanksgiving after deliverance in battle. We may be obliged, instead, to reckon with a very expansive type of imagery in which one sphere of experience can stand for another and in which, moreover, no distinction is drawn between material and spiritual, but even the spiritual appears in objective, this-worldly images. This is important if one is to avoid thinking naively that linguistic elements, taken from warfare and revolution, apply only to war and revolution.

The last line of verse 19 (quoted above) leads us to quote a few more verses from Psalm 18. The traditionally minded Christian reader will find them irritating, with their linking—on the one hand—of sin and forgiveness and—on the other—distress and deliverance. The psalmist is asking, in fact, why Yahweh has saved him in so marvelous a fashion. His answer runs thus:

> 20. Yahweh requites me as I act justly,
>   as my hands are pure so he repays me,

21. since I have kept the ways of Yahweh,
    nor fallen away from my God.

22. His judgments are all before me,
    his statutes I have not put from me;

23. I am blameless in his presence,
    I keep sin at arm's length.

24. And Yahweh repays me as I act justly,
    as my purity is in his sight.

Let me say at once: This is not always the tone of a lamentation and thanksgiving song. Distress is often seen to result from one's own sin and forgiveness of sin is implored. Fundamentally, it is assumed that removal of guilt and deliverance from distress are identical. But this psalm (and a few others) shows that things can be otherwise. And so for the Israel of the psalms there is no necessary connection between sin and distress, between forgiveness of sins and deliverance, salvation, redemption. This fact is not without importance for either the salvation-historical soteriologies of the Old Testament or their offspring, Christian soteriology.

Statements about Redemption from the Sion Ideology in the Jerusalem Liturgy

Who gave expression on behalf of Israel to what is described as "salvation" and on what occasion was it done? When one feels one's way from the key words and affirmations of the hymn of lamentation and thanksgiving and gropes toward other texts, one soon encounters new catchwords, notably *beraka* (blessing) and *salom* (peace, well-being). In addition, one finds a few words that are exceedingly difficult to translate, words like *sedaqa* (righteousness, order, innocence).

If we remain within the Psalter, there too we find songs which sing the praises of a reality that is felt to be righteous. This is constantly related to groups of affirmations which, in biblical theology, are described as reflections of the Sion ideology. These are texts that speak of Yahweh's throne on Mt. Sion and of the blessed rule that he, or the king he has appointed in Jerusalem, exerts from that place.

We will find these notions making a deep imprint upon the later exilic and postexilic expectation of a worldwide redemption effected by the action of Yahweh. Several studies of this Sion ideology have appeared in recent years and the most diverse conclusions have been reached, especially on the age and ancestry of these notions. This demonstrates that the entire field still eludes our comprehension. At the moment, however, we are interested more in the content than the history or tradition of Sion ideology.

In this ideology, the word "blessing" links up with motifs of plenty and fecundity. "Peace" is made concrete in the divine rule that flows from Jerusalem. First, all resistant peoples will be subjugated. All weapons will be destroyed. Men are filled with joy and burst into song. God, enthroned at the center, radiates his light on all.

Here we again recognize individual features of primitive mythology, such as the throne of God in the high north, the throne of the Creator. Other features derive from Israelite traditions, such as the worthlessness of human weapons in face of the power of Yahweh.

This is the point: Israel describes its salvation as an earthly salvation, but it uses mythical language to describe what is earthly. When Israel assembled for a festival and everything in the land was going well, Yahweh was enthroned in Sion, from whence he showered blessings on all peoples, who filled the earth with laughter and the clapping of hands.

To do justice to this kind of language, hermeneutics must say that such final and absolute affirmations could be made only if, in essence, they said principally that Yahweh himself, as the One who is present for Israel, is Israel's salvation. Accepting such an interpretation, however, one must never forget that Yahweh is fully existent for Israel, to the extent that the world is wholesome.

Education and Its Theory of the Connection between Actions and Reward

As early as the second millennium B.C., the whole of the ancient Orient had accepted a philosophy which believed in a relentless law that was woven into the fabric of events. At the creation, fixed ordinances had been embedded in the cosmos. If, in their actions, men adhered to these laws, they reaped blessings from their actions. If they departed from these laws, they brought upon themselves—and upon the whole world—a curse, misery, and premature death.

Through proverbial wisdom, the doctrine of a connection between action and reward had long since penetrated the common conscience. The educated found it in their school textbooks. Only in comparatively late Wisdom literature in Israel do we find the factual basis for this universal conviction's being called in question and contrary conceptions proposed. Job clung to the unfathomable greatness of God; Qoheleth, the preacher, abandoned himself to the blessings of the moment; the Wisdom of Solomon looks for a just settlement beyond the grave. But in earlier times Israel had accepted as law a connection between action and reward—and what is more, *in this life*.

As far as Israel's understanding of salvation is concerned, this means that salvation is bound up with morality; that before bestowing his blessing, Yahweh could demand righteousness. This is the starting point for the social preaching of the prophets. Deuteronomic theology translates this philosophy into the category of a contract between Israel and God. In Assyrian culture at that time, such categories were in the air. The ritual of concluding a treaty and regular acquaintance with treaties and contracts impressed these concepts on all.

These ideas sharpened moral awareness but also heightened perplexity, for Israel had obviously failed to keep Yahweh's law and had broken his covenant, and as the destruction of Jerusalem proved—that is, the destruction of Sion, which was the throne of God in redemption imagery—all hope of salvation was lost. From this perplexity the largest and most significant parts of the Old Testament developed. Perplexity was overcome, however. Eyes were turned toward the future, from which was expected a new, incalculable, and greater redemptive action of Yahweh.

But this leads finally to texts on soteriological theories—to some extent, to broad historical sketches—and our discussion of important institutionalized experiences of salvation is more limited. We stress the importance of these experiences. Israelites could relive them over and over again. They could repeatedly interiorize—make their own—what was offered to them as experience in their educational systems, in traditional speech and rites. Fundamentally, these socially buttressed experiences carried more weight than the texts we will now discuss, which are largely no more than literary pieces.

Who were the people who read what the Yahwist wrote? Did even a deutero-Isaiah enjoy the prestige we now accord him? Later, certainly, because they were recited as "holy scripture" within the liturgy, these writings, too, became the mediators of a common experience. All that survives for us are these texts, and not the laboriously created original institutions and the mediation of religious experience which they provided.

Redemption—Story Additions to the Narrative Books

In what follows I do not propose to describe an evolution from simple to ever more perfect soteriological systems. There is no such thing. The early Yahwist already stands alone on a summit. Deutero-Isaiah was writing at the same time as the priest-writer, but both set about writing in a totally different manner. Hence we shall present only a few types of soteriological schemes, and not in their historical sequence. Nor is the typology, oriented principally towards the modern slogan, "liberation," complete.

The first and most obvious type is the transposition of the popular lamentation ritual into the form of a story, occasioned by an actual incident of deliverance.

The second genre, narrative, is already one of the elements in the thanksgiving hymn. In the hymn, however, it is, as a rule, elevated into a type—to the plane of myth, in fact—as the example from Psalm 18 has shown. It is bound to be used, it is true, in connection with many concrete events, as soon as the prayer becomes a prayer formula. However, when a writer creates a narrative about a deliverance, it becomes concrete. It focuses attention upon a historical event in its uniqueness.

The story of a deliverance may be quite short and yet demonstrate, by its very language, that it is derived from the lamentation ritual—for example, a story of deliverance at the beginning of the Book of Judges:

> The Israelites cried to Yahweh, and Yahweh raised up for the Israelites a deliverer who rescued them, Othniel son of Kenaz, Caleb's younger brother. The spirit of Yahweh came on him; he became judge in Israel and set out to fight. Yahweh delivered the king of Edom, Cushan-rishathaim, into his hands, and he overcame Cushan-rishathaim. [Jg 3:9f]

In the later, Deuteronomic revision of the Book of Judges, the interpretation of the old stories, very often arising originally from sheer delight in story telling, becomes much clearer with the help of the lamentation ritual. An important fact is that several such tales could be told one after the other. Being saved from distress, and especially deliverance from the attack of enemy armies and conquerors, did not happen only once and never again; unfortunately, oppression by enemies came repeatedly. And so Israel was forever crying out to Yahweh, and Yahweh again and again sent deliverers and liberated his people.

The story of deliverance from Egypt, too, originally belonged to this simple type of soteriology. Certainly this was the first deliverance of all

Israel, and the incident was stylized as an act of deliverance by Yahweh at a very early date and with particular clarity. Nonetheless, the deliverance from Egypt takes its place as one in a series of Yahweh's acts of deliverance. In the Yahwist stratum of writing, it was already described in the well-known phrases from the lamentation liturgy as the redeeming act of Yahweh. For from the heart of the burning thornbush, Yahweh says to Moses:

> I have seen the miserable state of my people in Egypt. I have heard their appeal to be free of their slave drivers. Yes, I am well aware of their sufferings. I mean to deliver them out of the hands of the Egyptians and bring them up out of that land to a land rich and broad, a land where milk and honey flow, the home of the Canaanites, the Hittites, the Amorites, the Perizzites, the Hivites, and the Jebusites. [Ex 3:7f.]

Although the Yahwist described all the events in the exodus from Egypt as a single act of liberation, he composed a special tale of deliverance from the story of the destruction of the Egyptians in the Sea of Reeds. According to Exodus 14:14, the Israelites were terrified when they saw the Egyptians approaching, and they *cried out* to Yahweh. At the end, the Yahwist sums up the story: "That day, Yahweh rescued Israel from the Egyptians" (Ex 14:30).

We cannot, on the basis of the old Pentateuch documents, point to an Old Testament soteriology that is founded upon a single redemptive act at the very beginning of the nation's history. But is is precisely that which Deuteronomy tried to do, and did, moreover, in the "little historical credo" and again, in a different way, in the priestly writings.

The Once-for-All Exodus Act

The confession of faith in Deuteronomy 26:5-9, according to the law in the framework in which it comes down to us, was to be recited before

Yahweh by the Israelite at the harvest thanksgiving festival. Apart from the first sentence, the text rests upon the key theological concepts of the old Pentateuch stories. The allusions to the lamentation and thanksgiving liturgies are plainly developed, and history is consciously interpreted as a liberation—and redemptive—event:

5. [Prehistory] My father was a wandering Aramaean.
   He went down into Egypt,
   lived there as a stranger, few in numbers;
   but there he became a nation, great, mighty, and strong.

6. [Distress] The Egyptians ill treated us,
   they took our rights away
   and inflicted harsh slavery on us.

7. [Cry] But we called on Yahweh, the God of our fathers.
   [Yahweh hears] Yahweh heard our voice
   and saw our misery, our toil and our oppression.

8. [Intervention and help] Yahweh brought us out of Egypt
   with mighty hand and outstretched arm, with great terror,
   and with signs of wonder.

9. He brought us here
   and gave us this land, a land where milk and honey flow.

In Deuteronomic language, "this place" ("here") is none other than Jerusalem, where stands the temple, in which this confession is recited. Thus Yahweh's intervention runs like a great arc across the centuries—from the wonders worked at the exodus from Egypt down to the time of David and Solomon, who had, respectively, conquered Jerusalem and built the temple there. The arc stretches further, indeed—to the very moment in which this particular Israelite presents his gifts and recites this prayer; for, following the key phrase, "where milk and honey flow," the confession turns into the prayer:

Liberation

> 10. Here then I bring the first fruits
> of the produce of the soil that you,
> Yahweh, have given me.

Only at this point, at the harvest thanksgiving festival in progress at this precise moment, does the redemptive event, begun in Egypt, come to an end. The land has yielded its blessing; men live by this blessing; the cry of lament, rising from the slaves in Egypt, has been fully heard. This conception knows only a single redemptive act of Yahweh on behalf of Israel: liberation; but this liberation is realized in present well-being.

The problem posed by this conception is that it occurs within the framework of the Deuteronomic law, in which there is a conditional blessing and a conditional curse. Blessing or curse depends upon whether Israel obeys the law. Israel is saved, through no action of its own; but whether it remains in this blessed state depends entirely upon Israel itself.

This soteriological conception appears in the exilic and postexilic period and again in the priestly chronicles of the Hexateuch. According to this conception, it was being brought out of Egypt that first constituted Israel, the people of Yahweh. The goal of that deliverance was to lead them into the land of Canaan (Ex 6:2–8), and all of this is encapsulated in Yahweh's covenant promise to Abraham (Gn 17:7–8). This assures Abraham's posterity possession of the land of Canaan *forever,* for this is the significance of the phrase "from generation to generation." As the stories of sins in Numbers 13f and 20 show, a whole generation can be excluded from this promise, but in succeeding generation the promise can be restored and the people can set foot in the promised land. God's redemptive design for Israel outlasts any apostasy of the people. Here we see the weakness of the Deuteronomic conception overcome by a new version of the theology of the covenant.

If in this theology the word "exodus" is replaced by "Christ event," the conception of many Christian theologians is not very different, except that in Deuteronomy everything is much more concrete, for the substance of redemption is inhabiting the land and eating its fruits, unmolested by enemies.

The Yahwist and Curse and Blessing in National History

The Yahwist may have stylized the exodus simply as one deliverance among many others because, for him, redemption no longer presented itself as a question concerning Israel alone. With him, it achieved a wider horizon. He never doubted that Israel, as the people of Yahweh, was in a state of salvation; but he posed the question of redemption with his eye upon all the peoples of the world. In this, if our usual dating is correct, he is the far-seeing man at the court of David and Solomon, when, for a brief moment, Israel had risen to the height of a great empire.

The Yahwist makes no contact with the lamentation ritual. He uses it only to interpret Israel's destiny. He is guided much more by motifs from Sion theology or its precursor, and also by motifs in Wisdom literature.

In his primeval history, the Yahwist speaks of the situation of all mankind. Mankind fell progressively under a curse because it committed more and more sins. With his call of Abraham, Yahweh—God of all peoples—casts a ray of light into the world's darkness. They key text is Genesis 12:1-3:

> Yahweh said to Abraham, "Leave your country, your family and your father's house, for the land I will show you. I will make you a great nation; I will bless you and make your name so famous that it will be used as a blessing.
>
> > "I will bless those who bless you;
> > I will curse those who slight you.
> > All the tribes of the earth
> > shall bless themselves by you."

This text is followed by the sagas of the patriarchs, which show in a concrete way how Abraham and his posterity were able to mediate a blessing to other peoples. They prayed for them, as Abraham did for the righteous in Sodom. They made peace treaties, as Isaac and Abimelech

Liberation

did, instead of waging war over waterholes. They helped starving people find bread, as Joseph did in Egypt. All of these things are totally this-worldly. The mythical codes of Sion theology are to some extent translated into concrete terms by an authentic interpreter.

Yet another point is worth noting, and Gerhard von Rad in particular has drawn attention to it in his commentary on Genesis. In the Yahwist narratives, men do not really understand the way in which they will be used as instruments of Yahweh's blessing. They constantly get into difficulties as a result of their decisions. But Yahweh knows how to bestow his blessing in spite of men. Here the Yahwist, having recourse in part to the more realistic views of the old proverbial wisdom, goes beyond that philosophy—which had guided him to begin with—and follows the strict sin-curse logic of his primeval history.

Both of the first two types of soteriological thought that we have examined present a completely static view of the world: situations of distress were sicknesses that had to be healed. With the Yahwist, world history for the first time is set in motion. And so it is with this type of soteriology: for the first time, it becomes possible to draw parallels with a modern, this-worldly-oriented theology of salvation.

However, two typical modern elements are lacking in the Yahwist's concept. He takes no account of the possibility of man's being able to alter the world; it is Yahweh who does this, cutting across man's good, yet false, intentions. And it never occurs to the Yahwist that man might be able to alter the fixed structure of reality, perhaps restoring a lost paradise.

It seems to me that he slants his story toward the problem of the unity of mankind, which existed in paradise. At the Tower of Babel, men wanted to create that unity themselves, through the power structure of a mighty empire that would bind mankind together. The tower and the city are the symbols of this. But the enterprise collapsed, and men were scattered over the earth and disunited. The blessing Yahweh has in mind for men is of a different sort. He does not annul the diversity of peoples.

Thus modern theologies of peace could appeal to the Yahwist only with reservations, for they count on a peace that men themselves can create. Whoever wants to establish peace by force of a supranational political system is contradicted, moreover, by the story of the Tower of Babel. And a "theology of revolution" would get short shrift from the Yahwist.

Eschatological Soteriology and World Structures

Suddenly, the Babylonian Exile brought affirmations of redemption that were oriented toward the future. It was these affirmations, above all, that were able to resolve the crisis of a static belief in redemption, which the fall of Jerusalem had precipitated.

We must not, however, allow the poetic genius of a deutero-Isaiah or the motifs of the futurist Sion ideology (which blossomed in the other prophets) to blind us to the fact that this orientation toward the future did *not* inaugurate a new type of soteriology.

In the moment when these oracles were sounded, Israel was in deep distress. Hymns of lamentation resounded throughout the diaspora and among those who had been left behind in the homeland. It was still a feature of the liturgy of national lamentation to wait for the prophet to interrupt the lament and proclaim salvation, to declare that Yahweh had heard the cry and would soon intervene. That was all these prophets had done. But now they wrote it down, because their hearers were scattered over the face of the earth.

That the proclamation of redemption is not restricted to Israel likewise has its foundation in Sion ideology and, centuries earlier, had enriched the soteriological scheme of the Yahwist. In deutero-Isaiah, a new element may be that he cancels the once-for-all affirmation of the Deuteronomic Exodus theology and claims a once-for-all, final character for the redemption from Babel, which he preaches. But can we say that this is more than a telescoping of time, enacted in the cult—an example of a once-for-all being made present, which by no means excludes actual repetition?

Liberation

There may be yet another new element in Isaiah. For him, the return home of the nations under Yahweh's rule is effected by their amazement at the fate of Israel. Accordingly, Israel is seen as the nation that has become totally good for nothing as the servant of Yahweh, and that, by its own fault, has fallen into the deepest humiliation, from which Yahweh will have to save it. Even this idea was in embryo in the Yahwist's writings. All that has been said about deutero-Isaiah applies even more to the other prophecies about the future that belong to that epoch.

On the whole, the so-called eschatological prophecies that flourished from the period of the exile onward display, perhaps, only a few small features that might represent something typologically new, and one hesitates even about these. It is a question of statements of content. Fundamental structures were being changed.

As long as we are dealing with cosmic imagery, the usual mythical concept may persist, according to which nothing in the cosmos is secure. But now other features often emerge. In the Book of Ezekiel is a proposed constitution which divides the land of Israel in the future in a strangely geometrical—one might almost say inhuman—fashion (Ez 40-48). In deutero-Isaiah (Is 55:3-5) the old promises to David are consciously applied to the whole of Israel. In the coming redemption, will there no longer be a king? Something like this seems to be meant in a certain stratum of Ezekiel 34 (the meaning becomes narrowed in later accretions to the text), where Yahweh relieves the shepherds of his people of their office and makes himself their shepherd. Finally, in Jerimiah 31:31-34, we hear his incomprehensible saying about the "new" covenant, which is to be different from the old one:

> Deep within them I will plant my Law, writing it on their hearts.... There will be no further need for neighbor to teach neighbor, or brother to say to brother, "Learn to know Yahweh!" No, they will all know me, the least no less than the greatest" [Jer 31:33f].

Sayings of this kind may perhaps hint at the vision of a new society, founded upon a structure different from the one that prevailed at the moment. Here we might find pointers to such utopias as the "classless society" and to "nonauthoritarian communication." The proclamation, that is, of the rule of God as the abrogation of every kind of human rule and regimentation—a new immediacy, an end to all alienation.

If this interpretation is correct, and if the Old Testament, on the other hand, does not cease even here to speak of a this-worldly redemption, we might reach a point on which very basic modern theories of liberation and emancipation stand. But we only just reach this point, and there is always the problem of what to make of the fact that for these prophets it is always Yahweh alone—and never man—who brings salvation into the world.

Here we can look back and say that this last step had already been applied in the exodus experience, for a long period of laborious effort had to pass before this experience evolved. But perhaps we are right. At least in the spirit of later generations, who put the Old Testament together as a collection of writings and, in the process, conceived it as a unity, we may be allowed to read even the older types of soteriology with other eyes.

But we must not do this too quickly or too lightly. Moreover, when we do this we must be consistent and face the fact that, with an otherworldly hope and apocalyptic, we have to place yet another hermeneutic key signature in front of all the melodies we have already played. But this throws up new and difficult problems that cannot be solved here.

The People of God

The Old Testament and the Central Concept of the Council's Verbal Fireworks

Words are almost without number, but most of them are stored away in a drawer and scarcely ever brought out for use. Then one day some particular word has its hour. It is on all lips, and no one can do without it. Sometimes, within a few years, it becomes quite unexciting again.

Not many years ago the hour struck for the expression "the People of God." The new exegetes had started. In 1929 the Old Testament scholar Gerhard von Rad wrote his first book, *The People of God in Deuteronomy,* which immediately revealed the shape of this creature. Ten years later, Ernst Käsemann published his book, *The Pilgrim People of God.* The fact that others in Germany were making much use at that time of the word *Volk* may have exerted an influence. Then came publications that used the slogan "People of God" in ever rising crescendo. Most of all in ecumenically active theological circles, it became a key theme. Among Catholic theologians, it was launched as a counterbalance to the view of the Church as *Corpus Christi mysticum.* The pastoral liturgical movement, especially in France, took a great liking to the new expression in the fifties. Bishops carried it like a banner into the sessions of the Second Vatican Council. From there, for several years, it was unfurled before the whole Catholic world. As postconciliar euphoria died out, its popularity waned. Still, however, it stands in many documents, synodal texts, pastoral letters, and liturgical formulae. It is still dear to many preachers and to many groups on the fringe of the official Church. Letters addressed to "the People of God" still emanate from Taizé.

The People of God

Everyone was using it, but not in exactly the same way. It was sweet to some and sour to others. Individuals gave it different meanings. I observed this most clearly in 1968 and 1969 in the arguments I heard at close range concerning the congregation at Isolotto (Florence).

We are not concerned here with details. A priest, Don Mazzi, had built a truly living parish in a new workers' housing development, while the wind of the Council and biblical heurmeneutics was blowing. Because of the new shape of the liturgy, the style of lay participation, the content of religious instruction and, finally, the congregation's public attitude, tensions arose with the cardinal-bishop of Florence. In the public argument which soon followed, the slogan was constantly sounded: "the People of God." The cardinal represented the thesis that, as a people, the people of God possess juridical structures. Among the people of God, the *Codex Juris Canonici* applies and, as a pastor, Don Mazzi ought to obey his bishop; an archbishop does not receive delegations from a parish that holds popular assemblies and has "democratized" itself. Against this, Don Mazzi and his parishioners said: We are poor people, poor people who have heard the message of Jesus and believed in it and are, therefore, the People of God for whom, the archbishop exists. He should come to us and listen to us; otherwise, the hierarchy betrays the People of God. At first the archbishop did not come; then he came with a police escort. The parish got a new pastor, but many followed their former pastor into the "underground Church," which is still a feature of Catholic Italy.

Where in these tragic and, on the whole, representative events *were* the people of God? With the cardinal or in Isolotto? It is obvious that very disruptive dynamite can be detonated against the Church in this concept, "the People of God." Therefore it is reasonable to try to discover its origin.

We might begin by asking what the relationship was of "the people of God"—in the original sense of the expression—to the structures and institutions of Israel. We must ask whether we must assume that there was originally a connection between "the people of God" and the poor and oppressed. Also, we must not evade the question whether, from the start, "the people of God" contained the notion "democratization" that is so readily attached to it today.

Today we use the phrase "the People of God" to describe the Church. Thus we place the Church, which comes from Jesus of Nazareth and is attested by the New Testament, in continuity with the Israel of the Old Testament. In doing this we assume that Israel designated itself "the People of God." But it is precisely at this point that we must begin to question common convictions.

"The People of Yahweh," Not "the People of God"

A correction that must be made—not the most important, but well worth noting—is that the exact expression is "the people of Yahweh" and not "the People of God." This makes the religious-historical context plain, within which the following discussion must be conducted.

The God of Israel had a name; he was called Yahweh. But there were other gods, and Yahweh could be distinguished from them only by his name. Theoretical monotheism appears only with the Persian era. It is true that in early times men already called Yahweh *ha'elohim*, "the Godhead," and did so frequently. And in Israel, no one dared worship any god other than Yahweh; this is the First Commandment of the Decalogue. But there were those other gods; and so one identified one's God by his name, Yahweh. In the phrase we are now considering, which we render "the people of God," the identification of the Godhead by name seems to be important. For the expression virtually never occurs in the form *'am ha'elohim*, i.e., "the people of God," but almost always *'am JHWH*, i.e., "the people of Yahweh."

This is proved by purely statistical considerations. The expression "the people of God" is found twice in the Old Testament, the expression "the people of Yahweh" seventeen times. Besides this, we must note that the expression occurs principally when Yahweh himself is introduced into the dialogue, for example, when a prophet speaks in his name or when people address him in prayer. In such cases it is obviously "my people," "your people," or even "his people." If we probe the context, we discover that these expressions always stand for a presupposed "people of Yahweh" and not for a presupposed "people of God." This occurs in 303 passages. There is the so-called covenant formula: "You will be my people, I will be your God," in which the expression "people of Yahweh" and not "people of God" is always presumed. This is documented thirty-four times. In the Old Testament are 354 examples of "people of Yahweh" and two examples of "people of God." The deviation in the latter examples (Jgs 20:2 and 2 Sm 14:13) can be explained by special circumstances. Hence on statistical evidence we may say that Israel spoke not of "the people of God" but "the people of Yahweh."

It had to speak thus, because as well as the "people of Yahweh" it obviously knew the peoples of other gods. One of the oldest texts in the Old Testament is an Israelite hymn of victory over the Amorites of Heshbon. In this hymn is mentioned, to some extent in contrast to the victory over the Amorites, an earlier victory of the Amorites over another nation, the Moabites. The god of Moab was called Chemosh and the defeat of the Moabites is portrayed in these words:

> Woe to you, Moab!
> You are lost, people of Chemosh!
> He has turned his sons into fugitives,
> his daughters into captives. [Nm 21:29]

As the Israelites are Yahweh's people, the Moabites, Israel's neighbor on the east, are Chemosh's people. Whether the Israelites in their early period were convinced that every people was the people of a particular god and that, conversely, every god had a people that belonged to him, is not quite certain, but there is much evidence for this. And the later notion of "angels of the peoples" could well be tied up with this idea. Perhaps the Israelites presumed this sort of analogy to their own relationship with their God only when they knew it was in accord with the views of the people in question. The postexilic chronicle gives expression to the general theory that each people is the people of a particular god (2 Chr 32:14-17).

In any case, the old story in Nm 21 immediately gives a new slant to the notion.

"The Family of Yahweh" Not "the People of Yahweh"

In the text quoted above (Nm 21:29), the Moabites are first described as the "people" of Chemosh and then, without transition, are spoken of as the "sons" and "daughters" of Chemosh. The god Chemosh is thus the "father" of the Moabites. We ask, therefore, if "people" is the correct translation of the Hebrew word *'am*, which underlies these expressions. Because Hebrew poetry follows the laws of *parallelismus membrorum*, might not such translations as "family," "clan," "relatives," be nearer the mark?

This conjecture gains strength when we discover the same parallelism in a series of other places, where the Old Testament speaks of "the people of Yahweh." So runs the celebrated opening of the Book of Isaiah:

> I reared sons, I brought them up,
> but they have rebelled against me.
> The ox knows its owner
> and the ass its master's crib,
> Israel knows nothing,
> my people understands nothing.
>
> [Is 1:2f]

In the very late Wisdom of Solomon, written in Greek, the expression *laos sou* (your people) still occurs, accompanied almost always by expressions such as "your children" or "your sons." In fact, our translation of the expression *'am JHWH* as "the people of Yahweh" follows the ancient Greek tradition of translation, but the word *'am* possessed great breadth of connotation and could mean many other things besides "people." The corresponding Arabic word still denotes the uncle on the father's side—that is, one's father's brother, a most important person in the nomadic family. This may be the original meaning of the word, but by the time Israel's history had begun, *'am* in Hebrew had attracted a series of expanded and derivative meanings. Not just the uncle on the father's side but every member of the family—every connection, even the entire extended family—could be described as the *'am* of a man. In this sense we read, for example, that the patriarchs, after their deaths, were buried and so "were gathered to their *'am.*" Repeated expansion of the meaning of the word then led from "family" to "people"; and yet even in this case our translation of the word by "people" is misleading, for the Israelites regarded a people as a kind of superfamily, in which each is related to everyone else, at least back to the first ancestor of the people. In the case of Israel it was Jacob, who for that reason received the second name "Israel." Another development in the meaning of the word *'am* led to the meaning "army" or "troop."

In the periods of the history of the Hebraic language that are accessible to us, all of these meanings exist alongside one another. The context has to determine which meaning predominates in a particular case. If we apply this methodological rule to the examples we have of *'am JHWH*, we arrive at the following conclusions.

In early times two meanings must have been attached to the expressions, each having, perhaps, a different origin. In the world of the martial song, the expression *'am JHWH* meant "the army of the Lord." There are only three instances of this but they are sufficient to make this meaning certain. One instance is found in the very old Deborah Song; otherwise, *'am JHWH* means "the family of Yahweh." In this sense, however, the expression is not applied universally, without distinctions, but is found in popular lamentation songs, intercessory prayers, and prophetic oracles.

At a later date, both of these meanings were extended and we find them in other contexts. An obvious consequence was that the meaning "army of Yahweh," which could not be abruptly discontinued, declined.

A further point we must make is that the expression, when used in the sense "the family of Yahweh," did not always apply to the whole of Israel, as we shall demonstrate but when it *did* refer to Israel, which became more common as time went by, the denotation was "a people." And so "the people" of Israel was identified with "the family of Yahweh," through use of a word that was often used simply to describe Israel as a people. Within this usage of the expression we must take account, therefore, of a gradual weakening of the original meaning. As the old Greek translation of the Old Testament proves, people in a later period often thought simply of "the people" of Yahweh. But the older sense, "the family of Yahweh," seems to have lived on, and if the context gave encouragement, the meaning was easily reactivated.

An example may illustrate that many passages in which the expression is used take an entirely different tone if one translates by "family of Yahweh" instead of "people of Yahweh." In the Book of the Prophet Joel, the whole population is called to take part in a penitential liturgy because the land is in deep distress from a plague of locusts. On this occasion the supplicatory prayer of the priests is quoted:

> Between vestibule and altar let the priests,
>   the ministers of Yahweh, lament.
> Let them say,
> "Spare your people [relatives], Yahweh!
> Do not make your heritage a thing of shame."
>
> [Jl 2:17]

The people for whom this prayer was offered could rely upon Yahweh's help for the very reason that they belong to him. They are able to say to him: You simply cannot allow your own relatives and your own family inheritance to be destroyed!

That "the family of Yahweh" is preferable to "the people of Yahweh" was maintained by Otto Procksch in 1950 in his *Theology of the Old Testament*. Unfortunately, this thesis, like much else in his excellent book, was scarcely noted. Georg Fohrer was the only one to take up the idea, in some of his essays, in which he points out that here we have a clear example of the survival of an ancient concept from Israel's nomadic past. In this view, the tribal god of a nomadic group was regarded as its first ancestor and a kinsman as one who would come to its aid. These ancient mythological concepts are evidenced elsewhere, in a series of names of persons from the early period of Israel, for example, in the name "Abraham," in which the Godhead is described as "father."

"The Family of Yahweh": Used Only in Special Situations

It is most significant that this expression was not freely and universally available, as the expression "People of God" seems to be today among Christians. Even a statistical analysis of the Old Testament shows that this was so.

The expression is completely absent from the Wisdom books written in Hebrew; the Wisdom teachers, therefore, did not use it. It is found in books of laws only in special cases; the jurists, then, scarcely used it. It occurs 150 times in the narrative books, but except in ten special cases, the narrators did not describe Israel as the family of Yahweh. Only the prophets and a few other persons, who figure as speakers, speak in specific situations of "the family of Yahweh." There are some 150 evidences of the expression in the prophetic books, and the Psalter contains about fifty more.

Whereas among us, every Tom, Dick, and Harry uses the expression "People of God" at every opportunity, in Israel the expression "family of Yahweh" belonged principally to the language of prayer and prophetic preaching, a language that had its own special stamp and was not everyday language. Prayer is speaking to God and prophetic preaching is speaking about God, is God himself speaking to men through the mediation of men. In Israel the expression "family of Yahweh" was used essentially within the dialogue between God and man, and very seldom in conversation between or about men.

But we can come even closer to the matrix of this expression, at least in its beginning, which is the situation of distress. The evidence we have from the times of Samuel, Saul, and David show that in time of distress, people addressed Yahweh, telling him that those who were in distress were indeed his relatives and that Yahweh, promising his help, was motivated by the knowledge that he could not leave his family in the lurch. The archetypal situation for the use of "family of God" can be broken down into four situations: the cry of the people, the intercession of a mediator, the announcement of deliverance by a prophet, and the raising up of a human deliverer commissioned by Yahweh. Let us look at an example of each situation. Because of the complicated text and for the sake of greater clarity, we will have to adduce texts that are later but obviously had parallels in the time of David.

In times of distress, people assembled for lamentation liturgies. They fasted and wept; they recited, or sang, prayers which today are classified by scholars as the "hymns of complaint of the people." A series of these hymns is found in the Psalter and the first verses of Psalm 60 will serve as an example. They presuppose that there has been an earthquake.

> God, you have rejected us, broken us;
> You have been angry, come back to us!
>
> You have made the earth tremble, torn it apart;
> now mend the rifts, it is tottering still!
>
> You have allowed your people to suffer,
> to drink a wine that makes us reel.
>
> [Ps 60:1-3]

By describing themselves as Yahweh's family, the complaining people intensified the urgency of their complaint.

The People of God

It is clear that, very early on, the representative prayer of an intercessor could have had its place beside the common lament. We do not know exactly whether, in the early period, this intercession was the responsibility of the priest, or the prophet, or another group of men. We quoted above a priestly intercessory prayer from the Book of Joel. The prayer formulae of the prophetic intercession may correspond to the prayer the Pentateuch puts into the mouth of Moses after the people have sinned:

> "Yahweh," he said, "why should your wrath blaze out against this people of yours whom you brought out of the land of Egypt with arm outstretched and mighty hand? Why let the Egyptians say, 'Ah, it was in treachery that he brought them out, to do them to death in the mountains and wipe them off the face of the earth'? Leave your burning wrath; relent and do not bring disaster on your people."
> [Ex 32:11f]

This intercessory prayer thus comes under the umbrella that is denoted by the catchword "family of Yahweh."

It may have been the prophets who recited the intercessions; it is certain that they proclaimed deliverance. As an example, we may take the occupation of the land by the Philistines in the eleventh century. Saul, the peasant's son, along with a servant, was searching for some strayed she-asses. At length they visited the seer Samuel, who uttered an oracle for them concerning the she-asses:

> About this time tomorrow I will send to you a man from the land of Benjamin; you are to anoint him as prince over my people [family] Israel, and he will save my people [family] from the power of the Philistines; for I have seen the distress of my people [family] and their crying has come to me.
> [1 Sm 9:16]

The expression "my family" occurs here thrice, and the situation is plain. The Israelites are being oppressed and exploited by the Philistines. They have cried to Yahweh, using popular lamentation hymns and intercessions. Yahweh now sees the distress of his family and commissions the seer to place a *nagid*—that is, a charismatic leader— over his family. This *nagid* is promised that he will be able to rescue Yahweh's family from the hand of the Philistines. In the sequel, Samuel carries out Yahweh's commission. Anointing the *nagid,* he again speaks of Yahweh's family, which Saul is to deliver from distress.

This leads to the last part of the situation. The deliverance promised by Yahweh through the prophet came about—at least in the early period and for political distress—through a human leader. In the period before David he was called a *nagid*. Above all else, the *nagid* was an army leader, and from the office of *nagid* devolved the monarchy under Saul and David. The full title of the *nagid* would seem to have been "*nagid* over Yahweh's family and over his heritage." And so the concept "the family of Yahweh" entered into the title that originally belonged to the deliverer himself.

The whole context of popular lament, intercession, proclamation of deliverance, and appointment of a *nagid* may have been the first and oldest *Sitz im Leben* of the expression "family of Yahweh" that is still accessible to literature: man's distress and Yahweh's help. Starting from this context, the expression must have slowly, from about David's time onward, gained ground. But a connection with the original situation in which it was uttered is always evident. The expression forced its way from popular lamentation into other types of song and dominated the whole language of prayer.

Through the process of development during the period of the monarchy, as the prophets changed more and more from preachers of salvation to preachers of judgment and punishment, the expression "family of Yahweh" also forced its way into the language of the threat of catastrophe and underlined the horror of Israel's sin of children against the divine Father, of a family against the divine kinsman. In this category belongs the opening of the Book of Isaiah, from which we have quoted.

The People of God

Through the Yahwist, the expression "family of Yahweh" also got into the language that describes salvation history. But with and after the Yahwist, apart from a few very late deviations, it is always connected with a single event: the liberation from Egypt. The Yahwist wanted to give theological interpretation to this event from the old narrative tradition of Israel, and he did this by stylizing it as oppression, crying out to Yahweh, and proclamation of deliverance by Moses and liberation through him. Thus the Yahwist superimposed the schema of the distress-deliverance situation, as experienced in David's time, upon the old traditions. One of the linguistic means at his disposal was the expression "family of Yahweh," which was typical for this situation. Commissioned by Yahweh, Moses goes to Pharoah and demands: "Let *my family* go!"

In later texts concerning the liberation from Egypt, Yahweh is regarded as Israel's *go'el,* its "rescuer." In the family system presupposed here, the *go'el* is that relation—often the uncle on the father's side—who has the obligation to rescue a member of the family (in the case, for example, of his becoming enslaved). From the word *go'el* is derived our word "redeemer." And so our catchwords "people of God" and "redeemer" have a common origin.

In all the contexts we have mentioned thus far, the concept "family of Yahweh" has fulfilled no function that links it with salvation history. In a few later texts, most of all in the priestly historical narratives of the Hexateuch, it assumes this function as well. According to the priestly writing, Yahweh made the Israelites into his family precisely by freeing them from slavery in Egypt (Ex 6:7). According to the Yahwist, however, and the great bulk of texts, the converse is true: because these men are Yahweh's family, Yahweh intervened to bring them out of Egypt, and will intervene to bring them out of any distress, which moves them to call to him for aid. "Yahweh's family" is the title that provokes God's salvific action in history. The simple plea is that one is a member of Yahweh's family.

This relationship is so thoroughly relied upon that in some texts it is explicitly linked with the order established at the creation of the world. For example, in the Song of Moses we read:

> When the Most High gave the nations
>   their inheritance,
> then he divided the sons of men,
>
> he fixed their bounds according to the
>   number of the sons of God;
>
> but Yahweh's portion was his people [family],
> Jacob his share of inheritance. [Dt 32:8f]

The expression "family of Yahweh" points to an ultimate, deeply mythical, and free, gracious turning of the Godhead toward certain men, an action that precedes all history and hence all human decisions and prayers. When these men gain consciousness of all this, they are already Yahweh's family. Hence when they are in distress they may, and ought to, appeal to this fact.

And who are these men? Are they to be identified simply with "Israel"? The Song of Moses and many other texts do this. But does it apply universally?

The Family of Yahweh and Mankind in Poverty and Distress

For a start, it is doubtful whether in the early days the whole twelve-tribe confederacy gathered together to call upon Yahweh in distress-deliverance situations. This holds true even if one considers those theories false, which claim there was no twelve-tribe confederacy before David's time. Saul was the first *nagid* to be elevated *nagid* over the whole of Israel, thus becoming king. Historically, it is highly doubtful

The People of God

whether the title *nagid* was used from the start in respect of the whole of Israel. There are some indications that from time to time it was used of the Israelite groups that actually found themselves in distress and then became the "family of Yahweh" of the songs of lament, the intercessory prayers, and proclamations of salvation. Later, too, this must often have been so, in natural catastrophes, outbreaks of fire, and similar disasters which did not affect the whole country.

We must, however, proceed a further step. In the original distress-deliverance situation, distress was precipitated either by natural catastrophe or enemies—that is to say, by non-Israelites. But in David's time there are a few cases of the use of "family of Yahweh" when the distress arose within Israel. Sufferers from distress are designated by Yahweh as his relatives and family, in contrast to other Israelites who are not in distress—who, indeed, may be the very people who brought distress upon their compatriots.

The law in the so-called Book of the Covenant, forbidding interest, may be one such case. "If you lend money to any of my *'am* [relatives], to any poor man among you..." (Ex 22:24). Here we find a poor man in contrast to a rich man being protected—as a relative of Yahweh—by a law.

According to 1 Samuel 2:24, Eli, the priest at Shiloh, corrected his sons because he was forced to listen to the complaint from "the family of Yahweh," that they were defying tradition and exercising their priestly office to enrich themselves at the expense of the worshipers. Clearly, those who were exploited by the priesthood are here described as members of Yahweh's family.

This use of the concept "the family of Yahweh" continues thereafter in the prophetic books, which speaks of Yahweh's family when the rights of Israelites are protected against priests, officials, lawmakers, kings, and even false prophets. A single example suffices, an oracle of Isaiah against officials in Judah:

> O my people, your rulers mislead you
> and destroy the road you walk on.

> Yahweh rises from his judgment seat,
> he stands up to arraign his people.
>
> Yahweh calls to judgment
> the elders and princes of his people:
>
> You are the ones who destroy the vineyard,
> and conceal what you have stolen from the poor.
>
> By what right do you crush my people,
> and grind the faces of the poor?
>
> [Is 3:12-15]

And so the Judge of Peoples turns against his own people, against the leading groups within that people, and, in contrast to them, takes the genuine people under his protection, for *they* are his family. It is precisely this text that makes full play of the various connotational possibilities of the word *'am*.

Obviously, in most examples from the prophetic books the whole of Israel is designated "the family of Yahweh." Obviously, it is in harmony with the will of Yahweh that Israel possess structures and institutions and that there is authority within Israel. The title *nagid* already proved this to be so. In the period of the monarchy, the so-called covenant formula developed from the concept "the family of Yahweh." Its very use demonstrates a close connection between the concept "the family of Yahweh" and the two guarantors of Israel's structure, that is, the king and the law.

In spite of this, the cited examples show that the thrust of the expression "family of Yahweh" was not directed precisely at Israel as a structure. Even the question about democratization—in contrast to authoritarian structures—evaporates. "Family of Yahweh" is directed toward the mystery of the divine inclining toward those in distress—the poor, the oppressed. In its origin and throughout almost the whole of the Old Testament, "the family of Yahweh," formulated as a slogan, is not an ecclesiological but a soteriological concept. The object to which it addresses itself is taken up most unequivocally in the New Testament, when Jesus shows his care for the poor, the sick, the social outcasts, and gathers them into a new Israel. It is like a translation of the old expression into a more intelligible language, when Jesus speaks to these people about their Father in heaven, whose children they do not have to become, for they are already his children.

"The People of God" Today

Turning our attention again to the expression that has become so common today, we might sum up this way: "the people of God" is not a universal mode of speech in the Old Testament but an expression that was attached to specific situations and contexts. It was heard in dialogue between Yahweh and men, and was connected with distress and deliverance from it. In fact, the whole of Israel was usually denoted, but on closer inspection we see that the expression could also be used to the exclusion of groups within Israel, even involving the deposition of those in authority. The real meaning of the term is "the family of Yahweh," at least in its primary sense, and this sense largely prevailed throughout. It comes from the mythological thought of Israel's nomadic prehistory, and is a concept that belongs to soteriology and the theology of grace, rather than ecclesiology—unless one asks whether ecclesiology ought not appropriately be treated as a department of soteriology. But where would that lead us!

Does this mean that we dissociate ourselves from the fathers of the Second Vatican Council and their use of this concept? Not at all, for the Bible is not everything in theology and in the Church's history. We may not disallow the use of biblical terms in senses other than those they originally possessed. Just as the biblical concept "the Son of God," which was originally a Davidic title for the king, has served since the great councils to express the doctrine of the hypostatic union, so, obviously, the term "family of Yahweh" can come to mean "the people of

God," conceived primarily in a salvation-historical, sociological, and juridical sense; and this concept of "the people of God" can then, perhaps, at a particular phase in Church history, become a key ecclesiological concept, acclaimed by all. This is all the more possible because the Old Testament itself attests its beginnings, especially in the theology of the covenant. The people-of-God ecclesiology of the Council, therefore, has a right to be heard and expounded within its proper context, whether or not it is correct to link it with biblical linguistic usage.

But having conceded this point, we must resume our critical inquiry, for clearly the intention of the Council fathers in using the concept "the People of God" was to reach beyond unbiblical (or at least biblically one-sided) concepts of the Church to the richer and purer terminology of both testaments, a terminology that would have antedated or cast off the bias conferred on them by a long theological history. That is why the concept "the People of God" was pushed into the foreground.

The Council fathers wanted to say what the Bible says, even if, perhaps, they did not see all that the People-of-God concept brought with it. They had a praiseworthy, Christian, primitive trust in the Bible. To put this in a popular way, they were ready—almost to buy a pig in a poke. Then the fathers came home, and when they opened the poke for the faithful, out came the biblical pig—and it was not quite what they had expected. It even began to snort aggressively.

Going back, then, to our opening example, to Cardinal Florit and his adversary Don Mazzi: it cannot be concealed that the poor people of Isolotto understood the biblical term "people of God" to mean more than their biblically more literate bishop understood it to mean. The choice of this ecclesiological slogan has in fact led us further away from the juridically constituted Church than was originally intended. What does that matter, if thereby we have come closer to the central matter of the Bible, to that region where the talk is about God and man, about distress and deliverance?

Today, in this light, we may wonder why the concept has lost some of its earlier popularity.

God

The Polytheistic and the Monotheistic Way of Speaking about God in the Old Testament

Religion is back again. Right in the middle of a liturgically numb and intellectually anemic ecclesiastical milieu, spontaneous prayer is breaking out. "Youth religion" proliferate in the cities, because the traditional churches clearly have nothing to offer youth, hungry for conversion. Because the pundits of the West no longer know how to find the way into the interior man, the perplexed turn, in the midst of life, to Eastern meditation, to Yoga and Zen. A "new" word is in vogue: "experience."

Conscientious Church leaders may continue in the future to ask their doctrinal commissions to discuss the question whether or not best-selling theological authors are using the Christological names for God correctly. Their children, who have cleared out from home, or who may still be loitering crazily at home, are bothered by quite different problems of language. Spiritual hair is still untidy with the disheveling wind of the God-is-dead jargon. Now we hear tentative, sweet, pious murmurings about "friendship with God." God lives, because they have seen him, and might well bump into him again on the next street corner; or they are struck dumb before the ineffable depths in their own being; or they dance ecstatically for gods and demons which, only very recently, they assigned to primitive stages in human development. The structuralists in Paris are working on a theory about this. Bultmann's assertion, that one cannot simultaneously make use of electric current and believe in a myth, is being disproved. There are far too many who can.

Perhaps this state of affairs makes it possible for us to look again at something to which, for centuries, theologians have consistently closed their eyes, because they could not bring themselves to look in that direction. I speak of the polytheism of the greater part of Holy Scripture. This compels us to discuss the interchangeability of a polytheistic and a monotheistic way of speaking about God. Today the question is about many other ways of speaking about God, but the juxtaposition of polytheism and monotheism is a model case, which the Bible itself has worked through. It may therefore be taken as representative of others. The most stimulating key phrase is "the jealousy of Yahweh," whose meaning I shall try to explain.

Yahweh Is a Jealous God

After Moses had led the Israelites out of Egypt, they journeyed through the wilderness until they came to the mountain of God, where the God Yahweh appeared to them. He revealed himself in a burning fire and in the darkness of a cloud. Thunder rolled and rams' horns sounded. Yahweh proclaimed to the people the "ten words" that they were to make their rule of life. These words begin thus:

> I am Yahweh, your God, who brought you up from the land of Egypt, out of the house of bondage. You shall have no other gods beside me. You shall not make for yourselves any image of God, of anything that is above the heavens, or upon the earth, beneath, or in the waters that are under the earth. You shall not bow down before any such thing, and shall not obligate yourself to serve it. For I, Yahweh, your God, am a jealous God. [Dt 5:6-9]

In the Old Testament, the theophany at Sinai is regarded as the event which ushered in the covenant between the people of Israel and the God Yahweh. It is the center of the Old Testament. It sounds out the theme "Yahweh and the other gods," and this theme continues to resound throughout the Old Testament. All who read the Old Testament constantly see and hear this theme.

Yahweh forbids the people to have any other gods beside him. He himself describes this prohibition as emanating from his jealousy. This Vulcanlike God does *not* want that all men worship him alone and refuse to worship other gods. A jealous person is concerned only about what another, particular person does, and only in respect of this person does he refuse to tolerate a rival. Yahweh did not lure all peoples into the wilderness to his mountain; it was only this one people that he freed from slavery and this people alone to whom he revealed himself. And so it was of Israel alone that he demanded that no other god smell their sacrifices, no other god hear their prayers. Other peoples might happily continue to worship their own gods. Israel alone is Yahweh's people. But Yahweh is very jealous toward Israel.

> When you raise your eyes to heaven, when you see the sun, the moon, the stars, all the array of heaven, do not be tempted to worship them and serve them. Yahweh your God has allotted them to all the peoples under heaven; but as for you, Yahweh has taken you, and brought you out from the furnace of iron, from Egypt, to be a people all his own, as you still are today [Dt 4:19f]

Jealousy also denotes irascibility and passion. The Yahweh of Sinai is an excitable, harsh, and passionate God. He demands his rights; he fights for his rights. Hence the First Commandment in Israel is buttressed by unequivocal laws. If a prophet arises in Israel and urges people to serve other gods than Yahweh, he must be put to death, even if he has confirmed his message with signs and wonders. If his best friend or even his wife invites an Israelite to serve another god, witnesses must be called so that this person can be put to death by the assembly of the people. If a whole city apostatizes from Yahweh, the rest of Israel must wage a holy war on that city and destroy its population.

The laws in Deuteronomy 13 demand all this. All of these laws are addressed not to peoples of other religions but to the people of Israel. Perhaps the most gruesome god of the ancient East was Ashur; he, however, raged against other peoples, not against his own people.

God

Yahweh's jealousy, on the other hand, extended almost to the murder of his own beloved.

This is how the Deuteronomic historical writings see things. The normative redaction of these works dates from the period after the destruction of Jerusalem in 587, when the states of Israel and Judah had been destroyed, Jerusalem lay in ruins, and all the influential people had been deported to Babylon, so that the end seemed to have come for Israel. The Deuteronomic Chronicle explains the Babylonian Exile in terms of a historical triangle, extending over seven centuries: hence, Yahweh; there, the other gods; in between, torn this way and that, and finally falling away to the other gods, so that Yahweh condemns it to destruction, Israel. Other Old Testament texts, however, are convinced that Yahweh still cannot forget his ancient love for Israel, and that he promises to gather Israel from among the nations and lead it back to its own land.

The Common Interpretation of the Jealousy of Yahweh

All this sounds very anthropomorphic. However, we must begin by taking account of what we are really dealing with, especially as it occurs so frequently and so centrally. We must truly want to understand. What does "the jealous God Yahweh" mean?

The common interpretation is that here we encounter the beginnings of monotheism. what is said sounds somehow polytheistic, but what is really said is that there is only one God, and one ought to worship him alone. This is the traditional Christian, Jewish, and Islamic interpretation.

In this view, all peoples before Israel and around Israel had fallen into the delusion of polytheism; that is to say, they believed in many gods, which is an error. Israel, by contrast, since the time of Abraham, had known through revelation that there is only one God. And so Israel was monotheistic, and in consequence was permitted to adore only this one, true God. A monotheistic perception was not demanded of other peoples, at that stage in the development of revelation. Hence the monotheistic demand upon Israel could at first be clothed in the imagery of Yahweh, jealous of his "divine" neighbors. Later, this was no longer necessary. Then, for the first time, Christianity and Islam set in motion the universal proselytizing of the world to monotheism.

This traditional scheme of interpretation, however, is not quite satisfactory. The biblical affirmations about Yahweh's jealousy and his claim of exclusive worship, in contradiction of the tendency to worship other gods, turn out to be very different from merely clever, didactic devices or metaphors. They must have to do with something very different from theoretical insights into the objective structure of the transcendental sphere. What we encounter here can scarcely be described as the antithesis of a false, as opposed to a correct, theory concerning the number of divine beings. The battle of the jealous Yahweh with the other gods is much more than an invitation to accept the theory of monotheism, even if, at the end of Israel's history, we find theoretical monotheism established.

Things become much more problematic if we look more closely at them from the perspective of the history of religion. Polytheism and monotheism then disclose themselves as temporary categories. We discover that the so-called polytheism of Israel's ancient Oriental environment was much more complicated and closer to monotheism than we might at first suppose. On the other hand, we also discover that, up to the Babylonian Exile, Israel did not know of theoretical monotheism in the usual sense; so this cannot be the explanation of the antagonism between Yahweh and the other gods or of Yahweh's jealousy in respect of Israel.

Ancient Eastern Polytheism

All around Israel the world was polytheistic. This was true not just in respect of popular belief and the cult in the great temples but also of the thinking of the educated. From Egypt at one end of the Fertile Crescent to Babylon at the other, everyone worshiped many divine figures. The historian of religions is tempted to give up in face of the confusing multiplicity of cults and names; however, he soon discovers that the worlds of the gods seldom appear to lack a common structure. Often, lesser groups of gods are seen to have won a special position for themselves. Frequently a concept is developed of a pantheon of the principal divinities, at whose head stands (as a rule) a father and king of the gods.

Even the lowest social stratum, the nomads, were no exception. There are grounds, it is true, for supposing that nomads often worshiped only one god, the protecting god of their own clan, who had once appeared to their ancestor and now led his descendants upon their dangerous wanderings. But obviously, one knew that other clans had other gods. When one came to trade in the cities, one ingratiated oneself by making an offering to the gods of that city. There is no valid reason, therefore, for saying that nomads were not polytheistic.

At all events, the religion of this lowest stratum displays a feature which clearly stamped the polytheism of the ancient East and which has sometimes been called "monolatry," sometimes "henotheism" (following Schelling's terminology). There never was theoretical doubt concerning the multiplicity of gods. To this extent, it would obviously be false to see here a transition from theoretical polytheism to theoretical monotheism, as has often been proposed. It would be much more accurate to say that monolatry seems to be a frequently actualized inherent potentiality of polytheism.

In Egyptian art, for example, we are presented with a polytheism than which no crasser form can be imagined. The scene swarms with animals, plants, things, men, composite beings—all representing divinities. Every district had its own divinity. New gods were imported and worshiped, from every subjugated foreign country, and almost any of them could be addressed as "the only god, without equal." Each god could be designated "king of the gods" and "lord of all." This attitude reflects a change in thought, which seems to appear when people move from theological speech into prayer. The Egyptologist Erik Hornung, a rabid opponent of all theories of a monotheistic undercurrent in ancient Egypt, describes the phenomenon:

From the abundance of gods in his pantheon, the Egyptian, when worshipping, whether in prayer, in singing praise, or through ethical obligation, picks out *one* God, who, for the moment, means *everything* to him; the limited and yet tremendous power and greatness of God is focussed in the god addressed, beside whom all other gods sink into nothingness, and are at times written off altogether [*Der Eine und die Vielen,* Darmstadt, 1971, p. 232].

In the so-called Wisdom Doctrines, which were the foundation of the education of Egyptian officials, only in special cases were individual gods mentioned by name. Most statements have for their subject merely the word *neter* (god), which is far removed from theoretical monotheism. Each official, wherever he operated, had to operate with the god of that place. The doctrines expressed that which was held to be true of each god. For the worshiper—for the time being, in his particular situation—all that was divine was concentrated in this god.

In terms of these presuppositions, we can understand even the exclusive worship of Aton, established for a short period by Iknaton. This gave rise to such texts as the celebrated "Hymn to the Sun," in which it is said of Aton:

How immeasurable are your works! They are hidden from mortal sight, O you, the only God, who have no equal. You created the earth according to your good pleasure, you alone—with all its men, its cattle, and all beasts, all that dwells upon the earth, that goes on foot, that hovers in the heavens, that flies on wings, all the foreign lands of Syria and Nubia, and the plains of Egypt. Each one you set in his place, you create all that they need, each one has his food.

This text sounds utterly monotheistic to us, but it belongs totally within the framework of polytheistic language and prayer.

Things seem much the same with the polytheism of Mesopotamia. Basically, in the Sumerian city-states, only one god of the pantheon was worshiped: the "city god" at that particular time. Through the names and temples he received, he became identified with all the other cosmic divinities, so that he became the "universal god." The smaller local gods were his court—that is, his mediators and officials, who could only augment his splendor. But this does not alter the fact that the Sumerians believed in many gods, within their city and in other cities, and it was taken for granted that other cities had other city gods.

In the Syrian-Palestinian region, too, which provides fewer literary evidences, we find a similar picture of polytheism. A prayer from Ugarit begins with an invocation of the creator god and king of the gods, Ilu, who is then identified with the "circle of gods" and with individual foreign gods, who are named. All of this before the petitions begin.

Theoretical polytheism among Israel's neighbors, in practice, always left open the possibility of monolatry—the tendency, indeed, toward monolatry. Divine figures could split themselves up, then join together again. New gods could step in. Men were animated by a huge tolerance, an immense hunger, for new gods. But it always happened that the man who worshiped one of these gods more or less consciously summed up in that divinity all that godhead meant to him.

Monotheism in Israel

We come now to inquire about Israel's monotheism. On close examination, we see evidence of it only in a late period.

About the time of the patriarchs we can only make conjectures. The various groups that later blended to form Israel, we must presume, worshiped their particular "clan god." He might be called "the God of our father Abraham," or "the terror of Isaac," or "the bull of Jacob." This was normal polytheism, as described above. When clans confederated, the clan gods became identified with one another. When the clans settled in an agrarian land, the "God of their fathers" became identified with the Canaanite creator god, Ilu. When the group whom Moses led out of Egypt joined the rest, their God, Yahweh, became merged with Ilu. And Yahweh was a jealous God. From this time onward, no one in

Israel dared worship other gods, although for a very long time this commandment cannot have accorded with common practice. Even when the exclusive worship of Yahweh was accepted, no one thought of denying that the other gods existed, or of requiring other peoples to abandon their gods and worship Yahweh. To this extent, Israel's concentration of worship upon its one God, Yahweh, remained totally within the framework of the polytheism of the prevailing culture.

There is a tale from the period after the settlement of the land, recorded in Judges 11, which proves this point at a stroke. The Ammonites want to conquer Israelite territory east of Jordan. Before war breaks out, the Israelite leader, Jephthah, sends an embassy to the king of the Ammonites. In the middle of the "argument" in the message brought by the emissaries we find the following sentence: "Do you not possess all that your god Chemosh took from its owner? In the same fashion, whatever Yahweh our God took from the owner, that we possess too" (Jg 11:24). In the negotiations with the enemy, both gods are given equal value and are set side by side. The ultimate test was: In war, who is the stronger?

When praying to Yahweh, the same Israelites would obviously have confessed him in quite another manner, never suggesting that any other god was His equal. Perhaps we may regard the formulae of the Jephthah embassy as the polite language of diplomacy, but the ordinary folk spoke in the very same way.

The Book of Ruth reports a speech of the Israelite woman, Naomi, who wants to return home from exile, taking with her her non-Israelite daughter-in-law, Ruth, whose husband has died. Naomi leaves Ruth free to return to her own family in Moab and expresses herself this way: "Look, your sister-in-law has gone back to her people and to her god. You must return too; follow your sister-in-law." Ruth replies: "Do not press me to leave you and to turn back from your company, for wherever you go, I will go, wherever you live, I will live. Your people shall be my people, and your God, my God" (Ru 1:15f).

The concept that is voiced in this passage becomes even clearer in the youthful David's reproach to Saul, who is persecuting him:

God

Why does my lord pursue his servant? What have I done? What evil am I guilty of? May my lord king now listen to the words of his servant; if Yahweh himself has incited you against me, let him accept an offering; but if men have done it, may they be accursed before Yahweh, for now they have driven me out so that I have no share in the heritage of Yahweh. They have said, "Go and serve other gods." [1 Sm 26:18f.]

The "heritage of Yahweh" is the land in which Israel lives. Anyone who has to leave this land because of political persecution is, in David's view, and Saul's, cut off from Yahweh himself. He must then go and serve other gods, that is, the gods of the peoples among whom he lives.

By no stretch of the imagination can this be described as monotheism; it accords well with the picture we have of polytheism in the ancient East. We have no reason to doubt that in the liturgy David was accustomed to hear and to sing hymns in which Yahweh was adored as the universal God, as the Lord of all lands and all nations. He himself may have composed such hymns. In this type of polytheism, the god one was worshiping at the time made the universal, Creator God present; in fact he *was* that God. But this did not deny that other gods existed alongside him. In another land, and among another people, all of this happened, but with another god.

In view of these facts, biblical science has for a long time been prepared to regard theoretical monotheism as the great, new insight that appeared for the first time with the prophets. Elijah, in the ninth century, is often placed first in the line, but even this view must contain some misunderstanding. On Mt. Carmel, an ancient holy place, the altar of Yahweh had been demolished and an altar to Baal erected in its place. In the competition-sacrifice scene, Elijah challenges the Israelites: "How long do you mean to hobble first on one leg, then on the other? If Yahweh is God, follow him; if Baal, follow him" (1 Kgs 18:21). This, however, has nothing to do with monotheism. The point at issue is to whom does this mountain belong, and which god should be worshiped in Israel? The sequel makes this plain, in the prayer with which Elijah calls down fire upon the altar of Yahweh: "Yahweh, God of Abraham,

Isaac and Israel, let them know today that you are God in Israel, and that I am your servant" (1 Kgs 18:36). The fire of Yahweh came down upon the altar and the priests of Baal were slaughtered.

Following Elijah in the ninth century, Amos—in the eighth century—is often named as the first literary prophet to give evidence of monotheism. Like the author of the so-called Yahwist historical work before him, he sees Yahweh, the God of Israel, as the director of the history of the other nations as well. "Are not you and the Cushites all the same to me, sons of Israel? Did not I, who brought Israel out of the land of Egypt, bring the Philistines from Caphtor, and the Aramaeans from Kir?" (Am 9:7).

We have already shown that even within polytheistic thought it was possible to recognize, in the god of the time and the place, the universal Lord of the universe. Thus he is also Lord of all history. However, this does not rule out the possibility that one may concede the existence of other gods.

Is Jeremiah, at least, at the end of the seventh century, not a monotheist? He says such things as this: "What shortcoming did your fathers find in me that led them to desert me? Vanity they pursued, vanity they became. They never said, 'Where is Yahweh, who brought us out of the land of Egypt...?'" (Jer 2:5f). He describes the other gods as "vanity," as nothing. A few verses further on, these gods are said to be nonexistent: "Does a nation change its gods?—and these are not gods at all! Yet my people have exchanged their Glory for what has no power in it" (Jer 2:11).

But even here, one may ask if the nonexistence of the other gods is spoken of in the sense of theoretical monotheism. What is meant, perhaps, is that they have no power. They *are* not, because they can give no help. This notion is supported by the Song of Moses in Deuteronomy 23, which dates from the same period and displays connections with Jeremiah. In this song the gods of other nations are scorned in similar language (Dt 32:17, 21), but some of the verses make it obvious that their existence is accepted (Dt 32:8, 43 in the original text, as derived from Qumran fragments and the Septuagint).

God

We move on, then, into the sixth century, to the time of the Babylonian Exile. In the great author deutero-Isaiah (Is 40–55), prophet of salvation, we have a living object lesson, in which, with tremendous effort, the web of polytheism was broken in order—without any monotheistic system at hand to help—to begin to speak at last, in principle, monotheistically.

When he began writing his poems, deutero-Isaiah had to start on the assumption that there were many gods, all of whom were summoned to appear before a cosmic court of law, where it was proved to them that they do not rule over history, for they could not predict the future. It follows from this that they are powerless, which means that they do not exist at all. Against this background resounds Yahweh's hymn in praise of himself;

> I am Yahweh unrivaled,
> I form the light and create the dark.
> I make good fortune and create calamity,
> it is I, Yahweh, who do all this.
>
> [Kgs 45:6f.]

Even here, the language stems from the polytheistic tradition, in which a divinity such as Nanna in Sumer could present himself as unique and incomparable. Denial of the existence of the other gods in the pantheon was not required by such an attitude; but deutero-Isaiah intends to make such a denial. In the second half of his poem, the other gods have vanished. From now on, all pagan nations, if they strive for righteousness, can, as though they were a new people of Yahweh, find salvation in Jerusalem (Is 51).

After deutero-Isaiah's time, people thought monotheistically. Derision over the making of images of gods begins, and is introduced retrospectively into older books. When at last, for the first time, Greek philosophy becomes a vehicle of expression in the Wisdom of Solomon (chaps. 13–15), we have a monotheism which no longer faced problems of expression. A new language has asserted itself. But how late!

If I view things correctly, Israel reached monotheism only when it was emerging everywhere. At that time in Persia and Greece, the same fruit was growing on the tree. Zoroaster and the pre-Socratics may be regarded as contemporaries of deutero-Isaiah.

The specialty that Israel possessed, even within the polytheistic framework—that is, the jealousy of the God Yahweh—may have prepared Israel for monotheism, for through it Israel had long been accustomed in its worship to adore only one God. But that is all. Of itself, Yahweh's exclusive claim had done nothing to change the theoretical framework. Indeed, talk of Yahweh's jealousy could only make sense within the framework of polytheistic language. And so when monotheism won the day, it lost this significance. It became a metaphor. Following Aristotle, Philo of Alexandria aptly defined monotheism as the doctrine of "divine monarchy."

Two "Languages," Not Two Things

What we call polytheism is therefore by no means so "primitive" that, without further ado, we can brand it as error. Monotheism, on the other hand, entered the Old Testament so stealthily, so late, and so closely linked with broader rearrangements of human consciousness that it seems improbable that we can see in it the essence of Israel's religious message. Is the real message, for which the books of Israel still constitute the greater part of our Holy Scripture, not to be seen in something which lends itself to expression both in polytheistic and monotheistic, language?

We still have to determine what this message was. First, let us think through the notion that polytheism and monotheism may be only two "languages," each representing a different mental approach, but an approach to the same thing. This does not necessarily mean that both languages were equally at the disposal of the same people at all times. They may have been linked with certain epochs. Within a monotheistically speaking world, polytheistic language might become

God

"false." And the opposite could be true: monotheistic speech within a polytheistic religion could become "false" because it limited the divine and its accessibility to experience. In general, one must note that the matter concerns not just these two languages in respect of divinity. Much is to be said for the idea that the polytheism of the ancient Eastern high civilizations was a short-lived phenomenon, occurring late in the history of mankind. It may have superseded other "languages" (though this is very difficult for us to conceive) that may have been more akin to the subsequent monotheism than to polytheism (though it is wiser not to label the ancient primeval religion "monotheistic").

Perhaps the best way to classify the issue is to try, using the monotheistic language that comes naturally to us, to explain the way in which polytheism named and worshiped the divine, a way that was distinctive of polytheism alone.

Ancient Eastern polytheism was not characterized just by the fact that it spoke of many gods. Most significant also, as we have seen, was the way in which, in the religious act, divinity became concentrated in the particular deity who was worshiped at the moment. A controlling faith, therefore, was the dialectic of the many and the one. In "monotheistic" language, we may say that when the polytheist spoke of a "god," he was speaking not of God as he is in himself but, simultaneously, of the one God as he is in himself *and* as he is experienced by men in a particular set of circumstances. From time to time, knowledge of God through earthly realities comes within a concrete, specific, mundane experience. For men of the ancient world, this happened above all in his encounter with the cosmos: the starry skies, storms, the sea, the sun, the moon, the budding of spring, thunder, the fecundity of animals, the birth of a child. Likewise, special places and things played their part: mountains and hills, great trees, springs of water, special stones. Finally, there were the contingencies and events of one's personal life. If a man or a group found an experience of transcendence in some such concrete circumstance, and if behind this particular reality they sensed an infinite depth, an otherworldly grace, then the religious experience and its concrete occasion grew together into the form of a divinity.

I am speaking of the experience of what is otherworldly. Because there are many such experiences, there are many forms; and so there were mny gods. In addition, man is a social and historical being; he lives not just for the moment but recalls the past and preserves the present for the sake of the future. He lives not merely in his own experience but equally, or even more, in the experience of his fellow men, who reach him and condition him through speech and customs. In groups and in the exchange between groups, religious experience too is shared. In ancient times, the handing on of older and foreign religious experience was effected in the form of the names of the gods and in the cultic customs one learned in order to worship the various gods.

One would be justified in saying that a polytheistic divinity was never a being that existed in himself, but the name given to one concrete possibility, among many, of encountering the other world of the One, who is God. If that is the essence of a polytheistic deity, it immediately becomes clear why these gods were so variable, why they could split up and join together again, and why, in particular, a single god from among the many in whom men believed could suddenly, when he was worshiped, gather within himself—so to speak—all that is divine. It is in conformity with the system, then, that religious experience and religious practice in another life situation, or at least in another place and among other people, should almost necessarily be linked with another god.

This, obviously, is a description of a polytheistic experience of God, using the conceptual apparatus supplied by monotheism. One who is accustomed to polytheistic language would express himself differently, and for him it would be very simple. But conversely, it would be very complicated for him to describe, in his language, the extent to which monotheism, in contrast to polytheism, offers nothing substantially new.

One may ask why polytheism had to decline and monotheism to advance. But one should pose this question in detachment from the history of Judaeo-Christian revelation. Then one will come up against very basic rearrangements in the experience of the world and in the social conditions which we would be most inclined to designate as Hellenism, if one gives this word a slightly wider connotation than is usual. Objective thinking and logic must here have taken a role they did not play at an earlier date. And so the synthesis between the thing and the perception of the thing, which constituted the god of polytheism, was struck by a crisis. It is not necessary, however, to pursue this question further at the moment. We are concerned only to release both polytheism and monotheism from the labels "error" and "truth" and to display both clearly, as two in some sense equally valuable, if epoch-conditioned, ways of speaking about God.

The Jealousy of Yahweh as the Affirmation of a Special Revelation

The most obvious characteristic of the polytheism of the ancient world was its tolerance. Its extreme form, syncretism, though usually given a negative value by our religious-historical standards, is perhaps, in its context, the highest wisdom. Every new god can be a new and enriching revelation of the otherwordly, and ultimately unfathomable, mystery, and in the concrete act of worship, in the presence of the god who is worshiped at the moment, all things flow together. What does it signify if, within such a context, an intolerant God appears, who is jealous of his worshipers and keeps all other gods away from them?

This brings us back to our opening question, but now we may have better hope of finding an answer. The considerations that have meanwhile been raised have excluded the possibility of our seeing Yahweh's jealousy simply as a sign of incipient monotheism, not yet fully self-aware, which was beginning to protect itself against polytheism. Rather, we are forced to understand Yahweh's jealousy in terms of polytheistic language and, only then, to translate it into monotheistic language. That, however, is no longer such a difficult task.

If a polytheistic god is not only an objective reality, beyond this world's reality, but at the same time is also the way in which otherworldly reality is experienced by particular men in particular circumstances, then neither is Yahweh "simply" God—in the language of monotheism—but God insofar as he had been experienced by Israel at Sinai, in the exodus, and on other occasions, and as he would continue, over and over again, to be experienced in Israel's commemorative liturgy. If, then, Israel was forbidden to worship other gods, it was also forbidden to seek other ways of encountering God. Such a commandment implies a claim, for it makes sense only if the experience of God through Yahweh contains something for Israel which the experience of God through other gods did not contain. Yahweh must mean more than the knowledge of an encounter with God that is possible to each man in each age—more than the varied, yet always the same, perception of the one distant God "behind things," as was claimed.

In this way the relevant translation of the jealousy of Yahweh in monotheistic language is seen to be the theory of a special revelation given only to Israel. After a monotheistic way of thinking had appeared, this theory was advanced in the later books of the Old Testament—in connection, moreover, with the old Wisdom mythology and speculation. "Wisdom" means God's idea of the creation, his creative word, the intrinsic order of the created world, the laws which man can discern from the creation, and human action to the extent that it conforms to this order. All of this is connected and appears in Egypt as the goddess Maat; in Israel, it is personified as "the lady Wisdom." She is God's first creature, who at the creation played before God, and her delight is to be with the children of men (Prv 8:22-31). Whoever finds Wisdom finds life (Prv. 8:35). According to the Wisdom of Sirach, this Wisdom was present when the world was created, and so she can be discovered by all men, in all ages, throughout all creation. But she searched out for herself a special dwelling place and found it in the people of Israel. The manner in which she can be encountered there can be specified much more precisely: "All this is no other than the book of the covenant of the Most High God, the Law that Moses enjoined on us" (Sir 24:23).

In this we have the beginnings of a theology of revelation which has determined at least Christian theology up to the present. It distinguishes a general from a special divine revelation (one often speaks of a "natural" and a "supernatural" revelation). In the course of time, we find the theory appearing, as one might expect, in the most varied forms. It is present even when the term "revelation" is conceded only to special revelation; the terms "natural knowledge of God" or even "human self-explication in respect of God" are used of what is universally possible.

The jealousy of Yahweh—speaking monotheistically—is therefore to be linked with the idea of a special revelation, and perhaps we have to proceed a step further. The fact that exclusiveness is claimed indicates that what is special has to do with the meeting with God that took place within Israel. No new insights into the depths of God are mediated. For this, new gods would have to keep appearing. The really decisive event would seem to be the encounter with God, accepted at this particular point in time and in this place. This seems to be constitutive of "special revelation." If the transcendent, remote God approached men here, at this very point, the experience was no longer exchangeable, and had to be jealously guarded.

Conclusions

Today, religion is "in" again. Again, people pray quite naively; they bow toward the east; they believe in gods and demons. One gets the impression that it is possible to speak quite clearly, even as an atheist, of that mystery which is inadequately grasped when it is described by the word "God."

Perhaps the polytheistic language in the greater part of the Old Testament can make us realize that there are many "languages" with which to describe the one mystery, and that they can be translated into each other. At the same time, analysis of the jealousy of Yahweh should demonstrate that there is something which does not permit placing all religious experiences upon the same plane. At least the Old Testament makes this claim, and the New Testament carries it over into its Christology.

Today, Church authorities may not be far wrong, therefore, when they urge their doctrinal commissions to keep an eye on Christological, divine names.

Projections

On the Enemies of the Sick in the Ancient East and in the Psalms

From time to time we welcome illness. It had been approaching for a long time, but we were not aware of it. Now at last it is palpable, and we know where we stand.

Or life has piled up a heap of insoluble problems and there is no way out. Then comes an illness, perhaps not too serious, but it changes our whole situation. Because one is ill, many problems take on a new color, or they solve themselves.

All the same, to welcome illness is the exception. Normally it approaches as an enemy. It steals some of life's potential. It takes away freedom; inflicts pain; makes us a burden upon others. If it is the sort of illness we can do something about, we treat it as an enemy. The doctor looks grave and his eyes become keen. Medication is our weapon, our bed the battlefield. It may be that reconnaissance troops have been able to identify the enemy exactly and we now know it is this virus or that bacillus. And so our armory can be directed on the target until the enemy is defeated, driven out of our body, and totally annihilated. We are well again. Health is again our friend.

But health is not won back every time. There are illnesses that endure—minor illnesses and serious illnesses. Do they retain forever the status of enemy? For the sick, it seems, they chronically often lose their hostile aspect. One gets acquainted with them. One learns to go about with them, to live with them. Now and again a relationship, almost of friendship, develops between the sick person and his illness. One even meets sick people who, one guesses, could no longer live without their illness. Is it not possible for a person actually to grow fond of, to cater to, his illness? This, obviously, is an extreme case in the vast array of possibilities; but it happens.

However, this is not the end of the story about the enemy of the sick, for, besides the illness, the sick person finds other enemies too; and in what follows it is these enemies that interest us.

Every sick person is thrown upon other people. Someone who is confined to bed has to wait until another comes to him. When that person comes, the sick person—litterly—has to look up to him, from beneath. Nor does he know what others are saying among themselves outside the sickroom. Many sick persons do not know what is expected of them or what is really being done to and for them. They have to rely upon the competence of the doctor and those who nurse them, and upon their goodwill. This is taken for granted—correctly. But is such dependence and trust always valid or justified?

In short, illness can release spiritual mechanisms through which the sick person begins to suspect that this world, over which he no longer exercises normal control, is inhabited by enemies. The illness may no longer be regarded as an enemy—but in reality it remains what it is. It is painful, it limits life's possibilities, and it engenders feelings of insecurity and fear, but because it is now felt to be an everyday acquaintance, the enemy is seen as lurking elsewhere.

Suspicion grows—of the nurses, one's family, the doctor or the health service. The sick person senses enemies around him, which he himself has created by projection. This reaction is very common, and it is difficult to restore confidence and dispel these worries and suspicions of the sick person when, finally, he is able to express them in words. As a rule, the projections correspond to no objective reality. If the sick person fears enemies, he fears, in the last analysis, only his own illness. But he is unaware of this and senses that "enemies" intend to harm him.

Enemies of the Sick in the Ancient World

In ancient times this process must have operated even more powerfully. The man of those days was thoroughly bound up in his family and in the community of his city. Far more than ours, his spiritual harmony depended upon constant contact with relatives and friends, upon conversation and mutual recognition. Illness threw him back upon himself even more than it does us, and cut him off from all normal life, and so he developed projections of enemies on a vastly grander scale. What with us is often only incipient, we find in huge dimensions in ancient Oriental texts.

In a Babylonian text from the second century B.C. (*Ludlul bel nemeqi*), we find the complaint of a seriously sick official who is terrified by the thought that, while he is ill, his colleagues are set on undermining his position at court. The text builds the picture of a far-reaching conspiracy against the sick man, including the intention to use magic as a means of taking his life.

> Those at court are plotting against me. They gather together and speak godless things. One says: "I will use magic to kill him." Another says: "I will fix it that he gives up his position." Yet another says: "I will take his office myself," and a fourth: "I will steal his property."

Unfortunately, a piece of the clay tablet upon which this is written is broken off; so we cannot read what the fifth man says, or the sixth and seventh. But the text goes on thereafter:

> The gang of seven has joined forces, merciless as a demon.... They are of one heart and mind. They rage against me. They glow like fire. They act together against me with calumny and lies.

Enemies in the ancient East did not necessarily have to be human beings. One reckoned also with hostile demons and hostile deceased persons, and Egypt provides an example in a letter from a sick widower to his deceased wife. Convinced that she is to blame for his "evil condition," he writes to her:

> What crime have I committed against you, that I have fallen into this evil condition in which I find myself? What have I

> done against you that you have laid your hand upon me although I have committed no crime against you? Since I married you until this day, what have I ever done against you that I need to hide? What is there against me that has made me like one accused? What have I done against you? I will complain about you by word of mouth to the gods of the realm of the dead in the west!

After describing how he showered every benefit upon his wife throughout her life, the writer continued:

> But look, you will not allow my heart to be at peace. I will take out a suit against you. Injustice will be distinguished from justice.

It is impossible for us to determine the exact nature of this person's illness. Was it physical? Was it psychic? At all events, his deceased wife had become for him the archenemy, who was exercising an evil influence on him from "the realm of the dead in the west."

Often, a person did not know who the enemies were, whom he feared. To defend himself against them, he would make a long list of possible enemies, who were paraded in prayers and vows before the gods in order to obtain assistance. Very often we misinterpret such lists. At first sight, they look like lists of various diseases; in reality, they denote the demons who were thought to cause these diseases, for example, the following list from the Accadian Series:

> All that is bad, all that is harmful in my body, in my flesh, in my muscles; misery caused by bad dreams, signs and portents, misery caused by horrible, evil, harmful [acts], through manhandling, through the choking of a sheep... through what I see darkly... through what I tread upon in the street, and see by my side, the wicked Shedu-demon, the evil Utukku-demon, illness, headache, misery, distress, fear, quaking, sorrow, terror, weakness, woe, groaning,

humiliation, rending of the body, terror, affliction, fear, sin, calamity sent by the gods, wrath, banishment by oath of a god, by a written oath, sorcery, witchcraft, apparitions, machinations of evil men.

The whole world of wicked things, which might be responsible for the evil condition of the sick, praying person, is cited in every detail, because he was not sure exactly where the cause of his illness lay.

Enemies of the Sick in Israel

The people of Israel were part of the same civilization. Among them, however, such a list was scarcely conceivable. By its faith, Israel was bound exclusively to the one God, Yahweh. Fear of the dead and demons and terror at witchcraft were strictly forbidden the Israelite.

But prohibitions against overpowering fear and phantom enemies by no means released the sick Israelite from his fears and from the mechanisms which produced images of an enemy. It was merely that the framework of acceptable images of enemies was restricted. When the sick Israelite feared enemies, they had to be men—unless he happened to think of Yahweh, his God, the great enemy. But that bold intellectual step exemplified in the Book of Job, was taken only infrequently. Even this idea, in the end, had to be relinquished. Normally in Israel, the enemies of the sick man were his fellow men; hence the fantasies of the sick in Israel may be closer to us today than the other ancient Eastern fantasies. We, too, scarcely ever cringe before death, demons, or sorcerers, but our sick, nonetheless, are often compelled to objectify their fear.

The enemies of the sick Israelite are portrayed in the psalms, in the hymns of lament of the sick, which abound in this book of the Bible. In Psalm 22, for example, the description of the illness of the worshiper is permeated with references to enemies who are harming him. At first he puts his trust in Yahweh, then he begins to describe his illness and to complain about it; but almost from the start his picture of his illness turns into a picture of men who are evilly disposed toward him.

> Yet here am I, now more worm than man,
> scorn of mankind, jest of the people,
>
> all who see me jeer at me,
> they toss their heads and sneer.

After an expression of trust in Yahweh, a supplication, a request for help, follows. This is motivated by the observation that there is no man near at hand who is prepared to offer help:

> Do not stand aside: trouble is near,
> I have no one to help me.

Then follows a new, long description of his distress, but only in the middle of it is the illness itself described. At the beginning, as at the end, the words are exclusively about hostile men. The danger they threaten is expressed in images of wild and ravenous beasts.

> A herd of bulls surrounds me,
> strong bulls of Bashan close in on me;
>
> their jaws are agape for me,
> like lions tearing and roaring.
>
> I am like water draining away,
> my bones are all disjointed,
> my heart is like wax,
> melting inside me;
> my palate is drier than a potsherd
> and my tongue is stuck to my jaw.
>
> A pack of dogs surrounds me,
> a gang of villains closes me in;

> they tie me hand and foot
> and leave me lying in the dust of death.
>
> I can count every one of my bones,
> and there they glare at me, gloating;
> they divide my garments among them
> and cast lots for my clothes.

To this is attached the broadly formulated petition of the psalm. We discover, to our amazement, that it does not refer to the illness but only to the enemies, whom, in his terror, the sick man sees all around him.

> Do not stand aside, Yahweh.
> O my strength, come quickly to my help;
> rescue my soul from the sword,
> my dear life from the paw of the dog,
> save me from the lions' mouth,
> my poor soul from the wild bulls' horns.

Seldom do we find in so insistent form a sick person's transformation of the sense of his serious illness into the feeling of being surrounded by hostile men. At the end of his outpouring, all have become wild beasts, gathered round his deathbed. And in other lamentations in the Book of Psalms, which dwell longer on the actual illnesses, these adversaries are seldom absent.

Clearly, those who pray see the men who surround their sickbed as enemies. Perhaps all that is needed for this is that the visitors do not expect the sufferer to be restored to health, and the sufferer has only to get a hint of this, from what they say, to turn them immediately into enemies. Not so much their illness as the doubts of visitors is the great suffering of the sick. And so Psalm 6 concludes:

> I am worn out with groaning,
> every night I drench my pillow
> and soak my bed with tears;

> my eye is wasted with grief,
> I have grown old with enemies all round me.

There they are again. And now, if the psalmist's confidence that God will hear him wins through, he is able to express this confidence as a message of victory over the enemies who surround him:

> Away from me, all you evil men.
> For Yahweh has heard the sound of my weeping;
> Yahweh has heard my peition,
> Yahweh will accept my prayer.
> Let all my enemies, discredited, in utter torment,
> fall back in sudden confusion.

I wonder whether the enemies collapse and fall into nothingness because, when illness is past, the "enemy projections" lose their foundation in reality and visitors are seen again as their true selves. Perhaps in this way we might also arrive at a new understanding of the maledictory psalms—the prayers in which the curse of God is invoked upon the sufferer's enemies.

Faithless Friends

Let us pause to consider the way in which the sick in the ancient East, and especially in Israel, had a sense of being surrounded by human enemies. The most bitter enemy was the friend who had turned faithless; and the one-time friend, turned enemy, is a character found throughout the East. Here is what we read in an Egyptian song of lament from the third century B.C.:

> With whom can I now speak?
> My trusted friend has turned villain,
> The brother who worked alongside me has
> turned into an enemy.

> With whom can I now speak?
> No one remembers the past.
> Nothing is done now for him who once did good.
> With whom can I now speak?
> I am heavily weighed down with grief,
> for I have no one to confide in.
> With whom can I now speak?

We read the following in a Sumerian prayer of a sick man:

> My cattleman has invoked powers of evil against me,
> and yet I am no enemy of his.
> My companion speaks never a true word to me,
> my friend answers my honest speech with lies.
> A swindler is hatching a plot against me,
> and you, my god, do nothing to stop him.

The following complaint is found in an Accadian poem from the second century B.C.:

> I have become an outcast from all my relations.
> When I cross the street, they prick up their ears.
> When I enter the palace, they wink their eyes.
> My city gives me black looks, as if I were an enemy.
> Truly, my country is horrible and hostile.
> My friend has become my enemy, my companion
> a miserable wretch and a devil.
> My fellow shows me all his nastiness.
> My allies constantly whet their swords.
> My trusty friend puts my life in danger.
> My servant has cursed me publicly in the assembly....
> When my acquaintance sets eyes on me, he
> crosses over to the other side.
> My family treat me like a stranger.

All of these texts are very fatalistic. Little time is spent looking for a reason why, in time of illness or misfortune, friends turn into enemies.

Projections

This just is so; no one stays by a person in trouble. Hence one may take it for granted that when one is in distress, one will be forsaken by all. The world soon accepts the fact that it can continue, minus one person. One may even have to reckon with vicious enemies, who want to see the unfortunate person finished off with speed. An Egyptian proverb says: "In the day of misfortune a man has no friends."

In Israel, this does not seem to have been taken quite so much for granted. In the psalms of lamentation it is repeatedly stressed that former friends have become enemies "without any cause," which is not felt to be normal. All the more, therefore, when it occurs, does it become a subject for complaint.

In Psalm 41, for example, the worshiper first characterizes his enemies in general. They visit him, it is true, but when they have left his sickroom they wish for his death. Then he intensifies his description of their animosity by stressing that formerly they were his friends:

> My enemies say of me with malice,
> "How long before he dies and his name perishes?"
> They visit me, their hearts full of spite,
> They offer hollow comfort, and go out to spread the news.
>
> All who hate me whisper to each other about me,
> reckoning I deserve the misery I suffer,
> "This sickness is fatal that has overtaken him;
> he is down at last, he will never get up again."
> Even my closest and most trusted friend,
> who shared my table, rebels against me.

This motif is developed even more expansively in Psalm 55, where the praying person turns directly to his former friend and addresses him:

> Were it an enemy who insulted me,
>   I could put up with that;
> Had a rival got the better of me,
>   I could hide from him.

> But you, a man of my own rank,
> a colleague and a friend,
> to whom sweet conversation bound me
> in the house of God...

If we consider all the utterances in the psalms, a well-defined picture emerges. In Israel, the sick had the feeling that their friends had turned into enemies. Former friends suddenly drop them and avoid them, or they make it plain that they do not include the sick in their circle of friends. They treat the sick as men now worthless, or comfort them with empty phrases, or, instead of comforting them, mock them and indirectly reproach them for having either too little or too much trust in God. They give the sick much good advice, then shake the dust off their feet.

From this assembly of data we see that people who visited or had other personal contacts with the sick were suddenly felt to be enemies. The sick no longer trusted what others were saying and doing. They read hidden enmity into everything.

They may often have been right. The ancient East regarded a sick person as one rejected by the gods. In Israel too, as soon as a man became ill, the question was put: Has he sinned? Is Yahweh about to punish him? And the sick plagued themselves with the same questions. Presumably, if someone told them something different, they always found a reason for doubting the honesty of such words. They knew how one is accustomed to think in such circumstances.

Or were things not so simple? Did some visitors of the sick *not* think along these lines? If not, much that is said in the psalms about friends-turned-enemies would be projection and fantasy.

Conclusions

We find ourselves facing the same considerations with which we began. First, illness is felt to be an enemy. Gradually, however, one

Projections

makes friends with it. The fear it engenders, however, can become objectified in new "enemies," who are most easily found by the sick person in the people around him. This happens today; it happened on an even greater scale to men in the ancient East and, in a different way, in Israel.

The psalms of lamentation are by no means unique and spontaneous prayers. They are prayer formulae; they take their place in a large and official collection that was offered the sick as a form for their prayer. In Israel, one did not hesitate, therefore, to offer the sick the common projections of sick men. Through these formulae, indeed, and for the first time, the healthy person purposesly may have aroused them in the sick person.

Did people see them as the projections they really were? Perhaps to some extent. But perhaps people had a different kind of experience when they used them, and so adopted a different attitude toward them.

We are inclined to tell a sick person that he is deluding himself. We try to make him aware that his notions are projections, in the hope that, in this way, he will be freed from his fears and aggressions.

In contrast, those who were responsible for writing the psalms seem to have attributed more reality to the projections of the sick. They seem to have presumed that one freed himself of them more quickly the more he "verbalized" them. And so they encouraged the sick man to express these notions, and never contradicted him.

At all events, they led him to express his fears *in prayer*. To making conscious the sick person's imagined threats from enemies they linked the invocation of God. The sick person, while complaining about his enemies and thus openly declaring his fear, at the same time placed himself, with confidence, in the hands of God, whom he knew to be infinitely more powerful than any enemy.

We, too, often discover that we cannot talk a sick person out of his fears. In Israel, they taught their sick to express such fears in prayer.

Growth

The Priestly Document and the Limits of Growth

In 1973 the Club of Rome received the peace prize given by the German book trade. The winning book was a study of the precarious state of mankind; its title was *The Limits of Growth*. Shortly after, as if in corroboration, came the so-called oil crisis. From that time onward, ecological uneasiness, which had already begun in the U.S.A., became a reality in Europe as well. The Club of Rome was contradicted, but it published more books. Slowly, it was becoming clear to people that something really had changed. At the same time, however, it was becoming evident that everyone is deeply programmed toward growth.

Our minds are conditioned to accepting, as a law of nature, that this world cannot get on without growth. "Growth," "progress," "evolution" are linked concepts. We would feel that it was the beginning of the end if wealth were not increasing, if the indexes did not rise every year. A no-longer-expanding world is inconceivable to us, but what was recommended? Scarcely rising wages; an economy that is scarcely expanding; for several decades, perhaps, a planned retrenchment in the developing countries, while other countries deliberately aim at zero growth or even reduce their living standard, so that everything—population and quality of life—can oscillate at a level that would allow the earth to continue indefinitely; and then, within measurable time—in all intellectual activity, all areas of conflict, all technical progress within the whole world system—equilibrium, stable production; that is, no more growth. Our imagination simply cannot conceive such a state of things.

All of this proves how deeply attached we have become to the idea of growth. It is rooted in our being. If it is correct that we must now abandon this idea, the future of mankind, consequently, will be the concern not simply of politicians, economists, and computer experts. All of these specialists, irrespective of their desires, in the last analysis can only steer society in the direction desired by the majority. But today, in spite of much unease and contrary evaluation, that majority and normative will is unequivocally for growth.

The idea of growth inhabits those depths in man where myths live. It is itself a myth. And yet it is not a necessary myth; the myth of growth has not always obtained. It is something that mankind has acquired, that man has drawn to himself. Consequently, it is something he can discard.

But what a task! Who has the courage to take it up? Moreover, time is running out, and every ally is important. And here a question must be asked: On which side will we find the oldest and still most influential custodians of the myths of the Western world—the Christian churches and their older sister, the synagogue?

Christians and the Myth of Growth

Are these custodians perhaps the secret source of the "progress mentality," from which it will draw an ever new life force? Or might they become allies of a new education, which we see as the task ahead of us?

The question was posed long ago. It has even been posed insistently in respect of the book which supplies both Church and synagogue with their myths, the Old Testament. In German, the clearest discussion of the question has come from the pen of the Munich author and ecologist Carl Amery. In his book *The End of Providence,* he lays the major blame for the myth of growth upon Christians and Jews, and his argument traces back through two thousand years.

Even where the Christian faith has been abandoned, the virus, the idea of progress, has been passed on. Christianity was compelled to propagate the absolute dominion of man over the cosmos and the very first page of the Bible sounds the keynote, for in the so-called Narrative of Creation we read: "Be fruitful, multiply, fill the earth and subdue it." Moreover, man, to whom these words are addressed, is described as the "image of God." No other creature is granted such a privilege. Thus a great gulf is set between man and all the rest of creation, which is felt to be the proof of man's essential superiority. This feeling persists, and so Western man, though meanwhile he has become a confirmed materialist, is convinced he has the right to exploit this planet, regardless of the consequences.

Amery is not alone in making this analysis. Meadows, Toynbee, and many others said the same thing during recent years. Are they right?

Undoubtedly, man's apologists have all too long and all to readily proclaimed that modern man, who has taken his and the whole world's destiny into his hands, is ultimately motivated by the Judaeo-Christian impulse. It was not so long ago that Teilhard de Chardin's grandiose synthesis of Christology and the theory of evolution for the first time freed Catholic intellectuals from the fear of being out of date. It is also a fact that the ideology of growth first asserted itself in those sections of mankind which had been stamped by the Christian-Jewish tradition. Obviously, the cosmos had to be released from the spell of the powers and the gods of the ancient imagination before the attempt could be made to think in terms of radical, technical domination. The transcendent Creator God of the Bible was thus a kind of condition for the emergence of basic modern concepts. All of this may be conceded, though many distinctions must be made.

However, the condition of mankind may be too serious to allow us to leave the matter there, having cast a glance back at causes. In the last analysis, it is a matter of indifference whether and to what extent the impulse proceeded which generated the myth of growth in the souls of men, vis-à-vis the traditions of Jews and Christians. Jews and Christians alike regarded themselves as men who lived according to the Bible. Today, the only question is whether, given the modern mind and the possibilities of understanding that are now available, the Bible still compels them to adhere to the myth of growth.

The question has not been settled, either by the explanations of apologists, who would like to accommodate themselves to the spirit of the age, or by the indictments of newly converted environmental conservationists. We have to examine more closely what the Bible really says about growth and domination, and particularly what this much-quoted sentence from the creation narrative means:

> Be fruitful, multiply, fill the earth
> and conquer it. Be masters of the fish
> of the sea, the birds of heaven and all
> living animals on earth. [Gn 28]

What, in the light of modern biblical scholarship, is the exact meaning of this sentence?

It would serve no good purpose if we were to misinterpret that still powerfully operating potential in men who live by the Judaeo-Christian tradition or, without need, drive it into a false position. Should it turn out that the Bible does not legitimize the modern myth of growth, it would be possible, by education, to win over men who take their stand on the Bible and, separating them from this tradition, bring them to accept those guiding concepts which alone can promise a future to men today. It would not be easy—but it would be very much easier than, for the sake of saving mankind, inciting Christians and Jews against their Bible.

What, then, does the Bible, and Genesis 1:28 in particular, really say?

"Image of God" Is Not Necessarily Equivalent to "Domination"

Let us begin by looking at the affirmation in this context: man was created in the image of God. Does this separate man from all other creatures and set him in splendid isolation as absolute lord of creation?

The Bible does not expound the affirmation. However, the literature of the ancient Oriental world helps us a little.

The literature of Mesopotamia, like that of Israel, when describing the creation of mankind by the gods speaks of the image or likeness of God. That there is a similarity between divinity and humanity is thus part of the ancient, prebiblical, human traditions concerning the creation. In the Mesopotamian documents, however, this does not imply that man is placed in a position of dominion, for in the same texts that speak of man's creation in the image of the gods, the purpose of their creation is said to be the performance of slave labor.

The Mesopotamian picture of man is by no means bright and optimistic. Within the cosmos, a fixed amount of labor—forced labor—simply has to be done to keep the cosmos going. And to get this done, and not leave it to the gods, men were created. There is no mention of lordship. The fact that man resembles the gods makes no difference.

Similarly, we may not draw false conclusions from the Bible when it states that man is created in the image of God. The Bible gives man higher status within the cosmos than the Mesopotamian world gave him, but this cannot be inferred from the assertion that he is made in God's image. One must also acknowledge the Mesopotamian conception of man as the "great slave" of the gods.

Amery was too little acquainted with the cultural context from which the assertion derives, that man is made in the image of God. Besides, he was wrong to think the Bible says that man is the only creature who is made in the likeness of God. The literary work to which the creation narrative at the beginning of the Bible belongs—that is, the so-called Priestly Chronicle of the Pentateuch—contains, attached to the account of the events at Sinai, a long report of the erection of the sanctuary of Israel in the wilderness. In a certain sense, this sanctuary is the completion of the whole of God's creation; it comes about as the work of human labor and technique. But *so* it can come about, Moses must ascend the mountain and be shown the heavenly model for the earthly sanctuary. Thus we will not be far off the mark if we maintain that the heavenly model is nothing other than heaven itself. Not only is man created in the image of God but so is the whole of creation, in all its beauty, though accomplished through the industry of man—that is, as the reflection of God's radiant presence, of his heaven.

In the thought of the Bible, therefore, the "image" idea does not lead, as Amery believes it does, to a deep gulf between man and the rest of creation, but serves to establish the concept of man and creation as a might unity and a coordinated system. This may be affirmed without going into detail on the meaning the Bible puts upon the saying about man's likeness to God.

Commandment or Blessing?

For the present, we will do better to apply ourselves to the decisive text of Genesis 1:28, "Be fruitful, multiply, fill the earth and conquer it." In these words God addressed the first men after he created them. But perhaps first of all we ought to make clear that we are not dealing here with a commandment addressed to men by God, though this is a very common view. Such an interpretation of these words is possible, but we have only to read the sentences that lead to these words to see the real point:

> God created man in the image of himself,
> in the image of God he created him,
> male and female he created them.
> God blessed them, saying to them, "Be
> fruitful, multiply, fill the earth"... [Gn 1:27f]

We have here, therefore, not a commandment but a *blessing*. Having created man, male and female, God infused into them the power of multiplying and expanding over the earth. In ancient Semitic thought, a blessing presupposed a purpose: accomplishment of a meaningful, desirable, even necessary and commanded enterprise. Nonetheless, it was primarily a blessing, a gift that one accepted gratefully, and not a commandment to which one conformed by compulsion or, possibly, even against one's better judgment. One should not, therefore, talk glibly about such things as "the *commandment* to be fruitful and multiply at the dawn of creation." We ought rather to speak of "the *blessing* at the creation."

The Blessing of Fecundity: Only for the Birth of Nations

Even the latter phrase is misleading. It comes close to such a phrase as "order of creation," by which theologians usually understand things that are given to men as men, are given to all men at all times, are given to men in creation itself, so to speak, as their "order." Is the blessing of fecundity in Genesis 1:28 meant to be a blessing upon all men in all ages? Or does it apply, perhaps, only to particular periods of man's history?

The text imposes no limitation, which would seem to argue that it applies to all men at all times. But the context prompts caution. Shortly after, God issues dietary prescriptions to men and beasts; he tells them what they may eat. Astonishingly, the first chapter of the Bible provides only vegetable nourishment for man and beast. Therefore I ask any theologian who asserts that the saying about fertility applies indiscriminately to all men in every age if he also thinks, according to the biblical view of the ordering of creation, that all men in every age ought to be vegetarians. Very few have pondered this consequence.

In fact, the problem of vegetarianism, built into the order of creation, very soon solves itself, as soon as one notes the context of the literary work into which the creation narrative fits, that is, the priestly chronicle. According to this, shortly after the creation violence arose among men and beasts; undoubtedly this points principally to crimes among men, to murder and manslaughter. Tales like that of Cain and Abel would have been well known to the author of the priestly writing (though he did not use them), but, linked to this, he was clearly concerned with the fact that neither man nor beast had continued in the paradisical state of peace which the Creator had willed should prevail among all living creatures, and which found expression in a vegetarian rule of diet. Beasts began to eat one another and men began to kill and eat animals. This distorted the original world order so badly that God sent the Flood to enable a new world with a new order to arise. Immediately after the Flood, God issued a new dietary order, which permitted men to eat the flesh of animals.

A very great deal could still be said concerning the context of this symbolic narrative, but that would lead us away from our theme. The important thing is this: the vegetarian dietary commandment, issued by God at creation, does not, according to the priestly writing, apply to all men in every age. At a later date, moreover, God himself replaced it by another, nonvegetarian, law.

For this reason, one ought to be more hesitant about asserting that the fecundity blessing is meant to be a blessing on all men in all ages, precisely because it occurs within the creation narrative and contains no verbally expressed limitations. The real question is how the priestly chronicle as a whole understood the fecundity blessing.

Just as the human race received a fecundity blessing at the dawn of creation, so, after the Flood, it received a new blessing. Mankind had shrunk to a single family and badly needed the blessing again. Then, in the course of the chronicle, a blessing is repeated several times in almost exactly the same words, and always when it is hoped a whole people will grow from a single ancestor—for example, Abraham and Jacob, the ancestors of Israel. This shows that the blessing has to do not with human fecundity in general but with expansion, in specific cases, of a small number into a larger population—as, for example, the expansion from Jacob into the people of Israel.

This interpretation is confirmed by the narrative technique of the priestly writing, according to which the course of history is accompanied by an extraordinary number of divine utterances: announcements, commands, promises. Each utterance is quoted verbatim, and then follows (immediately or later in the story) the report of the narrator:

that God's word has been fulfilled. With the notice of fulfillment, the theme is completed.

Now let us deal with the blessing of fecundity. This, too, has a clearly recognizable note of fulfillment. After Israel had dwelt some time in Egypt and had developed from an extended family into a great people, the narrator affirms:

> ... The sons of Israel were fruitful and grew in numbers greatly; they increased and grew so immensely powerful that they filled the land. [Ex 1:7]

With this, the blessing given to Jacob had reached its end. In the sequel, the motif of fecundity is not taken up again. Obviously, the Israelites continued to have children, but only as many as were needed to maintain their number. This, however, had not been the theme of the fecundity blessing, which was growth into the people that belonged to God, and in such numbers as God had predestined.

In many respects, the priestly writings tell the story of Israel as though it were an example of what applies to all peoples. And the notice of fulfillment of the fecundity blessing upon Jacob contains several formulae which allude to the fecundity blessing at creation and after the Flood. From this we may conclude that these blessings are to be understood in the same way as the blessing upon Jacob. It is not a question, that is, of mankind's reproducing itself, but has to do with that intense increase which was necessary if the initially few men were to become the many peoples, in numbers, which God had predestined.

As soon as the predestined number had been reached, the fecundity blessing had fulfilled its function. This makes it very plain that the fecundity blessing at the dawn of creation, in the sense that the priestly chronicle gives it, is not to be regarded as a blessing upon all men for all time. It is aimed at the establishment of the peoples, and so it flows directly into the phrase "and fill the earth."

When the human race, originally small, increased, it had to cease living together in one place. It had to spread out and fill the world. This is clearly a programmatic, preliminary sketch, in the form of a blessing, of the first phase of human history. We must proceed from this conclusion when we interpret what remains of Genesis 1:28.

The Peoples Take Possession of Their Territories

"Subdue the earth and rule over all the animals"—in this fashion we might translate the second half of Genesis 1:28, abbreviating and following the customary interpretation. If in the first half of the verse we see a command to man forever to increase his numbers—a kind of divine sanction of a population explosion—we see the second half as commissioning man to be unrestricted ruler over nature; we see the legitimation of technology, the transfer of control of the world from God to the inventive hand of man—put it whatever way we like.

Following this line of thought, scientific biblical commentaries can rely in some degree upon the Hebrew original and say that the Hebrew words that are used here, *kabas* and *radah*, are expressions that denote the hardest and most brutal forms of ruling. *Kabas* means "to trample upon"; so we would have "trample upon the earth." *Radah* means basically "to stand upon something," "to stamp something into the ground." And so we would have "stamp the animals into the ground," which, obviously, is to be taken metaphorically. Both words signify the absolute right of man to dispose of the material and animal world. Nonetheless, the graphic but brutal expressions show how strictly this right is conceived.

This, then, is the widespread comment upon both sentences—a presupposition (which we have already questioned) that they have to do with a fundamental assertion concerning all men in all ages, with a command of the Creator to all men. What is the real state of affairs?

The translation of the two Hebrew verbs is not entirely false, but closer inspection of their use in the speech of the Old Testament yields other conclusions. The common theory seems very largely to have been the result of wishful thinking. Legitimation was needed for man's claim to dominion over nature and the animal kingdom, and so the etymology of the two words was made the occasion for interpreting them accordingly.

Behind the word *kabas* stands an image of "putting one's feet on something," and one thinks of the throne of the pharaohs, known to us from pictorial art. Seated upon his throne, Pharaoh placed his feet upon a footstool, attached to the throne. This footstool was decorated with prostrated symbolic figures that represented the countries over which Pharaoh ruled. In the carving, they lie prostrate beneath the feet of pharaoh, which indicates that these countries, with their inhabitants and all that was in them, belonged to Pharaoh. He neither stamped them into the ground nor trampled upon them; they were simply his possession. The phrase "to place his foot upon something" could be equated with "to lay hands on something," both of which rest upon a symbolic gesture; but when using them, one does not advert fully to the actual gesture. "To place one's feet on something" means "to take possession of." In the priestly writings the phrase is used with special reference to taking possession of territories.

The most obvious interpretation of our text is that it is a continuation of the preliminary sketch of the early history of mankind, begun in the first statement. The human race, at first few in number, was supposed to multiply. When its numbers increased, the descendants could no longer stay together in one place and had to spread out, until they filled the whole earth. And when population growth had reached that stage (now we come to our present text), the separate peoples were to take possession of their territories, so that, finally, one could say that mankind had taken possession of the whole earth.

The priestly chronicle does not recount the tale for the whole of mankind but exemplifies it in the story of a single people, Israel. Abraham, its ancestor, was promised by God (Gn 17) that his posterity would receive the land of Canaan in perpetual possession. Here, quite plainly, we find the notion that each people has its own appointed, particular territory. When Abraham's descendants became a people, they found themselves in a different land, in Egypt, where they were exploited. Then God took up their cause, remembered his promise, and brought them out of Egypt and led them into the land of Canaan, which he gave them as their own possession (cf. Ex 6:8). The priestly chronicle ends with the partitioning of the land among the tribes of Israel, recorded in the Book of Judges. The text concerning the partitioning of the land is introduced by the sentence:

> The whole community of the Israelites assembled at Shiloh, and the Tent of Meeting was set up there; the whole country was now subdued and at their disposal. [Jos 18:1]

At the very end of the chronicle the word *kabas* crops up again, for the first time since it appeared in Genesis 1:26. It provides a framework, as it were, for the whole work. What was announced at the beginning has happened, at least in respect of Israel: a people has taken possession of its territory and now is able to partition it among its members, who can dwell there in peace.

Dominion over the Animal Kingdom

Concerning the period following the possession of the territories by the various peoples, Genesis 1:28 speaks of man's dominion over the animals. What does this mean? Does the word *radah* mean that they may be trampled down, when the very next verse contains a vegetarian dietary precept? Can this otherwise rational author make such a contradiction?

Only one text, Joel 4:13, may support the brutal connotation of the word *radah,* and this is uncertain. Instead, the word might very well be a similar-sounding form of the verb *jarad* (to descend), a view that was accepted until the second half of the last century, before people became interested in giving *radah* (in Gn 1:28) the strongest possible meaning. The real root meaning of *radah,* moreover, may be "to lead about," even "to lead about together with other living creatures." The sense "to rule" should then be derived not from the idea of trampling but from that of guiding and leading. The array of connotation thus includes "to accompany," "to posture," "to lead," "to govern," "to command." The "sense context" becomes even clearer when we note that in the ancient East the shepherd served as a symbol of the ruler. Kings as "shepherds" of their peoples was a perfectly normal notion.

Our text undoubtedly indicates a kind of shepherding and guiding function of man in respect of animals—*all* animals, not just domestic animals. According to the priestly document, man had not gradually domesticated animals; from the beginning, animals had been created either domestic or wild, as we learn from Genesis 1:25. In Genesis 1:28, the various groups of land animals are not classified; they are embraced by the single phrase "all living animals on the earth." Earlier, the fish of the sea and the birds of the air, all ruled over by man, were named. The writer has in mind, therefore, a universal directive function of man over all the animal world, and this is not coextensive with the domestication of certain species.

This directive function in respect of all animals must have been very important for the priestly chronicle, for it was announced in the divine decree of creation in Genesis 1:26, where it is seen as the consequence of the fact that man is created in the image of God:

> Let us make man in our own image, in the likeness of ourselves, and let them be masters of the fish of the sea, the birds of heaven, the cattle, all the wild beasts and all the reptiles that crawl upon the earth. [Gn 1:26]

To clarify the matter further, we have to read on in the priestly chronicle. After the Flood, the fecundity blessing is renewed, and taking possession of territories is not mentioned. Only with Abraham does it become thematic. However, the theme of the rule of man over all the beasts also is absent, and does not become thematic in the whole of the subsequent priestly writings. But a passage in the middle of the blessing (after the Flood) deals in a different manner with the relationship of men to animals:

> God blessed Noah and his sons, saying to them, "Be fruitful, multiply and fill the earth. Be the terror and the dread of all the wild beasts and all the birds of heaven, of everything that crawls on the ground and all the fish of the sea; they are handed over to you. Every living and crawling thing shall provide food for you, no less than the foliage of plants. I give you everything.... As for you, be fruitful, multiply, teem over the earth and be lord of it." [Gn 9:1-3, 7]

Here, God uses the language that was spoken in Israel in time of war and in oracles concerning war. We cannot avoid interpreting this as though, after the Flood, a kind of state of war ensued—in the priestly chronicler's view—between men and animals. This seems to be the background to extending the dietary arrangements of Genesis 1:29 to allow men to eat the flesh of animals.

It looks as though this figurative state of war replaced the earlier, predestined rule of man over the animals. We cannot ignore the connection that links the two statements with the dietary order which immediately follows each; but this means that the last declaration of Genesis 1:28 became irrelevant for mankind after the Flood. After violence had entered the world, and brought the Flood upon it, man was no longer the peaceable ruler of the animal world, but the adversary of the animals. The relationship that God originally envisaged between man and the animals must have meant, by contrast, a paradise of peace for animals. The priestly document had prophetic texts in mind, which describe this peace in the animal kingdom in eschatological statements. For them, it is the lost paradise—a possibility offered to creation, but forefeited.

Of the final statement in Genesis 1:28 we may say, therefore, that what is affirmed is anything but a deep gulf between man and subhuman creation. A paradisical, peaceful unity in God's likeness to man, as understood by the priestly document, was at first meant to be realized. Absolutely nothing of what our generations devise by way of devastation among animal species on various continents, and among fish in the sea and an infinite number of birds and insects, in the name of transforming and exploiting the face of the earth for the sake of man, finds legitimation from this blessing at the dawn of creation.

It says the exact opposite of what is usually read into it. It justifies no population explosion, it says nothing about an alleged right to destroy the landscape and to exploit all supplies of raw material in the course of a few generations; it sketches a vegetarian, paradisical peace with the whole animal world. This blessing compels no Christian or Jew to swallow the myth of growth or to cling to it from loyalty to the Bible.

Open Questions

At the end of our analysis, nevertheless, several questions remain unanswered, and they must not be brushed aside.

One of them pertains to the fact that the priestly document introduces the postdiluvian state of war between man and beast as a new, revised order of creation. Not Genesis 1:28, it is true, but another passage in this system of affirmation—one that is more important for us today—seems to legitimize the exploitation of animals by man. And it cannot be denied that this is meant to be understood as a divine ordinance. Does this not enable us to provide a Christian basis for what is being done to animals today, even if the theoreticians who are interested in these things have hitherto overlooked this passage and so have not made use of its argumentation?

In my opinion, we reach the limit of possibility in interpreting the priestly document. It leaves the matter with its affirmation of the state of war between man and beast, and does not return to the topic in the course of the entire document. The affirmation serves to legitimize eating the flesh of animals, as was in fact customary, and that is all. The hostility image may have been suggested chiefly by the fact that in ancient times hunting and warfare were conducted with similar weapons, and the two pursuits were felt to be akin. What is happening

Growth

to animals today, however, is far beyond the scope of the priestly document, and so it is wrong to identify it with the state of war in the biblical saying.

But these observations lead to a further, much deeper question. Is not the whole experience of the world, which is depicted in this ancient document of Israel, so harmless and so closely linked with nature that one must disclaim all competence in respect to our modern problems of population explosion, industrialization, and ecology? To answer this question, we must undertake a fresh inquiry, which can only be indicated.

The priestly document does not presuppose the totally naive and small-dimension, happy world, such as this question implies. Our arguments may not have made this clear, but the world of the priestly document knew about overpopulation, discussed it thoughtfully and practically, and took a stance on the issue. The world at that time knew the problem of work and exploitation, and it pondered the problem posed by the transformation of nature by human techniques. On this, too, the priestly document (especially its later parts) represented a very definite viewpoint. All of this was contained within less harmful dimensions than we know today, but the core of the problem was there, and therefore it seems to me permissible, indeed demanded, that we transpose the affirmations of the priestly document about these problems into our own world.

As for Genesis 1:28, I hold to the view that this sentence need prevent no one from ridding his mind of the myth of growth.

The Future

Biblical Witness to the Ideal of a Stable World

The great accomplishment of ancient Israel, especially its prophets, was its reversal of man's outlook in the ancient world. In the ancient world, man lived in a cyclically revolving but stable world. Gods ruled over nature. There was confusion, war, natural catastrophe, plague; but these could be overcome. The mighty orders, which had been established at the beginning of time, remained. The proper thing to do was keep within them, preserve them, foster them.

The prophets, as it were, threw a bomb into this world. They turned men's eyes to the future. The world could change; it could become better; and man could hope for everything. But it was not man's deeds that would bring great things about (only in modern times did such a thought emerge); it would all be accomplished by God.

Although the Middle Ages lived by the Bible, still, in the manner of Israel's eschatology, it hoped for the end of this world and the ushering in of a new world. Nonetheless, the ancient sense of stability in the world had reasserted itself, or rather it had never disappeared. Although the rafters kept creaking and new cracks constantly appeared in the walls, man's worldly dwellingplace in the Middle Ages, on the whole, was stable. It was the advent of the modern age that tumbled his dwelling place about him. Then the full force of worldly dynamism was felt, and it kept on increasing.

Men no longer awaited the coming of God; they took the future into their own hands. And so today we find ourselves in an "exploding" world. We often use the term "population explosion," but we might use the term of other spheres as well, for example, the world of economy or commerce. And as no one is any longer capable of controlling a

The Future

genuine explosion, this world threatens to get out of control. We are no longer sure where the terrestrial dynamic, which we have released and in which all join, is leading us, because it has long since permeated the structures of our world. Does a better world really await us, or only the rotting smell of a spent planet?

Bible—what have you brought on us? Prophets—into what state of affairs have you led us?

Obviously, you did not mean things to turn out like this. You spoke of a future molded by God, and God would never destroy his own creation. All the same, you brought us a dynamic and set the future before our eyes. Did you not see the terrible dangers you were conjuring up?

Even in the Old Testament there was—it seems—a reaction against this motivating of men toward the future. I find it in the view of history expressed in the priestly document of the Pentateuch, which dates from the last years of the Babylonian Exile or the first years after the homecoming. Glowing visions of the future, such as those of deutero-Isaiah, had already been written, and it is evident that the priestly author knew them. Thus the stable world of the priestly document has polemic significance, and we see in it a harking back to a more ancient feeling about life—to developed ancient myths, indeed, but not because the writer closed his eyes to what was going on around him. Rather, he shrank from the risks involved in dynamizing the world, as his optimistic contemporaries were doing.

The priestly chronicle is at odds with the Mesopotamian view of the world, as were such prophets as deutero-Isaiah, during the Babylonian Exile. As in the whole of the ancient world, in Mesopotamia the world's stability was founded upon myths of the gods. No Israelite could adopt them, and so the author of the priestly document faced the appalling task of creating a myth of a stable world without the gods. Deutero-Isaiah removed the gods from the world at the expense of stability; so he was compelled to dynamize history. But the priestly document tried to debunk the gods without falling into the trap of dynamism.

A generation that is beginning to doubt the value of a world becoming more and more dynamic may find it rewarding to analyze the contribution of the priestly document. As we have had sufficient acquaintance with the prophets of Israel, let us begin our analysis by extracting the priestly document's concept of history from its most important literary source in Mesopotamian literature, the Atrahasis Epic.

The Atrahasis Epic

The Atrahasis Epic is a poem whose best-known version contains 1,245 verses. For over a thousand years it formed part of the educational heritage of Mesopotamia. The largest extant body of texts is derived from cuneiform tablets made by the scribe Ku-Aja in the seventeenth century B.C., and most of the fragments we possess are parts of various copies made in the seventh century B.C., that is, shortly before the production of our priestly document.

Only very recently have we been able to make a comparative study of the Atrahasis Epic. As early as 1853, tablets containing texts of this epic were excavated. The earliest deciphering of the story of the Flood, which is part of the epic, aroused great interest as early as 1672. It was in 1969, however, that a Danish scholar first reconstructed the threads of action that link the various fragments together. This led to identification of further sections of the epic. Only since 1969 has an English edition of the greater part of the epic been accessible to those who are not scholars of Assyriology. (There is as yet no German version.) An understanding of what this epic of primeval times is all about came even more recently—in 1971 by William L. Moran of Harvard University and, quite independently, by Mrs. Anne D. Kilmer of the University of California (Berkeley) in 1972, in short philological articles. Strange as it may seem, this epic is about the problem of overpopulation and the limitation of population growth, with a view to maintaining cosmic equilibrium.

The action begins in the existing cosmos, but before the creation of man. Only the gods inhabit the cosmos. But "slave labor" has to be done. The more powerful gods have forced the lesser gods to do all the jobs that are necessary for the life of the gods and for the cosmos. This they do on earth, where Enlil, god of the winds, has his palace, while Anu, god of heaven, lives on high alone, and Enki, god of the deep waters, lives deep below the cosmos. After forty years, the working gods can stand it no longer They go on strike, burn their tools, and demonstrate in front of the palace of Enlil, who calls on the other great gods for help. Enki, who figures throughout the epic as the most cunning—the fixer—discovers how to resolve the conflict. Men will have to be created. (Let us note well: the purpose of man's existence was to do the drudgery that had to be done in the cosmos.) What they had in mind was feeding the gods through sacrifices.

And so Enki and Nimtu, the mother god, created men. From clay, the blood of a slaughtered god, and the spittle of all the gods they formed seven men and seven women and established the mechanisms of human reproduction. The human race reproduced at such a rate that, after 1,200 years, Enlil could no longer sleep in his palace because the noise that men were making was so loud. To reduce their numbers, he sent a plague; and now, for the first time, Atrahasis appears—obviously a king. He stands in a special relationship to Enki, god of the deep waters, and asks him for help. Following his advice, men concentrate their efforts on making sacrifice to the god who is responsible for plagues, and they mollify him. Soon, however, the number of men is again so great and their noise so loud that, again, Enlil cannot get to sleep. So he stops up the rain and a famine ensues. Once again, men begin to die. Enki advises them to concentrate on sacrifice to the god of rain. Thereupon, this god secretly sends dew in the night, so that, despite the absence of rain, the fruit ripens.

At this point the text becomes very patchy. However, when Enlil sees that he cannot halt man's propagation by more or less conventional means, he gets all the gods to agree to annihilate mankind with a flood. Enki refuses to provide the primeval waters of the deep; so Enlil brings a flood upon the earth by means of a seven-day rainstorm. Enki has warned Atrahasis in advance, through a dream, of the threatening danger, and Atrahasis builds an ark. The rest of mankind looks askance at what he is doing; but Atrahasis and his family and the living creatures they take into the ark survive the flood. While the flood is raging, the gods are overcome with hunger and realize that, with mankind, they have also destroyed their sacrifices and the foundation of their own existence. We hear the moving hymns of lament of the great goddesses. After the flood, Atrahasis offers his sacrifice, and the gods come buzzing around like flies. They discover that there have been survivors.

This precipitates the climax of the epic. At a grand assembly of the gods, Enlil tries to put Enki on the spot for having frustrated the plan of annihilation; but most of the gods stand by Enki. At length a compromise is struck between the divine parties. On one hand, the continued existence of mankind is to be assured, so that the gods can retain their slaves to provide them with daily nourishment through sacrifice. On the other hand, the scheme ensures that men will not exceed the number that is useful for the gods—and that, of course, means useful for the cosmos. Toward the end of the epic the text again becomes fragmentary; however, we can make out part of the formula of compromise:

> Furthermore: there are to be only one third of the men there were formerly. There shall be amongst mankind infertile as well as fertile women. Among mankind the demon of death shall snatch small children from their mother's lap. Install Ugbabtu-priestesses, Entu-priestesses, and Igisitu-priestesses. Because intercourse with men is tabu for them, they shall be incapable of bearing children. [III, VIII, 1-8]

And so biological, demonic, and social measures are prescribed (today we would classify the demonic as biological, for it has to do with infant mortality). By these measures the number of men was to be kept steady—much lower, indeed, than in the labile period at the beginning. By this postdiluvian compromise the balance of nature is restored; the cosmos is stabilized; the epic comes to an end.

We may be astonished to discover that such a seemingly modern problem as overpopulation had assumed such importance in the second millennium B.C.; but let us consider. The highly organized canal-and-city civilization of Mesopotamia emerged because the land could not otherwise have supported the people who already lived there. And so, at an early date, that region must have known the problem of a too rapidly increasing population; the techniques of the time could provide assistance to only a limited extent. Nomads from the marginal lands, between the agrarian regions and the desert, aggravated the problem with their surplus population. The number of men could be felt to be a key problem for nature herself—in mythological terms, a problem for the gods. It makes sense, then, that although there were other well-known cosmogonic themes in Mesopotamia, this problem in the Atrahasis Epic overshadowed all others and became the one, dominant theme in a cosmogony.

We have to agree with William L. Moran when he describes the epic, as a whole, as a cosmogony. The cosmos *seems* to be in full existence when the story begins, but that is an illusion; it had not yet attained the stable form in which it now exists. It was extremely labile, and able to find equilibrium only after a process of trial and error by the gods. This process reached its climax in the compromise of the gods after the flood.

When equilibrium is achieved, the epic ends. From then on, there is no more to be said on this plane. Such a cosmogony tells the story only of dynamic and unstable origins. The implicit thesis runs: From the flood on, the cosmos is stable. The form it then received is its enduring form. One can find one's way around in it, so to speak. One can rely upon it.

The Priestly Chronicle

There is probably a double dependence of the priestly document upon the Atrahasis Epic—one through the chief literary model of the priestly document, the so-called Yahwist historical work. It is commonly supposed that the latter originated in the courts of David and Solomon and thus was several centuries older than the priestly document. The works have come down to us interwoven and enriched with other narratives and legal texts (the Pentateuch, for example).

Evidence that the Yahwist historian must have known the Atrahasis Epic, either directly or indirectly, is his construction of primeval history, which begins with the creation of man, in an already existing cosmos, and reaches its climax in the Flood and Noah's sacrifice. Even such details as Eve's designation—"the mother of all those who live" (Gn 3:20)—have parallels in the Atrahasis Epic. While the priestly document was conceived as a book that was to supersede the Yahwist history and replace its interpretation of world history and Israel's history with a fresh interpretation, the priestly document was forced into indirect confrontation with the Atrahasis Epic. The author of the chronicle seems to have been aware of this, and seems to have referred directly to the Atrahasis Epic, which obviously he knew.

He "borrowed" important elements which the Yahwist had not passed on to him—the motif, for example, of the increase of the human race. Even in small details, his knowledge of the epic is manifest: use of the plural, for example (for which the Yahwist could have no motivation whatever), in the narrative of the Creator of man, which recalls the assembly of gods in the Atrahasis Epic before the creation of men (Gn 1:26: "Let *us* make man in *our* image, in *our* likeness"). In contrast to the Yahwist, whose dependence on the epic is much more external, the former seems, above all, to have accepted (with certain modifications) the cosmogonic, fundamental conception of the epic and to have made it the fundamental conception of his own work. Let us examine this thesis.

The priestly narrative begins at an earlier time than does the Atrahasis Epic. There is only God—and primeval chaos (Gn 1:2). By forcing back the primeval waters and other acts of separating things out, God builds a vaulted space, a kind of cosmic dwelling house whose walls hold back the waters of chaos, which press upon it from outside. He furnishes the interior of this space with sun, moon, stars, fish and birds, land animals, and, finally, human beings. He creates mankind as man and woman. Men are to multiply, take possession of the territories of the world, and rule over the beasts in paradisical peace. After this six-day operation, God declares the seventh day to be holy and rests in it (Gn 1:3-2:4).

In contrast to the Atrahasis Epic, the creation of man is not preceded by a dramatic dispute among the gods. This is all the more evident when we consider that the source of the narrative is recalled by use of the plural. For the priestly document, any strife between gods was unthinkable. Its God was not just one of the powers of the cosmos, who had to contend with other powers; he stood out against all others required no human slave labor, and defined man in terms of his lordship over the animal kingdom. What remains—produced by the fecundity blessing—is the motif of the increase of the human race. With this, the priestly document seems consciously to take up the themes of the Atrahasis Epic.

As in the Atrahasis Epic, mankind thrives. The literary device, employed by the priestly document to express this thriving as a result of the fecundity blessing, is the genealogy, one of which follows immediately upon the week of creation (Gn 5). This brings mankind from its first parents down to Noah, the hero of the Flood, which receives ample treatment. In the priestly document, moreover, the Flood appears as an exact antitype of the creation of the cosmos (Gn 6:9-22 and parts of Gn 7-8). If in this representation the cosmos was in some measure portrayed as a hollow dam in the midst of the waters of chaos, we now see the waters of chaos breaking in and destroying the cosmos, until a halt is called and the cosmos is reconstituted.

The effect of the Flood is thus the same as in the Atrahasis Epic. The human population is reduced to a small remnant—accomplished, however, by a mere rainstorm, though on an extraordinary scale. The "waters of the deep" played no part in it. Here, however, by contrast, the existence of the cosmos is threatened.

In the last analysis, the recasting of the story is probably connected with a difference of views about the relationship between God and the world. The priestly document denies the eternity of nature. More clearly than in the first sentences of the Bible, here, in imagery and antitypal imagery, in the six days of creation and in the Flood it is affirmed that

God created the world from nothing and that it depends, unconditionally, upon him. To build up this double picture, the storytelling in the priestly document had to start at an earlier point than did the Atrahasis Epic, for which the cosmos existed when its story begins.

What brings the cosmos to the brink of extinction? Certainly not the fact that mankind has increased too greatly in number (no such thing is mentioned). Rather, all living things, God's "good" (indeed "very good") handiwork, had become "corrupt." The story of the Flood begins with this affirmation:

> The earth grew corrupt in God's sight, and filled with violence. God contemplated the earth; it was corrupt, for corrupt where the ways of all flesh on the earth. [Gn 6:11f]

In the typically repetitive style of the priestly document, the matter is reformulated shortly afterward, when God commands Noah to build the ark:

> The end has come for all things of flesh: I have decided this, because the earth is full of violence of men's making, and I will efface them from the earth. [Gn 6:13]

The Atrahasis Epic is basically amoral and purely physical-biological in conception. In contrast, the priestly document sees sin and the behavior of living creatures among themselves as the threat to the cosmos. "Violence" is a sin against God, insofar as it is destructive of his good creation.

After the Flood, however, the instability that is implied in the possibility of violence was overcome—as was the instability of the cosmos in the Atrahasis Epic—by a postdiluvian compromise. This is surely how we have to understand Genesis 9:1-17. In the beginning, God had given flesh—men as well as animals—permission to eat only vegetation (Gn 1:29-30). The violence which called down the Flood must be understood to mean, at least, that men and animals had eaten flesh—in violation of God's decree—and so had been killing living things. By the compromise after the Flood, man was granted the flesh of animals, in addition to vegetation, for food (Gn 9:2-3). Thus the killing of animals by hunting or slaughtering ceased to be considered violence; but the killing of men was still violence, and God himself saw that it would be avenged (Gn 9:5-6). However, the possibility of violence is now so limited, in comparison to former times, that vengeance can be taken upon the guilty without involving the whole cosmos. And so God is able to swear an oath that he will never send another Flood (Gn 9:9-17). The compromise has thus brought stability to the cosmos.

The compromise after the Flood brings the Atrahasis Epic to an end. Stabilizing the number of men stabilized the cosmos itself. But the compromise after the Flood is not the end for the priestly document; it continues with the history of the peoples and, in particular, the history of Israel. Does this mean the history of a stable world?

Here we have reached a point whose understanding depends a great deal on our interpretation of the priestly document. It seems to me that in the priestly document the "Flood compromise" brings a limitation of the extent of violence, so that the edifice of the world, as such, is stabilized. That which in the Atrahasis Epic was the driving force of the cosmogony, that is, the enormous propagative power of the human race, is introduced at the very beginning by the priestly document, but it does not play a part in the course of the story. Certainly this was not what provoked the Flood, as it had in the Atrahasis Epic. Correspondingly, human fertility is not restricted by the Flood compromise, as in the Atrahasis Epic. Quite the opposite. The text of the Flood compromise is introduced by the exact repetition of the original fecundity blessing: "Be fruitful, multiply, and fill the earth" (Gn 9:1).

The newly granted permission to eat the flesh of animals seems to have the effect of increasing human powers of reproduction, adding, so to speak, more animal vitality. In conclusion, in Genesis 9:7, the fecundity blessing is repeated, with the addition of a word hitherto used only of animals, the verb "to teem." "Be fruitful, multiply, *teem* over the earth."

No doubt this is where concern with the problems of human increase begins. As long as this increase does not come to a halt, the same thing that we described as "cosmogony" in the Atrahasis Epic is in process in the priestly document. And because in Genesis 1:28 other things, too, were linked with the increase of the human race, most of all the various peoples' taking possession of the parts of the earth allotted to them, a further dynamic has to be looked for before a totally stable world can emerge.

Immediately, after the Flood, the new fecundity blessing showed its power. In Genesis 10, genealogies indicate the growth of the new human race and its penetration into the various regions of the earth. In contrast to the Atrahasis Epic, whose world seems to be Mesopotamia, the priestly writer no longer depicts the second phase of the cosmogony on an international horizon. From now on, all its breadth is constrained within the example of one nation (here the priestly document follows its chief source, the Yahwist chronicle). We may leave the question open whether he took Israel merely as an example of what happened to all peoples or whether he saw in Israel the real, critical point in the second cosmogonic phase.

At all events, the more expansively developed family tree of Shem soon brings us to Terah, Abram, and Lot (Gn 11:10-27). The narrative is picked up again at this point. Terah has no settled home; he wants to move from Ur in Chaldaea to Canaan, but stops halfway there in Haran. After his death, Abram and Lot proceed farther; but other people already live in Canaan. Besides, Abram has problems about posterity, for Sarai, his wife, is barren and he can have a son only through her slave girl, Hagar. Then the problems, which will have to be solved in the second half of the priestly document, are named: the increase of people and a land to possess, which must also be provided for Abram's line of mankind. Additional problems will emerge along the way.

The stories of the patriarchs in the priestly document give a very concise treatment of Isaac and Joseph, concentrating on Abram and Jacob. In the story of each, a great revelation of God stands at the center (Gn 11 and 35). At these revelations they again receive the fecundity blessing of the dawn of creation and the morning after the Flood, especially for the benefit of their groups (Gn 17:6-7, 15-20, 35:11). This is so great that not only Israel but other peoples also will stem from Abraham. These others, however, are soon dropped from the narrative, which follows only the destinies of the chief line. To the promise of increase is added by oath the gift of a defined geographical region to Israel: Yahweh will give Israel the land of Canaan (Gn 17:8, 35:12). A third promise remains at first unexplained: "I will be your God and the God of your descendants" (Gn 17:7, 8).

The fulfillments of these promises and blessings follow one after the other. The fecundity blessing is the first to show results. The fulfillment or execution of a divine word is always recorded in the priestly document, and almost in the same words in which God had spoken. The record of fulfillment of the increase of Israel is at the beginning of the Book of Exodus. In the meantime, the descendants of Jacob have once more gone far away from Canaan; they are in Egypt.

> But the sons of Israel were fruitful and grew in numbers greatly; they increased and grew so immensely powerful that they filled the land. [Ex 1:7]

None of the formulae is missing, not even those parts that were added after the Flood, and a new part is added: "they ... grew so immensely powerful." And so the business of increasing has been finished. The blessing has been fulfilled. Israel has its quota of men; it is a powerful people; it fills the land.

But not its own land—it is in a foreign country. Instead of the Israelites' being masters in their own land, the Egyptians make slaves of them and oppress them. In the Atrahasis Epic, slave labor was the purpose of human life; here it symbolizes the miserable and unjust intermediate state of a cosmos that had not yet achieved harmony. God will have to intervene and rescue Israel from slavery and lead the people into their predestined land.

This program, the second stage in the fulfillment of the promises made to Abraham and Jacob, is formulated in Exodus 6 in the revelation given by Yahweh to Moses. The liberation from Egypt, regarded in other parts of the Bible as the most fundamental fact in the history of Israel, appears in this place—in any interpretation put upon it—as an interim scene on the way toward stabilization of the world.

The program formulated in Exodus 6 corresponds to what happens in the sequel. With signs and wonders, Israel is led out of Egypt. On trek through the wilderness, it discovered, in connection with the miracle of manna, the rhythm of the week, with the sabbath as the day of rest, and at Sinai the sanctuary was established. Then retrograde factors emerge. The sins of Israel (Nm 13f) and its spiritual leaders (Nm 20) require in retribution the dying out of the exodus generation. The next generation will be the first to enter Canaan, after the elapse of forty years.

But eventually they get there. The two leaders of the new generation are installed: Eleazar, the spiritual leader (Nm 20: 25-28), and Joshua, the secular leader (Nm 27:15-23). Here, as with the compromise after the Flood, there is a modification of the hitherto prevailing order. With Moses and Aaron, the priest was subordinate to Moses, and God conversed with Moses. From now on, Joshua will be subordinate to the priest, for Joshua did not receive all of Moses' dignity but only some of it (Nm 27:20), and through the oracle, Eleazar conversed with God (Nm 27:21). Aaron had died (Nm 20), and now the last of the sinful generation, which fell into the sin even of unbelief, Moses himself, dies—on the threshold of the promised land (Nm 27, Dt 34).

We scarcely need tell more. The priestly presentation of history is almost finished and breaks off just as the Atrahasis Epic broke off, when, through the compromise after the Flood, that condition of the world was assured which guaranteed harmony and stability.

And so a conquest of the land is not recounted, because basically the priestly document knows of no war, apart from the mythical destruction of the Egyptians in the sea (which was the work not of Israelite troops but Yahweh). Only one or two sentences tell us that the Jordan was crossed and a paschal festival immediately celebrated in the land (Jos 5:10). The supply of manna ceased and from then on men lived from the fruits of the land (Jos 5:11f). The whole land is in the possession of the Israelites, and they build the sanctuary at Shiloh (Jos 18:1), where they divide the land among themselves (Jos 19:51). All this is a succinct indication that normal life is beginning in their own land.

In spite of this brevity, the priestly chronicle is interested ultimately not in the tale of the traveled road but in the goal now reached. It tells of the stable cosmos as it has become and will remain, filled with inhabitants who live peacefully and healthily on their own portion of earth. The priestly document also describes the world epoch before this condition was reached, and to that extent describes an unstable world with dynamic processes. This epoch constituted what we now call "history," as the world found its way to a better future.

It would be a misunderstanding of the priestly document, however, to read into it the notion that, once Israel occupied its land, the process would continue. Neither the Atrahasis Epic nor the priestly document, both of which run twice through the cosmogonic arc—first to reach a stable world edifice and then to accomplish a stable distribution of the population—means to compose an ongoing cosmogony.

Once, there was increase—which does not mean there should *always* be increase. The objective of increase was that the peoples would take their origin from families, and now that this has been accomplished, the fecundity blessing of the opening stage has achieved its goal. Once, whole peoples wandered across the face of the earth; but people must not forever wander about, without a homeland. The object of wandering was simply to distribute people over the earth, until each arrived at its own territory. Now they are there, and the blessing concerning possession of the land, belonging to the early stage, has achieved its end. From now on, the world can and should remain the way it is. A sanctuary has been set up in the land, in which God dwells in the midst of his people. After cosmogonic world history comes the epoch of cultic joy. Further historical narration is superfluous.

The Priestly Document and Instability

This is the way one has to understand the priestly chronicle, if one recognizes the close connection of its narrative structure with that of the

Atrahasic Epic, and uses this connection as a basis for interpretation. This interpretation, admittedly, is new, but only because the Atrahasis Epic has only very recently become known to us. There are still great uncertainties in interpreting the Atrahasis Epic, and additional uncertainties of great magnitude necessarily emerge when we compare two literary works from such diverse cultures; therefore one must always be prepared to question and to revise such an interpretation, in its details or even in its totality. But in light of the data available at present, this interpretation seems to me to be demanded.

If this is so, one must risk making it. Such a comparative interpretation undoubtedly leads us further than one that, because it rests solely upon the text of the priestly document, seems to make no presuppositions, but, in fact, secretly (as it were) reads into the text modern categories of interpretation, evolutionary notions, and what is essentially a dynamism of the future. Is this not what has always happened, insofar as people have given any thought to understanding the history in the priestly document?

If our interpretation is correct, the priestly document deliberately set itself against any emerging eschatology. The future was unnecessary for it, because all is contained within the present. This is shown repeatedly in its transformation of the traditional concept of the covenant, which had been a kind of contract between Yahweh and Israel. A contract can be broken; it *had* been broken, and the consequence was the exile; thus God's relationship with Israel—and everything else—was called into question. The prophets had to invite men to forget what had been and to hope for something new from Yahweh. The disciples of Jeremiah produced their text about a "new covenant," which Yahweh would inaugurate and which would infinitely surpass the "old covenant" (Jer 31:31-34). Not so the priestly document; it transposed the covenant of Sinai, where the covenant concept traditionally originated, to Abraham, the father of the promise, and made from this an "eternal covenant." Individual generations might drop out of the covenant relationship through sin, but succeeding generations revived the covenant and Yahweh made good his ancient promises, which culminated in his being their God and dwelling in their midst. For the priestly writer, nothing

The Future

can be more sublime. In the ordinances of the cult, the transcendent God has become immanent.

This provides the answer to an objection that is bound to be made at this point. According to the priestly document, after the Israelites entered Canaan the stable epoch in world history arrived. But it did not—and the most striking proof of this is the fact that, in the very moment when the priestly document was produced, the occupation of the land by Israel was *500 years in the past*. In all this time, the world had known no peace, and the people of Israel, in particular, had had a very rough history. Of all the twelve tribes, Judah alone remained, on a miserably reduced territory; and then Judah was driven out of its territory, to live in exile in Babylon. It was almost like Egypt all over again. The real world, as experienced in the time of the priestly document, was thus the very opposite of stable. Does this document, and this author, simply ignore the fact?

Taking account of a wide variety of indications in the text of the priestly document, exegetical scholarship has very recently come to see that, in this document, the distant past—before the entry into the land of Canaan—is very definitely stylized, with an eye on the situation of the Jews in the Babylonian Exile. Hence the purpose of the pronouncements in the priestly document was seen as arousing a "hope of homecoming" among the exiles. By reference to the somewhat archetypal events of the time of Moses, they were told what could still happen between the people and their God, if the people would be prepared to accept it.

I think that this is the correct interpretation; and it fits the picture of a stable world exactly. It may happen that this stability is upset, but this represents a retrogression to the intrinsically conquered instability of the cosmogony that once was. That is why the situations which then emerge so clearly recall the intermediate stages of the once unstable world, recorded in the history in the priestly document. And that is why Judah, in Babylon, remembered Israel in Egypt. But the covenant which guaranteed the stability of the world—the "Noah covenant" concerning the edifice of the world and the "Abraham covenant" concerning the typical nation—is an everlasting covenant. People can in effect reject the covenant relationship, but it is offered afresh to the next generation. If a breakdown of the equilibrium of the world and the nations occurs, the ancient history of the world, which had not yet achieved stability (as told by the priestly document), provides a model for the restoration of harmony. The fundamentally stable world of the priestly document therefore allows typological correspondence to the troubled, primeval stage of the world, when there still was history and evolution, but it finds no place for any genuinely new history of its own.

For this very reason, the priestly document refrains from urging its readers to look toward an ever greater future. It is able to convey this restraint and yet give hope—hope of returning home. This means a real homecoming, not escape into the unknown.

Because everyone is mentally conditioned to look forward eagerly toward the future, such a vision also fills us with fear of emptiness and boredom. What is a man to do in a world that has found tranquillity and is no longer preoccupied with thoughts of change? Would life not become dreary?

The priestly document seems to avoid this question by breaking off its narrative at the point where stability is achieved. But that is not quite relevant. It has discovered an instrument of narration which enables us to direct our attention to the perfected shape of the world. By anticipation it allows Israel's most important institutions to be established, in the period of the wandering in the wilderness. In the wilderness, what will give meaning, light, and joy to the posthistorical, tranquil world was already disclosed.

After the exodus from Egypt (Ex 12:40f, parts of Ex 14), Israel journeyed to the wilderness of Sin (Ex 15:27, 16:1), where the miraculous feeding with manna and quails began. Through this, Israel discovered the mystery of the "time rhythm" that was built into the cosmos. The sabbath governs time. As soon as the world achieves stability, there is no longer a pressing forward; time becomes structured by the week, with its benign cycle of work and festivity. Work ceases to be hectic. On the sabbath, it becomes possible to celebrate a holy festival, which sheds light upon the entire week.

The Future

From the wilderness of Sin, the Israelites moved to the wilderness of Sinai (Ex 17:1, 19:1f), where God instituted Israel's sanctuary and gave it its cult: the presence of God among men. The most important passage runs thus:

> I will remain with the sons of Israel, and I will be their God. And so they will know that it is I, Yahweh, their God, who brought them out of the land of Egypt to live among them; I, Yahweh their God. [Ex 29:45f]

As the Atrahasis Epic (but by no means that alone) makes plain, their cult of the gods gave meaning to life for the men of Mesopotamia, and that cult was conceived as the human slave labor which kept the divine cosmos going. For Israel, too, in the view of the priestly document, the world and human society—within a cosmos that has become stable—reach their summit in the cult. But this cult is based on the drawing near of God, who comes freely and bestows his presence. It is this cult alone that makes the world, now at rest, truly lovable. This is what was meant when God said to Abraham: "I will be your God, and the God of your descendants," and again when the sentence, expanded, was repeated to Moses: "I will adopt you as my own people, and I will be your God" (Ex 6:7).

The priestly document had a curious fate. It was woven, with other documents, into the Pentateuch, so that its well-defined understanding of history became almost invisible. All the same, it provided the framework for the Pentateuch, and the prophets were regarded as no more than commentators on the Torah, so that we may say that in Palestinian Jewry it remained the final norm. Perhaps that is why in postexilic Jewry interest became so minimal in the production of historical works that carried the story further.

Apocalyptical writing was the first to resume the thread of the prophetic dynamic of the future. Within the framework of its expectation of the end, the primitive Church saw Jesus as the fullness and the end of time. But this meant that Israel's entry into the land of Canaan no longer constitutes the point at which the history of the world reaches its end, which is the appearance of Jesus of Nazareth. On the whole, does this not again present a concept of a stable world, as the priestly document does? Will any Christian dare affirm that God still has something even greater to offer than his own Son—that is, himself?

In view of this fact, one is bound to ask why Christians today do not find more difficulty with the "prophetic evolutionism" that is currently in vogue.

Leisure

The Work Week and the Sabbath in the Old Testament, and Especially in the Priestly Chronicle

There is work and there is leisure, and both are part of man's life. How are they distributed in the world?

The ancient world made a clear-cut distribution of work and leisure. Work was for slaves and women; leisure was the substance of a man's life—a free man's life. Also, the medieval system of education, as well as the Humanist educational ideal, were determined by the ancient distinction between the "liberal arts" and the "mechanical arts." The humanistic gymnasium (grammar school) and Humboldt University were the last repercussions of this system of distribution of work and leisure: work for slaves and women, leisure for gentlemen.

This held true not only of the Graeco-Roman world but applied also to the ancient East, and we must bear this in mind if we want to understand how great a revolution was the "Sabbath Commandment" of the people of Israel, for in this commandment the distribution formula of work and leisure among those "above" and those "below" was scrapped. A new distribution of work and leisure was proclaimed for all men, and in terms of a temporal cycle. "For all" because everyone is addressed, and "in terms of a temporal cycle"—because the commandment runs: "For six days you shall labor and do all your work, but the seventh day is a sabbath for Yahweh your God. You shall do no work that day" (Ex 20:9f, Dt 5:13f). And to make it quite clear who had the right—the duty, indeed—to keep the day of rest, the following list is added: "You shall do no work that day, neither you [that is, the free man, who is addressed] nor your son nor your daughter [i.e. the family of the free man], nor your servants, men or women [i.e. those "below"], nor your ox nor your donkey nor any of your animals [i.e. even the subhuman creatures on the farm], nor the stranger who lives with you [even the framework of the group is burst through]." So that the explosive factor in the revolution in the distribution of work and leisure would become quite clear, there follows yet another statement: "Thus your servant, man or woman, shall rest as you do" (Dt 5:14).

It was still assumed that there would be slaves, but the foundations of a slave-owning society were seriously undermined, for the distribution of work and leisure to different classes of men is rejected. Moreover, the freeing of slaves is already in sight, for in at least one of the versions that contains the Ten Commandments the new distribution of work and leisure is based upon the fact that Israel had once been a nation of slaves and was rescued from slavery only by its God. The text runs: "Remember that you were a servant in the land of Egypt, and that Yahweh your God brought you out from there with mighty hand and outstretched arm; because of this, Yahweh your God has commanded you to keep the sabbath day" (Dt 5:15). He who has known the harshest exploitation and then been able to move into the ranks of the fortunate, who have received the gift of leisure, ought to appreciate the difference. He ought to feel within himself an impulse toward change. He cannot be content with the ancient distribution of work and leisure. He must reach the point where he wishes every man to have work—and leisure.

The Status of Man and the Life of the Gods

This revolution was so powerful that it changed even the concept of God. Just as in human society there were those who worked and those who enjoyed leisure, people explained the relationship between men and the gods in the same way, especially in the Mesopotamian culture. The gods, above, were beings who enjoyed sacred leisure; men, below, on the contrary, were beings of work. It came from the differentiating character of man, that he was to do the slave labor that had to be done in the cosmos.

The Atrahasis Epic, well known in the ancient East during the first and second millennia B.C., begins with the statement:

> As the gods, just like men,
> performed servile work, and suffered weariness,
> the weariness of the gods was great,
> their labour heavy, their exhaustion excessive,
> the seven great Anunnaki resolved,
> that from now on only the Igigu should suffer from work.

When the epic begins, the gods are divided into two classes: the seven great Anunnaki, who assure the portion of leisure for themselves, and the lower class, the Igigu, whose lot from now on will be to work. This is a divine reflection of human conditions.

For only forty years, however, did these heavenly laborers submit to their drudgery. Then they went on strike, burned their tools, and held a demonstration outside the palace of one of the Great Seven. This god called to the others for help, and one of them, the god of wisdom, saw a way out. He said to the mother god:

> You are the goddess of birth, the creatrix of men.
> Make men to be our yoke-bearers.
> He will bear the yoke, that the weather-god
> will give him,
> He will bear the weariness of the gods.

While the god of wisdom and the mother god were creating men from the blood of a slaughtered Igigu god, mixed with earth, the mother god triumphantly proclaimed to the other gods:

> I have taken away your heavy labor,
> I have placed your weariness upon men.
> You cried for men—
> I have freed you from the yoke, have given you freedom.

Leisure

At this point the history of mankind begins—man, the new cosmic slave, whose existence makes it possible for the gods to enjoy leisure.

This myth merely recounts in epic breadth what one learns over and over again from Mesopotamian texts of the most diverse genre, from widely different epochs. The purpose of man's being is to bear the yoke of the gods and do the necessary slave labor of the cosmos. Man knows no real leisure, which is the prerogative of the gods. If any class should acquire even a small share of leisure, it would rise above the genuinely human and become, more or less, like the gods.

One can interpret this definition of man's essence as one will. One may think it is an almost classic example of religion as the opium with which rulers dope their subjects so that they accept a system of exploitation. Or one might say that this is merely verbal articulation of the true experience: that freedom and leisure are not granted to men and that, in the last analysis, life is burdensome weariness. Perhaps both are true. At all events, the new distribution of work and leisure, proclaimed in the Third Commandment—not according to class but the days of the week—threw this definition of the essence of God and man on the scrap heap.

If all men are to work but are also to enjoy leisure, it cannot be that the gods are beings of leisure and men are cosmic slave laborers. I have said that the Bible gives us two versions of the Ten Commandments. In one, the Sabbath Commandment finds its *raison d'être* in the liberation from Egypt, where Israel itself had been a slave. The other version, by contrast, sees the *raison d'être* of the new distribution of work and leisure in the action of the Creator:

> For in six days Yahweh made the heavens and the earth and the sea and all that these hold, but on the seventh day he rested; that is why Yahweh has blessed the sabbath day and made it sacred. [Ex 20:11]

In the Mesopotamian texts, too, men were seen as created in the image of God. This meant, however, that men were to perform slave labor in place of the gods, and the latter thereby were released to become beings of leisure. For Israel, the Sabbath Commandment revealed its God as one who works as well as rests.

Did Israel's Sabbath Win the Day?

This was the great revolution the Third Commandment brought into the world. But today, it would seem, the spirit of this revolution is a thing of the past. Work and leisure are no longer distributed simply between those above and those beneath, the bosses and the bossed—except, here and there, as intrusions into our very different world of vestiges from slave-owning and feudal societies. On the whole, the Third Commandment has won the day. Everybody works and everybody has leisure. Indeed, many of those at the "top" work more than an eight-hour day—more, that is, than their subordinates—and many of them die before their time because they work themselves to death. As a class, they probably work harder than anyone else and undoubtedly as well.

And for everyone, leisure time increases. Closing time comes earlier in the day, and we no longer speak of "Sunday" but "the weekend." For many, the weekend begins about noon on Friday, and an ever lengthening summer vacation is guaranteed to all. Low-cost tours and excursions—to southern climes, exotic places, around the world—are available to most. In addition to all this, many are given leave for educational purposes.

It might appear, therefore, that the Third Commandment, with its message of the sabbath, has been victorious. It no longer commands the individual to take his stand against society and to follow his own, enlightened conscience. Society has made it a reality, accepted by all. If one did not accept the rhythm of working time and leisure time, he would be flying in the face of one of the most sacred laws of our society.

We almost forget that a divine commandment enforces or underlies this rhythm.

All the same, we are not really at ease with the Third Commandment. Despite appearances, changes have been taking place that again call everything into question.

Society assures the individual an ever increasing amount of leisure, but we have to ask, with growing urgency, whether this free time does us any good—whether, in our society, it really brings us time for rest, for leisure, for celebration. In fact, we may experience dread of free time because it threatens our lives with boredom and loneliness. Or we, like many others, seeking escape from boredom, may turn what should be leisure into a new type of activity, into a so-called hobby, which in reality becomes a form of servile labor that can stifle communication within a family. Or anxiety may appear as the achievement of excellence in sport, as participant or spectator; or we may become an "inveterate traveler." Or we may settle for nothing more than the dreariness of dragging through the weekend with the help of TV, fast-food meals, a few beers, and "extra" sleep. How often do we come to the end of a period of free time, worn out and jaded, unhappy, and looking forward to getting back to work!

Our distress over leisure is illumined from another angle also. Because work today is normally organized as "industry," there is reason to speak of a "leisure industry," which governs human leisure with much the same rules and standards as industry proper. The individual becomes a cog in the giant wheel of a system of organization, competing offers, modish pressures. People no longer do the pushing, they are pushed. Has leisure, therefore, not become a new form of enslavement? Through a dialectical transformation of leisure into a new type of work, we may be back where we started. Once again, men may be no better than perpetual slave laborers. We would not now apportion leisure solely to the gods in heaven but to a utopian paradise—a dream for the distant future. In principle, however, we would become Mesopotamians again. The Third Commandment would have been proclaimed in vain.

Consecrating Leisure

It seems important, as I see it, to pay heed in this situation to a small word in the Bible's sabbath ordinance, which we often fail to hear. The word is "consecrate" or "keep holy."

The Third Commandment begins with the sentence "Observe the sabbath day and keep it holy" (Dt 5:12). What does this mean? In biblical language, "to keep holy" means to remove some thing from the sphere of the normal, the common, the profane; to place it in relation to God through (for example) ritual or prayer or worship. Related to human leisure, therefore, the word means that his free time will become liberating for man, will bring him rest and enable him to be himself, only if it culminates in sacred celebration, in making contact with God, who in himself is tranquillity and blessed festivity.

If we read the Third Commandment carefully, we see it really means to introduce a day of rest for all men; but it goes a step further. At the same time, it wants to ensure that rest and celebration really come about; hence it clearly points out what man must pay heed to on the day of rest. He must see that he makes his rest a holy rest, which brings him close to God. This aspect of the sabbath ordinance is, as a rule, unknown to our modern society, and it may well be that here is the cause of the sickness that affects us when we try to cope with our leisure.

I suspect that something like this is the case: When we work we produce some sort of goods (which are used somewhere or other) which we lose sight of and in which we therefore lose interest. What interests us is the money we earn by our work, and then we use this money in our leisure time. The purpose of our work is thus found in our leisure time. And the purpose of our leisure time? Many think we must use it to become fit again for work. And so the purpose of our leisure time is work. The dog is chasing its tail. We work for leisure time and our leisure time gives us strength to work. The whole thing makes no sense.

But we *must* find meaning in life. If work has no other meaning (at least for many) than to give opportunity of leisure, then leisure must have more meaning, a meaning in itself. The concept of the hobby can help us here, in which a person does something for fun, and something he has chosen for himself. In leisure time we can be with our family, meet our friends, enjoy the arts, games, walking, nonutilitarian education—everything, indeed, in which we can become more ourselves, can bring into our lives that augmentation of meaning that we need. When we sense that what we are doing contains meaning in itself, we experience happiness.

It seems, however, that in all we have so far mentioned the experience of "meaning" is strangely endangered. Boredom can hang over friendship, art, even entertainment. The sense of meaning can retreat; everything can become empty; the world can crumble into a meaningless mosaic. Probably all the separate realities of our life preserve their meaning only if life itself is interiorly illumined by a fundamental meaning that embraces all.

If one wants to be assured of this meaning, one stands at the place where the Third Commandment of ancient Israel used the phrase "keep holy." In the ritual of worship, in common prayer and praise, we relate ourselves and our world to God as to a force which can give ultimate and secure meaning. It is always worthwhile relating to God and living in the light of his love. When, at some point in leisure time, we experience contact with this ultimate meaning, everything else acquires meaning, leisure makes men of us, and the danger is banished of leisure tumbling into empty boredom or into another form of what, in the end, proves to be meaningless work.

We merely affirm this, without adducing proofs. In the last resort, proof would be possible only through the experience of trying it out. Does the leisure time of a group become something different—provide a genuine antithesis to work—if the group makes it holy, opens itself to God and shapes itself with reference to him? There surely are such experiences, but we are not speaking about them at the moment. For the present, we prefer to treat of the myth through which, in the Old Testament, the message of the sabbath rest, as contained in the Decalogue, was unfolded for the Israelites and made to soak into their hearts. As a rule, we know only fragments of this myth, chiefly the opening chapter of the Bible about the creation of the world in six days plus one. But it is worthwhile grasping it as a whole. A myth cannot prove, but it can perhaps light values in our soul. It may even work more powerfully than any proof.

The Distinguishing Feature of the Priestly Chronicle

Myth is one of the principal narrative strands of the priestly chronicle in the Pentateuch. This source for the Pentateuch treats of the beginnings of the world and of man, immediately adding a prehistory of the human race. Toward the end of this prehistory, as in the older Mesopotamian prehistoric tales and in the Yahwist historical work, is the story of the Flood. After the Flood, the new human race spread over the face of the earth, and soon the story picks up a single thread in mankind's history, leading from the patriarchs Abraham, Isaac, and Jacob to the forming of the people of Israel in Egypt. Israel becomes enslaved in Egypt, then is liberated from Egypt by Moses, acting on the command of Israel's God, Yahweh. In the wilderness, especially on Mt. Sinai, Yahweh reveals himself in a theophany. His worship is instituted. Thereafter, experiencing miracles and often committing grave sin, the people journey through the wilderness until they reach the frontier of the promised land of Canaan, where Moses dies. The document ends with a brief mention of the entry into the land and its partition among the tribes.

To outward appearance, the priestly document tells roughly the same story as its older source, the Yahwist chronicle, but the language is different. Moreover, only selected events are recounted, and more expansively treated. The rest are either summarized or ignored. In his affirmations, the Yahwist author wanted to portray the past, while providing, by selection and editorial comment, a historical-theological interpretation. The priestly work, in contrast, prompts us to ask whether and in what degree its author was interested in imparting information about Israel's or the world's past. For him, were the sequences of events, reported by the Yahwist and other sources, and well known to men from these sources, more than the narrative raw material, with the help of which he formed new affirmations on a plane different from that of mere facts? Curiously, study of the priestly document came to a standstill last century, and resumed only very recently. The question about the didactic intention of this apparently historical work has not yet been satisfactorily answered, and no doubt requires much more research and discussion before it can be.

We are justified even at this stage, however, in assuming that the affirmations of the priestly writing aim far beyond the mere communication of facts. But this means that, because this writing makes affirmations through narration, the narratives are not mere reports but the portrayal of types and archetypal sequences, of myths and events that are true everywhere and in every age. This was in the author's mind when the priestly writing speaks of the myth of the sabbath rest.

"Work and rest" is by no means the only mythical theme of the priestly document. A great deal of what is treated in the priestly document will have to be ignored in what follows, but the theme "work and leisure" is always one of its central themes. And it is closely bound up in the narration with the other principal themes. Hence one may speak of the priestly document as containing a kind of mythical theology of work and leisure.

The Cosmogonic Work and the Leisure of God

Its starting point, exactly as in the Mesopotamian model in the Atrahasis Epic, is the story of creation. In the Atrahasis Epic, however, the cosmos and the gods are already there when the story begins, and only the creation of man has to be told. In the Mesopotamian myth, the becoming of the world and the becoming of the gods belong together. First, men are made by the gods. Israel knew but one God, and he made all things, beginning with light and darkness, proceeding with heaven, earth and sea, plants, stars and animals, and finishing with man. The remodeling of the theogonic cosmogony to make it a genuine story of creation is still discernible in the clumsy concluding sentence of the priestly narrative of creation: "Such were the origins of heaven and earth when they were created" (Gn 2:4a). "Heaven and earth" means the whole of reality. "The origins of heaven and earth" is the traditional name for cosmogonic narrations in which one thing is brought into being from another. The phrase is thus used again, but is interpreted by the addition "when they were created."

The gods of Mesopotamia were very largely symbols of the cosmos, of its numinous depth, and not of the truly infinite and transcendent. This alone made possible that change of distribution of work and leisure that the Atrahasis Epic relates, by which things were simply transposed within the cosmos. Work has to done; the question is simply Who is going to do it? All the gods, or the lesser gods, or freshly manufactured worker-beings, specially designed for the purpose, beings who are almost gods but not yet divine—that is, men?

As Creator of all things, the transcendent God of Israel stood against the world, so to speak. There is no place here for a power struggle over the sharing of work and leisure. God is not, in himself, part of the world; hence he cannot reserve for himself a part (even the pleasanter part) of the unity-in-tension that is work and leisure, delegating the former to a weaker being. The transcendent God, he is utterly beyond the tension of work and leisure or he has—in his divine fashion—a share in both. This is the logic we must infer from the genealogy of the cosmos and the gods, recast in the form of a creation narrative, when we analyze the problems of work and leisure. By no means, then, could man have been created in order to release God from work. In a story of origins, man's origin calls for a new, a different treatment.

We cannot fail to see this in the priestly narrative of creation, in which the world was created in six days and, on the seventh day, God rested from his labors. The "day refrain" gives structure to the whole story. First, from the primeval water chaos, light and darkness are separated from each other: "Evening came and morning came: the first day" (Gn 1:5). Then God created the vault of heaven, so that the realm of the world was hollowed out within the primeval waters, and thus "Evening came and morning came: the second day" (Gn 1:8). God separated earth from sea and caused plants to grow on the dry land: "Evening came and morning came: the third day" (Gn 1:13). God placed the sun, moon, and stars in the heavens and through them ordered the course of the seasons: "Evening came and morning came: the fourth day" (Gn 1:19). Then God created the animals in the water and the birds in the air, and "Evening came and morning came: the fifth day" (Gn 1:23). Finally, God created animals and men upon the dry land: "Evening came and morning came: the sixth day" (Gn 1:31). A conclusion has been reached, and the content makes it plain that, after man, nothing greater can come. This is also indicated by the formula of appraisal, which precedes the announcement of the day: "God saw that it was good." But before announcing the sixth day, the text intensifies this formula: "God saw all he had made, and indeed it was good" (Gn 1:31).

Thereupon follows the announcement of the sixth day, and following this climactic series of days, and in antithesis to it, the seventh day, proclaimed with thrice-repeated solemnity and linked to the preceding by the dialectically applied notion of completion: "Thus heaven and earth were completed with all their array." Completion is reached at the end of the sixth day (Gn 2:1) and yet it is not reached, for thus far all has been work; and so the statement about completion is at once corrected: "On the seventh day God completed the work he had been doing. God blessed the seventh day and made it holy, because on that day he had rested after all his work of creating" (Gn 2:2f). A most solemn formulation, playing upon Israel's well-known Sabbath Commandment from the Decalogue and deployed in stylistic counterbalance to the significant six-day labor of creation.

So God relates himself to his creation as one who works and as one who rests. He is no slave laborer of the cosmos, as the Mesopotamian gods were at first, until they discovered how to transfer their burden to men. But neither is God sheer rest nor a *deus otiosus,* as the gods of Mesopotamia wanted to be and were to become. God works and he rests; becomes engaged, then keeps his distance; gives of himself, then retires within himself.

Moreover, God penetrates his creation with the unity-in-tension of work and leisure. When the priestly document uses the word "bless," it usually has fruitfulness in mind. "Be fruitful, multiply"—so, a few verses earlier, ran God's blessing of the animals and men (Gn 1:22, 28). When God blesses the seventh day, it can only mean that he is infusing into his creation the power of making the seventh day fruitful, of bringing forth an abundance of seventh days: days of rest and consecration.

In contrast to the other, preceding days, no formula of execution follows "and so it was" (Gn 1:7, 9, 11, 15, 24, 30). This blessing hovers freely, as it were, in the space between God and his creation, without settling down upon it. Or, we might say, it rests deep within the creation and does not immediately manifest itself. With other elements in the account of creation, it is more a program and an announcement than an immediate reality. One thinks of the continuing blessing upon men: "Fill the earth and conquer it" (Gn 1:28). The spread of mankind over the earth is told only after the account of the Flood, and how a now numerous people eventually takes possession of the land assigned to it by God is described only at the end of the priestly chronicle, through the example of the people of Israel.

In the story of creation in the priestly chronicle we have, therefore, no finished doctrine of work and leisure—not by any means. There is no "theology of the sabbath" which one can extract from this text alone. Rather, the myth of the sabbath begins to emerge. Then quite different themes come into the foreground, and only in the story of the exodus from Egypt is this theme picked up again. Till then, the cosmic mystery of divine creation and divine repose has not become apparent. Then, however, the time is ripe, for human labor has been perverted by men.

Egypt: Alienated Work

The priestly document characterizes the world of perverted work in a typical summary, concisely and solemnly: "The Egyptians forced the sons of Israel into slavery, and made their lives unbearable with hard labor, work with clay and with brick, all kinds of work in the fields; they forced on them every kind of labor" (Ex 1:13f).

The work had to do with building and agriculture, representing the two chief areas of human endeavor: assuring life and transforming the world through civilization. (Both themes will return later, in their positive antitheses.) The work is slave labor (much clearer in the original Hebrew text than in translation). It is founded on compulsion; it is heavy; it makes the lives of men—and men themselves—bitter. And so the Israelites groan (Ex 2:23). They cry out to God, their cry for help rises to God (*ibid.*), and God hears them (Ex 2:24, 6:5) and rescues them from their slavery (Ex 6:6). This is the announced program of deliverance which Moses hears (Ex 6:2–8). It is the preface to the narration of the several so-called plagues and the annihilation of the Egyptians in the Sea of Reeds.

Egypt and the exodus from Egypt—this is the metaphor by which the priestly document describes how work is assigned by the masters of a land to a poor and subject people, so that their humanity is damaged. But God will not tolerate this, and he frees the slaves. The moment Israel leaves Egypt behind it, alienation is past. But has Israel found true life? Anyone who has studied the priestly account of creation knows what lies hidden for man in creation, but the men about whom the priestly author was writing do not yet know this. They have left Egypt behind them and now are in the empty wilderness. The time of learning and uncovering reality can begin. Now the Israelites begin to learn true work and true leisure.

Work as Gathering Up and the Discovery of the Sabbath

The first report by the priestly document of Israel in the wilderness is the miracle of the manna and the quails. When the Israelites reached the wilderness of Sin and had no food, they complained. Moses and Aaron, to whom they turned, directed them again to Yahweh, and in the depths of the wilderness, shining in a cloud, the glory of Yahweh appeared and promised them meat and bread. In the evening, quails flew in and covered the ground, so that the people could gather them up; and in the morning white manna lay on the ground, and it, too, was gathered up. Then, each day, each person gathered as much food as he needed and each found exactly what he required. A surprise came on the sixth day: everyone found a double supply and reserved the extra amount for the seventh day. On the seventh day, they found nothing on the ground and they ate what they had saved from the sixth day. They had discovered the mystery of the sabbath.

The work they were doing had changed, had taken a different form. They did no slave labor in the fields, wrung nothing from the soil that it was reluctant to yield; they had simply gathered what the cosmos offered them. And as they set about doing this, the world (as it were) revealed to them the hidden mystery of the seventh day, the mystery of rest, which interrupts the transformed labor of the preceding six days. Moses interpreted the discovery for them explicitly: "Today is a sabbath in honor of Yahweh; you will find none [no food] in the field today. For six days you are to gather it, but on the seventh day—the sabbath—there will be none" (Ex 16:25f).

They had discovered the sabbath, which can now recur every seventh day. The blessing that God bestowed upon the sabbath has become effective, but this is only the beginning of the history of the sabbath among men. There is the archetypal sabbath of God, of him who creates, and there is the sabbath of men. Are they different? Are they related as archetype to copy or is there more than that? Are they even more closely connected?

For the first time, the myth of the seventh day pressed forward to its climax with the story of Sinai, where the theme of the sabbath is revealed in the theme of worship. We could also say that the theme has changed from negative to positive. The account of the miracle of manna puts it laconically: "on the seventh day—the sabbath—there will be none." Is there really nothing to be found? There is already, however, the first hint of something positive, for the sabbath is described as "a day of complete rest, a sabbath sacred to Yahweh."

Leisure

Perfection of the World through Technical Skill and Worship

And so the Israelites journeyed farther into the wilderness of Sinai, where they encamped, and where something very great happened. There was an encounter between the other world and this world, between God and man.

It happened, in the myth, in a cascade of events. The transcendence of God became visible in a cloud, which contained the glory of Yahweh. The cloud descended upon Mt. Sinai, which at this moment is to be thought of as a mountain representing the world, the symbol of the whole cosmos (one is reminded of the Babylonian ziggurat), where communication takes place between God and Moses. Moses, who is called up the mountain, enters the cloud and beholds the heavenly sanctuary—or, better, beholds heaven as God's sanctuary. Then he comes down from the mountain and the Israelites built the earthly sanctuary, the "dwelling place" (the Tent of Meeting), after the model of the heavenly sanctuary. At the moment that this sanctuary was built, the cloud rose from the mountain and came to rest upon the sanctuary, filling everything with splendor and glory. Here it remains, in the midst of the Israelites.

Within this account, sketched at first quite roughly, all the lines in the theme of work and leisure are gathered together, so that it is hard to know where one should start. First, perhaps, with the external structure of the story. In both stages of the narrative the sabbath terminology shines through, in the terms that a reader of the priestly document will recall from the creation narrative. The play on "six" and "seven" appears at the center of the statement about the descent of the cloud upon Mt. Sinai:

> The cloud covered the mountain, and the glory of Yahweh settled on the mountain of Sinai; for six days the cloud covered it, and on the seventh day Yahweh called to Moses from inside the cloud. To the eyes of the sons of Israel the

> glory of Yahweh seemed like a devouring fire on the mountaintop. Moses went into the cloud. He went up the mountain and stayed there. [Ex 24:15-18a]

This is an archetype of what happens on the seventh day: man is called into the fire, into the light of God, which melts and devours the mountain of the world. The seventh day marks the touching of the world by the holy and the terrible, because it is so completely other worldly. Moses had to ascend the mountain to experience it.

But this meeting is meant to be shared by all men, and so this can happen the sanctuary is built and the glory of Yahweh fills the sanctuary forever. The text that describes the completion of the sanctuary also reminds us of the story of creation:

> So all the work of the tabernacle, the Tent of Meeting, was completed. In carrying it out the sons of Israel had done exactly as Yahweh had directed Moses.... And Moses blessed them.... The tabernacle was set up on the first day of the first month in the second year.... Thus Moses completed the work. The cloud covered the Tent of Meeting and the glory of Yahweh filled the tabernacle. [Ex 39:32, 43, 40:17, 33, 34]

One again recognizes the catchwords from the account of the sixth and seventh days of creation, and so it must have been obvious to alert readers of the priestly document that something smilar to the completion of creation was taking place with the completion of the tabernacle. And if the completion of creation was fully realized only in the rest of God, the same applied to the descent—that is, the resting or settling—of the glory of God upon the sanctuary. The resting of God, the resting of men; the meeting with God in the fire, the liturgical meeting in the sanctuary—all belong together and are meant to signify one and the same thing.

How, then, in this concluding piece, does the polarity of work and

Leisure

leisure appear? The story of the manna takes note of man's work only to the extent that it assuages his hunger, provides him with food. But as even the false world of Egypt had hinted, work serves not only to assure life but to create a culture, the transformation of the world, which is seen most plainly in architecture.

This aspect of work came into play when the sanctuary was built in the wilderness. Obviously, God's work of creation is completed in the building of the sanctuary. Human work is a continuation of the creative work of God. On the mountain, Moses was shown the model of the sanctuary—heaven itself. And so human work continues God's work by turning earth into heaven.

Clearly, this changes the nature of work itself. In contrast to the world of the slave laborers of Egypt, with the building of the sanctuary of Yahweh we have a working world that is characterized by free will, voluntary readiness, spontaneity, and the pooling of gifts. Moses' appeal for offerings for building the sanctuary introduces the appropriate phrases; he called upon those who could give "willingly" (Ex 35:5), whose "heart prompted them to give" (Ex 35:21). And when the work starts, the word "skill" or "endowment" appears—the same word which in other contexts means "wisdom" or "education" (Ex 35:26, 36:2, 4). And those who had various gifts assembled for the work because "their heart prompted them" (Ex 36:2). This is surely meant to describe the antithesis of the alienated labor of Egypt.

If there is so much enthusiasm, even joy in building the sanctuary, what of the leisure—or should we not say "celebration"—on the day of rest and festivity within the completed sanctuary! Of the first liturgical celebration in the sanctuary we are told:

> The glory of Yahweh appeared to the whole people—a flame leaped forth from before Yahweh and consumed the holocaust and the fat that was on the altar. At this sight the people shouted for joy and fell on their faces. [Lv 9:23f]

The work and rest of God have been completed through men. In the rhythm of work and rest, man not only reflects the divine rhythm, he carries if further—indeed, he draws God and his rhythm into this world. God's heaven is no longer somewhere or other beyond this world, and God's glory is *in* this world. Man's industry creates a dwelling place for him; man's leisure is holy communication with him. And from all this arises the unmixed sound of joy. In this way alone does the day of rest become holy. This alone is the guarantee that it is also a day of rest.

This is the biblical—more precisely, the priestly author's—myth of work and rest. He expounds through myth what Israel, by its sabbath precept, has to say to a slave-owning society. Our society appears to have heard Israel's message, for we assign work and leisure time to all men, no longer reserving work for those "beneath" and leisure for those "above." This, alone, demonstrates the historical resilience of the sabbath rest. But when we look closely at the precept and, even more, when we probe into the myth, we may discover that we have missed the decisive nuance of the idea and run the risk of losing all that has been gained.

The real vitality of the sabbath rest consists in its being able to become more than rest, to turn into celebration, into encounter with other worldly fire. How far removed that is from what we commonly call "free time"! Not until glory appears do we hear the unconstrained shout of joy.

Power

The Sin of All Mankind and the Sin of the Elect, according to the Priestly Document

Today if one wants to speak about sin and guilt, especially in a Catholic region, he finds himself in a peculiar situation. A deep undercurrent in the modern mind affirms that man is not free and that everything because of which man might otherwise be held guilty can be explained in terms of social and psychical presuppositions. And the Church, moreover, seems to be the society first penetrated by this view. The practice of regular confession has declined to a terrifying extent, and sin plays a much smaller part than it used to in preaching and in religious instruction. And this in a decade when protesting youth reject and want to change the society their fathers want to bequeath to them, and when all are becoming aware that an almost suicidal ideology of growth threatens to destroy our environment and render our planet uninhabitable.

During the same period, psychologists have introduced the phrase "the work of mourning," which every human ought to perform because of his past. Naturally, we Christians know full well what Mitscherlich means by the phrase. It is a new word for an old thing, formerly known as "contrition" and "repentance." Why do we like it so little?

One suspects that our traditional Christian speech pertaining to sin lost touch with reality and, for that reason, often became overly oppressive and tormented, whereas, *real* sin was not recognized as such, so that our tradition, explicitly and in detail, sometimes seemed to confound one with the other. Take the catchword "power"—from the rack to brainwashing, from institutional authority to passive resistance, what a pregnant word in our days! Are we aware that one document of the

Bible sums up the sin of all mankind in this word, then goes beyond this sin to name others that are worse, because committed by the elect?

So that our talk about sin may again make contact with reality, we allow our ancient documents to say, quite simply, what they have always said on the subject.

Sin in the Older Historical Writings

I invite the reader to turn his attention to the historical narratives of the Old Testament and to focus it upon a single work, the so-called priestly chronicle in the Pentateuch. In it we shall encounter that curiously differentiated view that distinguishes the sin of all mankind from the sin of the elect. Let us start, however, with a glance at the other great historical works of the Old Testament.

The first great theologian of history in Israel was the so-called Yahwist, who began his historical work with an account of original sin, the story of paradise, and the fall (Gn 2:4–3:24). It contains a complete doctrine of sin. (To some extent, all subsequent sins are prefigured in the first sin.) The Deuteronomist, the theologian of history for the beginnings of the period of exile, likewise began with a kind of original sin. In Deuteronomy 1 he recounts the sin of unbelief of the people of Israel at the oasis of Kadesh, which led to postponement of entry into the promised land for a generation. In this account, too, all subsequent sins of Israel are described in advance. (This, too, is an account of an original sin.)

Neither historian, however, lets the matter rest with the description of original sin. From the sources they are editing, they take a long chain of separate stories about the sins of individuals or the entire people and about the complicated vicissitudes of life, all proceeding from sin. Over and above this, however, by commentary and arrangement of material, they introduce themes that comprise what might be called "the history of sin."

For the Yahwist, primeval history becomes increasingly overshadowed by sin, so that the whole of humanity dwells in darkness; light and blessings are restored anew by God to Abraham and his posterity—but, according to divine predestination, for the sake of all peoples. In the Deuteronomist's historical work, sin comes even more into the foreground. It opens with the dying Moses proclaiming the Deuteronomic law to the people; this is a standard by which, subsequently, the whole history of Israel will be judged. Most of all, it is of the kings of Israel and of Judah that account will be taken, in terms of this standard, concerning the constantly increasing power of sin among the people of Israel. At the end, even the devout king, Josiah, is no longer able to extinguish the burning wrath of God. Jerusalem is handed over to its enemies and Israel is forced into exile. The Deuteronomist's history is basically a justification of God's action in allowing Israel to go into exile—where the author composed the work. Thus it is a long recitation of sins.

Then, after the Babylonian Exile or just as it was coming to an end, another great historical work was composed, which gives a fresh account of the history of the world, from the creation and Abraham until the entry of the people into the promised land of Canaan. This is the so-called priestly chronicle, upon which we will concentrate. The first caravans had probably arrived back in the promised land, following the edict of Cyrus in 538, but most of the exiles were still in Babylonia, having settled down, and were by no means poor any longer. Reports from those who had returned were not inspiring, for they returned to find depressing conditions that offered little hope of improvement. Precisely at this time, it must have been important for the authors of the priestly history to confront their people afresh with the past of the world and of their own people, and to recast, and give new accents to, the old Yahwist history, which in the period of the exile everyone knew well, from his childhood onward.

What role did sin play in this new work? What did it make, in its new conception, of the original sin of the Yahwist, of his many separate accounts of sins and his whole theology of sin? To what extent did the new work take over from the old; to what extent did it select and modify; to what extent did it construct a new and distinctive doctrine of sin?

The Priestly Document and Its Sources

If we compare the priestly document with its sources in respect of the theme of sin, we are struck chiefly by the fact that so much has been omitted. The story of paradise and the fall is gone. The account of Israel's breaking the covenant in worshiping a bull, immediately after inauguration of the covenant at Sinai—so important for the Yahwist—is deleted outright. Thus also with many others—Cain's murder of his brother Abel, the Tower of Babel, and all the evil that Jacob's sons did to their brother Joseph.

In many other instances the priestly document takes over the stories or the substance of stories it found in its sources, but the factor of sin is always removed. Thus, in the Yahwist chronicle, the story of the Tower of Babel provides a motive for the distribution of mankind over the earth. The priestly document, as we have said, omits the story of the building of the tower, and at the end of the list of peoples (in Gn 10:32) it contains the thoroughly objective announcement, meant to be taken as a reference to the divine blessing of fecundity: "These were the tribes of Noah's sons, according to their descendants and their nations. From these came the dispersal of the nations over the earth, after the flood" (Gn 10:32).

In his account of the annihilation of the two wicked cities of Sodom and Gomorrah, the Yahwist wove into the Abraham story a mighty guilt-punishment story. Through Abraham's intercession in Genesis 18:17–35, he had developed this account into a veritable piece of ideological catechesis. In the priestly document, all of this is contracted to the briefest announcement; it is aware of no sin and no longer describes Yahweh's action as the punishment of sin. "Thus it was that when God destroyed the towns of the plain, he kept Abraham in mind and rescued Lot out of disaster when he overwhelmed the towns where Lot lived'' (Gn 19:29).

In the Jacob saga, too, the Yahwist's hidden leading motifs of guilt and nemesis are discarded. Jacob no longer deceives his father, and the fraudulently acquired blessing becomes a father's normal blessing for a journey. The account of the bringing out from Egypt, according to the chief theme, had been a tale of liberation and redemption, but it was also the story of the guilt and punishment of the Egyptians. In the priestly document, all reference to this is carefully avoided. In the story of the wanderings in the wilderness, according to the Yahwist, the account of the miracle of the quails (Nm 11) was an account of the sinful murmuring of the people in the wilderness and of their punishment by God. In the priestly document, the miracle of the quails is combined with that of the manna (Ex 16), and the new narrative structure has a totally different dénouement. Its author is chiefly interested in the marvelous help God has given his people in their distress, and in the discovery of the mystery of the week and of the seventh day as the day of celebration and rest from work.

The priestly document would seem, therefore—in contrast to older presentations—to be set on depicting the history of the world and the people of Israel as no longer a history molded by sin. Do we see a reflection here that is similar to what we are experiencing today? Has the sense of sin waned, so that it is scarcely seen or detected anymore? It may be that the contemporaries of the priestly writer were in an analogous situation, but it would be false to draw such a conclusion concerning the priestly document and the purpose of its affirmation. The priestly document makes all the above rearrangements, seriously interfering with what were undoubtedly traditional narrative subjects, but not because it did not like to talk about sin. Its purpose was quite the opposite; it wanted to speak very pointedly and unequivocally about sin, and for that reason it confined the discussion of sin to three narratives, omitting everything that might distract the reader from these three decisive complexes of affirmation.

Two of these narratives are found in the earlier source, and both are tales of guilt and punishment: the story of the Flood (Gn 6-9) and the story of sending the spies from the oasis of Kadash-Barnea at the moment Israel was on the point of entering the land God had promised it (Nm 13-14). In the third case, the priestly document introduces the motif of guilt and punishment into a narrative context, which originally was not a story about sin. This is the account of the miracle of water in the wilderness, when Moses drew water from the rock (Nm 20).

The moment we look more closely at these three "sin narratives" of the priestly document, we notice that they are related to each other, complement each other, and, taken together, form a deliberate, systematic statement. The story of the Flood comes from primeval history, which treats mankind as a whole. This, then, is the narrative example of the sin of all mankind. The other two stories concerning sin come from the time of Israel's wandering in the wilderness; here, toward the end of the second part of the historical work, the narrative is no longer about mankind as a whole but about the "chosen people" of Israel. All of Yahweh's ordinances of salvation for Israel, save one, are there already; the covenant has been concluded with Abraham (Gn 17), Israel has become a nation by having been delivered from Egyptian slavery (Ex 1-14), with the miracle of manna, the mystery of the sabbath has been disclosed (Ex 16), and since the happenings on Sinai, Israel has possessed a sanctuary and God dwells in the midst of his people (Ex 24 ff). All that remains is for them to enter the land of Canaan, already promised to Abraham.

At this point the priestly narrative adduces examples of the sin of Israel. In the story of the spies (Nm 13f), it speaks of the sin of the political leaders of Israel and of the people who listened to them. In the story of the water (Nm 20), it speaks of the sin of Moses and Aaron—that is, of those who are God's mediators. In this way the priestly document clearly and systematically treats the sins of all men and also the sins of the elect. These three stories are not by any means, and certainly not only, accounts of any three events from the gray and distant past; they are exemplary narratives. They narrate a type. From the priestly narrative of the Flood we learn about the sin of mankind in general and from the other two narratives we learn—over and above this—about the sin of a chosen people.

The Sin of Mankind: Violence

When the Yahwist, in his historical book, came to the Flood, he had already told the story of many sins. He could therefore begin the story of the Flood (in Gn 6:5) quite simply, by saying that God looked down from heaven and viewed the earth. Because he saw sin, he resolved to annihilate the earth; but he saw the righteous man, Noah, as well, and planned to save him. Then begins the story of the Flood.

With the priestly document it is quite different. According to this document, at the end of his six days of creative work God looked at the earth and declared: "Behold, it is very good." Then comes a genealogy that, without going into details, spans ten generations, from Adam to Noah. Now the Flood has to be reported, which makes it necessary for the author to explain—before he can inform us that God looked down and saw sin upon the earth—how things have changed upon earth since the six days of creation. He does this by developing a theme of contrast between Noah and the rest of creation. In Genesis 6:9 he says this of Noah: "Noah was a good man, a man of integrity among his contemporaries, and he walked with God." The antithetical declaration of Genesis 6:11 runs: "The earth grew corrupt in God's sight, and filled with violence."

The words are carefully chosen. Sin is described as "violence," as *hamas*, a well-known Hebrew catchword; we hear it often in the lamentations of the prophets. It denotes arbitrary oppression and inconsiderate domination of his fellow man by one who holds power. The earth was *full* of this—*wattimmale*—another word used by the prophets (Ezekiel in particular spoke this way). Now the whole earth—men, beasts, plants: the whole edifice of the world—is "corrupted" by this violence.

We may be astonished to observe that in this carefully thought out description of sin, sin is not related to God, who only now appears. Nevertheless, all this has been happening *lifne 'elohim*—"in God's sight." In God's sight, the earth was corrupt.

The writer is expressing, in the language of the prophets, what all men regard as sin. Originally, the prophets had coined various expressions to denote the sins of their people, Israel, and had applied them to the sins of other peoples, but here the expressions deliberately designate the sins of men *qua* men, not the special sins of Israel. The sins of men as men consist in the injustice they do to each other, and the consequences of this injustice are that the whole cosmos, even subhuman creation, becomes corrupt, destroyed. To the extent that this happens, this injustice becomes sin in the eyes of God. It provokes the Creator God for it damages his creation, which he designed and created to be "very good." It is not particular actions that are sins against God. Sins against men are the only sins, but because they damage God's work they become sins against God.

God punishes men by sending the Flood, which threatens to reestablish chaos—a mighty piece of imagery. In reality, it expresses what has already been said conceptually: sin does damage to God's work.

For the rest, the priestly narrative of the Flood repeats the theology of the sin of mankind in its opening section. Having stated the fact that sin has entered the world, the author—so to speak—"allows" God to discover sin (Gn 6:12): "God contemplated the earth: it was corrupt, for corrupt were the ways of all flesh on the earth." Then follows the word God spoke to Noah to ensure his salvation, which starts with God's decision to punish mankind: "The end has come for all things of flesh [again, typically prophetic language]; I have decided this, because the earth is full of violence of man's making, and I will efface them from the earth." In his act of punishing, God does only what man has already done: he hands the world over to its corruption.

In the end, however, he stops short. For Noah's sake, he arrests the Flood and, in the so-called rainbow covenant, solemnly binds himself never again to send a flood on the earth.

In view of the threat that hangs over us today from destruction of our environment, do we grasp what an uncannily bold statement is contained within this promise never again to send a flood? In the last analysis, the biblical Flood represents what violence, the essence of all our sins, does to the world. But God says that his desire to preserve the world and men is stronger than any violence our sins can do to the world. This in no way diminishes the guilt attached to our violence, to our destruction of the cosmos. And yet it gives us hope which we often scarcely believe we have.

Do we Christians see it as our task to pass on to our world and our times this message about the sin of man and about the hope that, nonetheless, is given as well?

The Sins of the Elect: Disparagement of God's Gift and Unbelief

For the author and the readers of the priestly document, as the Babylonian Exile was coming to an end, the story of the Flood served chiefly to distinguish the special sins of Israel from the sins of mankind in general. When the prophets denounced Israel for violence and proclaimed that the loss of its homeland and the decline of its cities had been the consequence of this sin, Israel had to some extent fallen to the common level of humanity. If it had repented in exile, and no longer lived by violence but tried to be just and humane, both to its own folk and members of other nations with whom it lived in close contact, there was nothing very special about that. That which God specially desired of Israel had still not come to light.

Noah had walked justly and perfectly in God's sight, as the priestly document tells us. God required this of Abraham also (Gn 17:2): "Bear yourself blameless in my presence." But only after this had been said, and its acceptance taken for granted, did God speak to Abraham about the special role he had in mind for Abraham and his posterity: he spoke about the covenant in which Abraham received the land of Canaan and in virtue of which God would "become God" in a special way for Abraham's posterity. In view of this election, new dangers and risks emerge. Clearly, this is what interests the priestly document. It applies itself to this topic in the other two stories about sin, which are set in the period of Israel's wandering in the wilderness.

The ancient story of the spies was retold over and over again, and can be found in a highly developed form in the sources used by the priestly author. In spite of this, it had always been, and remained, a war story. Its conclusion is a tale of a holy war of conquest, desired by God, that Israel had refused to fight because of fear and unbelief. The spies brought back such terrifying tales about the military strength of the inhabitants that the Israelites lost heart; therefore God punished them with a defeat, and not until the next generation grew up could they enter the land. The priestly document appropriates this story but omits all connection with war, conquest, and victory or defeat. In its version, military necessity does not account for sending out the spies; God merely issues a command that a delegation take a look at the land and appraise it. In a tour that lasts exactly forty days (forty is the sacred number), twelve men travel throughout the land, from its most southern to its most northern point. The question is Israel's attitude toward Yahweh's last and greatest salvific gift, "the land of Canaan, that I will now give to the Israelites"; therefore there has to be a representative from each of the twelve tribes and each representative must be a leader of his clan (Nm 13:2). Everything depends upon what they say on their return.

Sin occurs, then, in their appraisal, their evaluation of Yahweh's salvific gift. In the story of the Flood, sin had received a precise name: *hamas* or "violence." Here, too, the same thing happens. The sin of the reconnaissance team is *dibbat ha'ares*, or "disparagement of the land," which is God's gift of redemption for Israel. And so the sin of the people's representatives is disparagement of God's salvific gift.

The text of the disparagement is given verbatim in Numbers 13:32. On their return, the spies explain to the assembled people: "The country... is a country that devours its inhabitants. Every man we saw there was of enormous size."

Readers of the priestly document were well acquainted with the catchword describing the land of Canaan as a "devourer of men." This then was found in the book they loved to read—Ezekiel, chapter 36, where God threatened the other nations with punishment because they mocked his chosen people and said of their land: "You are a maneater, you have robbed your nation of its children" (Ez 36:13).

From this, we understand the nature of the first sin of the chosen race: adoption of the derogatory assessment by other people of God's special gift to his own people. Presumably, this connection was supremely real. The reports back to Babylon from the first who returned to the homeland—perhaps even the reports of the official emissaries of the exile communities, who had been sent ahead to prepare a reception for the returning caravans—presented a depressing picture to those who were eager to return. And of course the people in Babylonia reacted accordingly; the call of the prophets to return home left them cold. They told them: We prefer to live here in a strange land. We have nothing to expect from this land of our fathers.

At all events, this is the "atmosphere" of the priestly narrative. The land-reconnaissance team dragged the whole nation into sin as Numbers 14:36 asserts. The people expressed the wish that they had died in Egypt or been destroyed in the wilderness (Nm 14:2), and their wish was fulfilled to the letter. In 14:28f, 35, God anounces that all will die in the wilderness.

Only Joshua and Caleb were not a party to this sin. They had contradicted the other spies and declared: "The land is very, very good" (Nm 14:7). In these men, the reader of the priestly document can see how one ought to live uprightly, as in the story of the Flood and Noah. Joshua and Caleb, therefore, will enter the promised land with the succeeding generation.

Nor had Moses and Aaron, the spiritual leaders of Israel, disparaged the land, but their hour of weakness was soon to come; and this brings us to the third tale of sin in the priestly document, the account of the water from the rock (Nm 20). In itself, this was a tale of the miraculous assistance given by God to the Israelites in their distress in the wilderness. Because they had no water, the community assembled and complained. Moses and Aaron went to the sacred tent and prayed, and the glory of God appeared. God commanded them to assemble the community in front of a rock and to speak to the rock; then there would be water. They assembled the people; Moses began to speak; water gushed from the rock; and men and cattle were able to drink their fill.

At two points in this miracle story, however, the unexpected occurs. Moses is to speak to the rock; things have gone so far, however, that he speaks to the Israelites. Instead of addressing the rock, he puts a rhetorical question to the Israelites that betrays his uncertainty: "Listen now, you rebels. Shall we make water gush from this rock for you?" (Nm 20:10). The water gushes, nonetheless, but the narrative closes at Numbers 20:12 with a judgment of God upon Moses and Aaron: "Because you did not believe that I could proclaim my holiness in the eyes of the sons of Israel, you shall not lead this assembly into the land I am giving them."

Here, too, the sin is given a precise name. Israel's spiritual leaders fail in their function of preaching. They do not give testimony to the marvelous power of God. By their manner of speaking before the community, they reveal that they themselves have no faith, no trust in God's ability to work miracles in seemingly impossible situations. We will not be wrong, I think, if behind this story about sin we discern the typical attitudes of the spiritual leaders of Israel after the end of the exile, priests as well as prophets.

Problems of Exegesis

At this point, however, a question arises that can lead to a final consideration. Precisely in its theology of sin, the priestly document has deliberately interfered with the traditional manner of narrating a story about sin and, throughout the story, has worked out an almost systematic theory of sin. There is the sin of all mankind and there is the sin of the elect—who are not individuals but a people, through whom God wishes to be glorified in the course of history.

The sin of all mankind is men's mutual damaging of rights, misuse of power, inhumanity, violence. It is sin against God because it damages God's creation. The sin of the elect is directed more directly against God; it is the deprecatory evaluation of God's redemptive gift of the land of Canaan, adoption of the value put upon that gift by the nonelect. It is unbelief—doubt that God has the power to lead them into this land and, in this land, make the incredible real: supply water from a rock.

But this double sin of the elect, so systematically developed and contrasted with the sin of all mankind, seems so concrete, so historically anchored, and so unique that we have to ask whether all this is more than a message to the priestly author's immediate audience, those who lived in the first years after the Babylonian Exile, when the new religious policy of Cyrus the Great again made it possible for the Jews in Babylonia to return to the homeland from which, seventy years earlier, Nebuchudnezzar had deported their grandfathers. Is there anything here for generalization? Do these tales really embody a typology of sin which can claim validity today? Transposition of the sin of all mankind into our world, as sketched in the priestly version of the story of the Flood, is easy, almost instantaneous, but transposition of the sins of the elect in the wilderness does not seem so simple.

We are tempted to go off into abstractions and make the disparagement of the land stand simply for scorn of God's gifts of salvation—the Church, the liturgy, the grace that God pours into our hearts. We might even be so bold as to draw an analogy between Moses and Aaron and the pope and bishops and affirm that, according to the priestly theology, the special threat to them is unbelief. But if we do, we begin to wonder if this is not just an intellectual game of allegorical interpretation.

In spite of this, I consider such interpretation appropriate, although the work of translation is no easy matter. It is correct, I think, that we, as the Church, as the congregation of God founded upon Jesus Christ, must claim that what was said to the congregation of the Israelites is said also to us, although the New Testament congregation is not bound up with a single nation or possession of a single land. It is correct that the sins which in the view of the priestly document threatened the Israelites are also the sins that threaten the Christian Church: disparagement of the land and unbelief in God's desire and power to work marvels.

We have to ask once again what disparagement of the land meant in the context of the message of the priestly document. My thesis is that Israel's relationship to its land was not a special relationship, although it had been the subject of the covenant with Abraham (Gn 17). The land is Israel's in exactly the same way as, in the priestly document, other lands are other nations' lands. On their creation, according to the priestly document, God at once conferred a blessing upon men, which to some extent contained a historical program: "Be fruitful, multiply, fill the earth and conquer it" (Gn 1:28). With this translation, one normally thinks of technical and similar skills, but my research leads me to translate along these lines: "Fill the earth and take possession of it." The image this conjures up is of the human race, at first small in number, propagating and giving rise to diverse peoples, who spread over all the earth, each occupying the territory predestined for it by God, where each was to live in freedom and happiness.

In this framework, the fact that God provided a particular land for Israel is not special. It does not constitute Israel's election—or at least it is not only that. Israel's election may well consist in fulfilling the exemplary function of living in this land the kind of life that God wants all people to live in their several lands. They are to live so that the glory of God lives with them and appears at the center of the community. Therefore Israel's election means it should live a life that is at once the most normal and the most unusual—the most "normal" because Israel is to do only what is expected of every man: live happily in his own land; the most "unusual" because this "normal" obligation is not fulfilled by any of the many peoples, and it would be a miracle if any people succeeded in this task. God chose Israel to perform this miracle, and Israel sinned, in respect of this miracle, by not trusting in the land assigned to it by God and by not expecting the miracles God promised.

If we accept this connection between normality and election, as presupposed by the priestly document, we can transpose this theology of sin into the contemporary Church of God in a much more concrete and disturbing way. Corresponding to the Israelites, who preferred to live as guests in a foreign land to returning to their own land, the land God appointed to be their normal dwelling place, would be the type of congregation and church that hands the world over to others and allows itself to become a segment of society. To them would correspond all who think they can worship God and know his presence, and enjoy all the happiness that flows from this, without concentrating on what is truly normal, without realizing that they must change the everyday world, without seeing that in every sphere of life they are obliged to live as examples of the life that God has decreed as normal.

Disparagement of the land—adopting the views of others about this world: the idea, for example, that society is wicked and no one can change it, that the decline of society is inevitable and there is no point in trying to create a better life in this world, so that God's glory may become visible—would be to think that the sum total of God's design for his chosen people was that they wander about the wilderness, taking with them a sanctuary contained in a divine cloud, leaving their predestined land uncultivated, so that it became despised by other nations. As for the unbelief of the priests and the prophets, this would be found in all stewards of the sacraments who know only what is spiritual and never dare preach to the elect that God wants to transform reality before their very eyes, so that finally God's world will appear. This is the unbelief of those who do not dare confess that God possesses the marvelous power to do this.

I hope that this will not be misunderstood. It is not a "horizontal" theology. Scarcely any Old Testament document is so theocentric, so "vertical," as the priestly document. Nothing happens in this account that is not first proclaimed and commanded by God. Nor does any other section of the Old Testament give such importance to the cult and festivals as does the priestly document. In addition, this is the first document to record the Passover festival, the first to reveal the sabbath, the first to report the erection of the sanctuary at Sinai and the subsequent descent of the glory of God to dwell in the midst of his people, after which the people are led out of the wilderness to the frontier of their own land and directed toward normality. But they are directed toward this life.

And when the priestly document asks what are the real threats to the elect, its answer is not They do not keep the sabbath holy or They do not offer the sacrifices in the sanctuary with due reverence, but rather: They forget about God's presence, granted to them long ago, and that they are supposed to live in a proper land, demonstrating to other peoples what genuine living in a proper land is. The priestly writing would answer further: The danger that threatens them is that, though their priests and prophets know how to walk with God, they do not have the courage to preach to the faithful that God can work the miracle of all miracles, can make water gush from sheer rock, can satisfy a dried-up and thirsting humanity with a good, wholesome, happy life.

Here, says the priestly document, lurk the sins of the elect. It says this no less to us than to its contemporaries.

Love

The Ethos of the New Testament: More Sublime than That of the Old?

In the Sermon on the Mount according to Matthew, we read six times in succession: "You have heard that it was said [to our fathers]." Then comes a quotation from the laws of the Pentateuch, followed by the statement "But I say to you"—and Jesus proposes a demand that exceeds the old law (Mt 5:21-47). There are, that is, six antitheses between the Old and the New Testament, in respect, moreover, of moral behavior. Is Jesus teaching another, a new morality?

It is not the function of an Old Testament scholar to determine the precise meaning of this antithesis. We can advert in passing, to the fact that Jesus refers only to laws that had been formulated in legal texts, and that a little earlier, when he was speaking about "the law *and* the prophets," he said he had come not to annul but to fulfill them (Mt 5:17). Perhaps what we have here is not the antithesis of New Testament and Old Testament ethics but of genuine ethics and a legalistically conceived pseudoethics. However, these antitheses in the Sermon on the Mount, and other passages in the New Testament, have encouraged the view that, in contrast to the Old Testament, the New has introduced *substantially new norms* for moral action. Let us see what light the Old Testament can throw upon this view.

The Historical Changing of Ethical Norms

The task is not easy, for the following reasons. It is not easy because of the modification the norms that we are comparing have undergone in the course of history. It is almost impossible because the formulations of Old Testament morality do not appear as such but only in other species of utterance, connected with other things.

The history of at least fifteen hundred years is mirrored in the Old Testament, and the social change in this span is enormous. At the beginning, we have tribal groupings of peasants and seminomads. At some point the stage of ancient Eastern high civilization is reached, with monarchical, civic, temple, and administrative centers, a feudal system of land tenure, and a standing army. At the end, we are dealing with a relatively autonomous population group, living partly in its own land and partly scattered throughout other lands, but within the framework of the Hellenistic world civilization.

It should be obvious that morality, once it has been formulated in concrete, presciptive propositions, in order to remain the same requires, as society changes, new and durable formulations. On this plane, therefore, the thesis of a substantial difference between New and Old Testament ethics cannot be discussed, for social change has likewise continued since the time of Jesus Christ. And certainly it is not affirmed that, meanwhile, the New Testament ethic became outmoded and has been replaced by something more exalted. The thesis has to look for a difference in principle at the highest level, that is, beyond the area in which constantly changing circumstances make constant reformulation necessary. At this level, is there evidence that Jesus performed a *volte face* in respect of all that had gone before him?

This question is even harder to answer because the ancient world, at least in the pre-Hellenistic period, was scarcely aware of social change—it tried, indeed, to deny it. It was part of ancient man's mechanism of mental stabilization to represent all that is as having been unchanged since time began. And so new precepts of behavior were seen not as new formulations but as modifications or new interpretations of well-known formulations. Yahweh had ordered all things at Sinai; through divine Wisdom at creation, the cosmos had been imprinted—although, in reality, one statement comes from this, another from that epoch, and all have changed their meaning many times.

The New Testament and the primitive Church, borne on the sense of "modernity" and, through the mission to the pagans, bursting through the framework of Jewish society, were in a position largely to discard the highly complicated language system which had gradually evolved to embody the inherited ethos, to leave it lying by the wayside (as a snake sloughs off its skin), and to formulate afresh its own ethos, using the building stones of the Jewish and Hellenic tradition. To the present day, Jewish orthodoxy—on the other hand—constantly integrating fresh changes, has continued to spin the web of the ancient language system. However, it would be utterly false to interpret this Christian discontinuity in the ethical language system as though it signified discontinuity in moral obligation.

The historical limitations of concrete moral precepts, which no longer bring their Old Testament background with them into the New Testament, make it extraordinarily difficult (as we have said) to find our way perceptively into that area of ethical content where genuine substantial change can be said to have occurred. Most of all, one must be on guard not to jump to the conclusion that a higher level of theoretical reflection implies a higher morality.

Generic Links in the Moral Teachings in the Old Testament

The subject is made even more difficult by the fact that, conceptually and verbally, the moral sphere is not adequately separated from other spheres of human behavior. This is true preeminently of the early period. Just as the head of the family of the seminomadic clan was, in one person, father and director of all business and education, as well as sacrificing priest and charismatic vehicle of divine guidance, so the instruction the clan handed down from one generation to the next (mostly in the form of short collections of sayings learned by heart) was a great many things in one: law, morality, educational material, wise sayings, *belles-lettres*.

Love

The more society merged into high civilization, the more differentiated its departments became. In the tradition that has reached us, we are able to distinguish three categories in which moral norms find verbal expression. In general, they correspond to the three main divisions of the Old Testament. Let us begin with the last of these.

Especially the education of the children of the wealthy upper class—but not only education—acquired its institutions slowly. Traditional texts evolved from these institutions, first orally and then in literature (one speaks of "Wisdom"). And we must take into account a living exchange with the corresponding institutions and traditions of neighboring peoples, notably the Egyptians.

In the Wisdom "teachings" and in collections of proverbs there is, as one would expect, a large number of ethical norms, but they are difficult to isolate from the other concerns of education. Most of all, the educator wants to put before the eyes of the young an ideal picture of behavior in all of life's situations, which may be different from the actual moral norm.

In public life, above all in political life, the moral norm was made known in a completely different fashion, because the prophets were the conscience of the nation. From some point or other onward, their message, too, was written down and handed on, so that we have it in the prophetic books. However, these norms are often concerned with specific and unique situations, for which behavioral directions are given. Behind them, in many cases, general norms are discernible, but frequently it is not easy to detach the norms from the specific imperatives. As a rule, we do not know the whole story of the circumstances which led to this (and not another) prophetic demand.

Justiciary and the law also formed an autonomous sphere. At some stage came the codification of law, which rests, settled in several layers, in the Pentateuch, where we find it today. Ancient Oriental law, however, was largely casuist—not systematic—in construction. And even if law and morality were not as clearly distinguished as is required in a modern understanding of law, we must ask if the concrete, traditional propositions of law give complete insight into the moral norms that lie behind them.

Besides, there are texts which present themselves as collections of laws but which, in intention, may not be laws at all. Many Mesopotamian collections were pieces of propaganda rather than codes of laws, even though they tried to appear as the latter. Indeed, at least a revised stratum of the Deuteronomic law may be part of a historical work, of the first-edition Deuteronomistic writing, which was designed to revive national and religious feeling during the Assyrian crisis.

This, however, has implications. The law that commands extermination of the population of the Canaanite cities on the conquest of the land (Dt 20:15-18) was not extant at the time the land was occupied; it was formulated five hundred years later for literary reasons and was no more than a gesture, modeled on Assyrian propaganda. (One may inquire, of course, about the ethics of such propaganda.) At all events, the historical book's portrayal of the Israelites' cruelty was set in the far distant past; more humane rules were enunciated for conduct of the war that might break out. Therefore, no one was allowed to think he could wage war in the former fashion. Thus one must be very cautious about asserting that a war of total annihilation was preached.

All of this is merely by way of example. In biblical laws, we must try not merely to search behind a law for morality but often, first of all, decide whether that which presents itself as law is something quite other than law.

The relationships between categories become even more complicated in the postexilic period, for now, in the more restricted life of Israel as an ethinic group within the Hellenistic world system, many differentiations, already gained, were annulled. Israel's Torah became the foundation of education; the prophetic writings breathed a new spirit into Wisdom. The late Wisdom literature, as well as the apocalyptic writings, can be analyzed as independent mixtures of the old categories, in terms of their latent moral demands, only with the greatest effort.

The road to knowledge of the real ethical content of the Old Testament, to grasping the guiding principle of its morality, is a hard one. Hence in attempting a comparison with the ethical content of the New Testament, one has to adopt a strategy of caution. I can see scarcely any other possibility than to leave it to the advocates of the view that the

New Testament contains a more sublime morality than the Old—to expound it themselves and then to check it out again. This will not lead to a positively proved, complete picture but merely to verification or refutation of the various assertions.

The Thesis of a New Ethic of Love

The view that the New Testament contains substantially more sublime ethical norms than the Old usually reaches its peak in the thesis of a higher ethic of love. This can appear (in detail) in various forms, most of which may be dismissed.

There is, for example, the assertion, which is forever coming to the surface—from the depths of goodness knows what regions of the subconscious, with almost anti-Semitic malice—that the Old Testament preaches an ethics of fear whereas the New preaches an ethics of love. Quite modern evidence of this is found in the translation of one of the verses of the hymn "*Tantum ergo sacramentum*" in the new Catholic unity hymnbook *Gotteslob*. The Latin "*et antiquum documentum novo cedat ritui,*" meaning "the old usage [viz. the paschal lamb] gives way to the new rite [viz. the eucharist]," is now translated in this manner: "The law of *fear* must give way, for the new covenant is here; meal of love without compare; partake of this in faith" (N. 544). Need more be said?

The love of God holds a central place in the Old Testament, in Deuteronomy 6:5, and in the time of Jesus this text formed part of the daily prayer of the Jews. It was always in their mind. The concept of "the fear of God," very common throughout the ancient East, does not stand in antithesis to this; it is the ancient Eastern word for "religion." At the core of its meaning is the notion of holy reverence which the creature, confronted by the Creator, feels in religious experience. He trembles before the Creator and yet, at the same time, is fascinated by and drawn toward him. "Love in place of fear" is not a formula in which to express the relationship of the New Testament to the Old in respect of their moralities. Just as inappropriate is the formula "morality in place of legalism."

Whoever presents this contrasting pair reduced the Old Testament to the collections of laws it contains, and probably has not even read them, for even they do something which one does not automatically expect of laws today: they often motivate their demands and try to persuade the reader or hearer. It is true that in later rabbinic Judaism we frequently find the attitude that all of God's laws are equally important, their content is irrelevant, and they are to be observed simply because the Lord of the World has issued them. Even this would not be legalism in the strict sense, and we would have to examine more closely the precise meaning of such statements within the more complicated Torah concept of this tradition. In my view, they are designed to turn attention from the thing and onto the person, from the moral act to the divine presence. However that may be, if we compare the New Testament with the Old we ought *to compare* them, and not confuse the Old Testament with its later Jewish extension—and least of all with a derogatory misunderstanding of the latter.

We are on more solid ground if we derive the morality of the Old Testament from the principle of righteousness and the morality of the New Testament from the principle of love. This is not to say that, in the Old Testament, love is not part of morality, or that righteousness has no place in the New Testament; we would simply say they are accorded a different status in each system. As I will prove, this point of view certainly merits consideration. However, to be able to regard New Testament morality as more sublime, one has to see an ethic of love as surpassing an ethic of righteousness. And to be able to do this, one has to work with a concept of righteousness such as Aristotle might have accepted, but not the Old Testament. And thus we may have come to an antithesis of linguistic systems rather than things. More details are bound to emerge if the problem is discussed in terms of what we shall call the "fourth formula," which maintains that the Old Testament knows only a particular command to love whereas the New Testament commands a universal love, culminating in love of one's enemies.

Love

In the Old Testament, it was commanded that love be shown (with one strictly defined exception) only to one's "neighbor," that is, one's compatriot. In the New Testament, the command is to love *all* men, and only when love is so conceived does it become the source from which every moral demand can be deduced. With this antithesis, one has to suppose that the same language is still spoken. This is certainly the case when we compare the New Testament with the community of Qumran, where it was explicitly commanded to love "the children of light," that is, the members of one's own community, and to hate "the children of darkness." This is not so with the Old Testament; hence it is often assumed that the sixth antithesis in Matthew 5:43 refers not to the Old Testament but to the community of Qumran and its interpretation of the Old Testament. And so, initially, the possibility of various language systems in the Old and New Testaments remains open. In addition, we must ask whether universal formulations of norms within each community and within their socially conditioned horizons of thought can be expected.

In the following discussion we shall take stock of the ethic of love in the Old as well as the New Testament. This will necessitate another look at the ethic of righteousness in the Old Testament.

Love of Neighbor in the Old Testament

By way of introduction, let it be said that the New Testament does not say that the command to love brings something new in every respect. With astonishing speed, Jesus picks up the same line of action as the lawyer who wants to test him, and who questioned him about the "first of all laws" (Mk 12:28) or a "great commandment in the law" (Mt 22:36). Quite simply, Jesus quoted for him, concerning love of God and one's neighbor, the two classic texts from the Old Testament, Deuteronomy 6:5 and Leviticus 19:18, and both are satisfied. According to Matthew 22:40, Jesus had not the slightest intention of infusing new content into the moral demand, for he says: "On these two commandments hang the whole Law, and the Prophets also." St. Paul says much the same thing in his Letter to the Romans: "All the commandments: You shall not commit adultery, you shall not kill, you shall not steal, you shall not covet, and so on, are summed up in this single command: You must love your neighbor as yourself" (Rm 13:9). Love—as it was not in the Old Testament—has now become the keyword, but its content remains the same as in the Old Testament.

This might well be an example of the reluctance of the men of ancient times to admit changes, of the technique of conceiving even what was new as though it were ancient and had always been. Therefore we should compare the statements more closely, beginning with the Old Testament.

The command to love one's neighbor in Leviticus 19:18 is the final summing up, the climax, of a series of commandments, which follows an older commandment, first quoted in Leviticus 19:15: "You must not be guilty of unjust verdicts." In the chain of commandments, the statement slowly detaches itself from the context of concrete judgments; in addition, and alongside external actions, interior dispositions are given ever greater prominence. The text goes like this:

> You must not be guilty of unjust verdicts. You must neither be partial to the little man nor overawed by the great; you must pass judgment on your neighbor according to justice. You must not slander your own people, and you must not jeopardize your neighbor's life. I am Yahweh. You must not bear hatred for your brother in your heart. You must openly tell him, your neighbor, of his offense; this way you will not take a sin upon yourself. You must not exact vengeance, nor must you bear a grudge against the children of your people. You must love your neighbor as yourself. I am Yahweh. [Lv 19:15-18]

It is clear that the commandment to love one's neighbor is the summit and the summing up of the law, but it is also true that the word *rea* (neighbor) is a synonym for *'amit* (clansman), *'ah* (brother), and *ben 'ammeka* (your fellow citizen). This becomes even clearer when, further in the same chapter on the law of holiness, the scope is widened to include another group besides one's fellow citizens, that is, the *gerim* or resident "strangers." (One might also call them "guest workers.") The law of love is extended to them also:

> If a stranger lives with you in your land, do not molest him. You must count him as one of your own countrymen and love him as yourself—for you were once strangers yourselves in Egypt. I am Yahweh your God. [Lv 19:33]

What we do not find, either here or anywhere else in the Old Testament, is a further extension of the law of love to embrace the *nokri*, the foreigner, whom one meets in one's own country or when one is abroad. The latter is governed by no law of love but by the traditional and very exalted ethics of hospitality.

As for the "enemy"—the laws have principally in mind the personal enemy among one's fellow citizens—he is included in Leviticus 19, even if the word is not used, and he is described as "brother." In other cases where the word occurs, "love" is not used. But it is specifically stated that one must help one's enemy when he needs help:

> If you come on your enemy's ox or donkey going astray, you must lead it back to him. If you see the donkey of a man who hates you fallen under its load, instead of keeping out of his way, go to him to help him. [Ex 23:4–5]

One could hardly say that "love of one's enemy," as it later came to be called, was lacking here. Is what we find in the Old Testament so different from what we find in the New?

Love of Neighbor in the New Testament

Perhaps too much universalism is often read into the New Testament statements about love; so an Old Testament scholar may be permitted to bring a few things down to earth. For the most part, he finds himself in the company of his New Testament colleagues, though not of all of them. Let us begin with the latest of the New Testament writings, in which we would expect to find the most advanced universalism.

In the Johannine writings, love of one's neighbor appears as "love of one another," as "brotherly love," and as "love of one's friends"; therefore the love that is emphatically demanded in these writings is love of members of the congregation for one another. Undoubtedly, hatred of those outside the congregation is not required—as it was in Qumram—but exegetical attempts to apply such texts as 1 John 3:14 ("We have passed out of death and into life, and of this we can be sure because we love the brothers") and 1 John 4:20 ("A man who does not love the brother that he can see cannot love God") to a love for all men, because otherwise such a love would be too stifling, is not convincing in the context of the Johannine letters. Thus in these late Johannine letters we have the same substance as in the Old Testament. In place of the national community we have the community of faith and, without prejudice to the attitude to be taken to outsiders, the word "love" is applied only to those within the community.

Things are quite different in the older Pauline letters, above all in the very important chapters 12 and 13 of the Letter to the Romans—though, on the whole, this too has to do with the congregation. In 12:9, the word "love" occurs for first time, and in the following verses is given an interpretation that keeps it within the household of faith. From 12:14 onward, outsiders, too, come into vision: first persecutors, then all mankind, then enemies, and finally the court authorities are mentioned in detail. In this passage, "love" does not occur, and one could argue whether it is still to be interpreted or whether new words and new formulations emerge from the logic of the subject. It reappears for the first time in 13:8, in the expression "mutual love." Is this to be given a universal connotation or is one still to focus upon the community of faith? At all events, from this point onward St. Paul becomes involved in Old Testament argumentation; so we might assume that he understands love of one's neighbor just as Leviticus 19:18 does—a text he quotes.

Undoubtedly, the heart of this text has an ethical universalism that almost recalls the Stoics, but the word "love" is not used here and the suspicion remains that, for Paul, this word did not have a sufficiently universal ring. Therefore, at the climax of his universal declaration, he prefers to quote another biblical formula: "Do all you can to live at peace with everyone." This is derived from the Greek text of Proverbs 3:4. And so I say that, in Paul, one senses (at most) that the word "love" is only becoming a universal ethical concept.

And now for the gospels. As we have shown, Jesus accepted the commandment to love one's neighbor in its Old Testament sense, But—unlike the Old Testament—he did not include all men in the concept "neighbor." Rather, he accepted the old concept of "neighbor," and only according to Luke did he extend it, in response to a question, by telling the parable of the Good Samaritan. But even this parable does not say that all men are to be included in the concept "neighbor." It says, simply, that a neighborly relationship can arise, in cases of distress, even outside one's group. We must note, further, that at the end of the parable Jesus did not say that the man who fell among robbers was a neighbor to the Samaritan but that the Samaritan, the man who had shown love, had become a neighbor to the man who was robbed (Lk 10:36f).

The neighbor relationship did not emerge from the distress situation but through love. In this sense, Jesus broke the objective reference of love for neighbor. Love is oriented toward the encountered distress and a neighborly relationship emerges through love. To this extent it can be called, in retrospect, "love of one's neighbor."

The phrase "universal love," which fits certain Stoic ways of thinking, is out of place here. Rather, Jesus directs love to the distress, which warrants it. This is undoubtedly a radical bursting of the bonds of love only of the group, which we find in the Old Testament, but is it more than development of what the Book of Exodus demanded by law in respect of the "wandering donkey" of one's personal enemy, even if the word "love" was never used?

When the gospels speak of love of one's enemies (Mt 5:43-48, Lk 6:27-36), are they speaking of universal love? If we attend to what is discussed in Matthew 5:38-42 or to what is interpolated in Luke 6:29f, it becomes clear that the evangelists are talking about personal enemies within one's group. There is nothing new in this, in comparison with Leviticus 19, where love of neighbor is discussed in the context of how to proceed against personal enemies. In Luke, something else, deriving from early Church experience, comes on the scene through the preceding verses (5:22f), as well as through many formulae in 6:27f, for example, "Bless those who curse you." Very probably, this has to do with the processes which preceded the definitive separation of those who believed in Jesus from the Jewish community of faith. Thus the discussion is about the very concrete challenge to counter, with every legitimate means, an incipient and slowly widening split in the community. Is such concern for the unity of Israel such a new thing, in comparison with the Old Testament?

There is only one point to be added: a foundation is provided which allows us to go far beyond the concrete cases of personal enmity and exclusion from the Jewish community. People are to prove themselves as children of their heavenly Father, who is good to all men (Mt 5:45, 48 and Lk 6:35f). This is figurative dynamite, but it was not detonated for the first time in the New Testament. At the end of the Book of Jonah it was made clear to the chauvinistic prophet of God that Yahweh must show mercy not just to Israel but also to Nineveh, where more than 120,000 people "cannot tell their right hand from their left, to say nothing of all the animals" (Jon 4:11). Only one thing is lacking here: in this context the Old Testament does not use the word "love"; it speaks of "showing mercy." The gospel, likewise, speaks of mercy at the end of the parable of the Good Samaritan (Lk 10:37).

Let us sum up. If we set aside whatever is conditioned by the changed times and situation, no difference can be shown in this matter between the Old Testament and the New. The guiding principles are the same; the only difference is linguistic usage. Use of the word "love" increases, even for cases to which the Old Testament does not apply that word. But there is variation in different strata of the New Testament. It is only with Paul that love is marked out as a kind of summary of morality, but even here, only the beginnings are evident.

Love

"Love" is not a normative word in the Old Testament. On the whole, the Old Testament saw no need to sum up morality in a single expression. However, the beginnings are not absent.

The Supreme Ethical Norm in the Language of the Old Testament

In ending our discussion, let it be said that only the commandment to worship Yahweh takes precedence over all other demands of the law, as it is found in the Decalogue or in the paraenesis of the Book of Deuteronomy. This is another matter, apart from love of neighbor, and is connected with the polytheistic presuppositions of early Israel. With regard to the supreme ethical norm, the following passage from the Book of Micah is the most important:

> What is good has been explained to you, man;
> this is what Yahweh asks of you:
> only this, to act justly,
> to love tenderly
> and to walk humbly with your God.
> [Mi 6:8]

The last injunction means to live, in a formal sense, in accord with the will of God. One might compare it with what the priestly document in the Pentateuch says concerning Enoch, Noah, and Abraham—that they walked with God (Gn 5:24, 6:9, 17:1). The "substance" of life, by contrast, is denoted by the other two catchwords, *mispat* (righteousness) and *hesed* (kindness and faithfulness). The same pair of concepts appears again in a summarizing passage in the prophet Hosea:

> Hold fast to love and justice (*hesed umispat*)
> and always put your trust in your God. [Hos 12:7]

Presumably, in this double concept we find the typical Old Testament formula for the comprehensive content of morality. The word *mispat* (right or righteousness) is much wider in connotation than the notion of justice that derives from Aristotle. The word *hesed* almost defies translation; it hovers between "faithfulness," "kindness," and "love." Not until after the Old Testament period does it mean "charity." In the expression *hesed umispat*, these two words supplement each other, giving rise to the keyword for morality, which perhaps justifies contrasting the Old Testament ethic with the New in terms of the ethic of righteousness (in contrast to the ethic of love).

But now it should be obvious that there is very little real contrast in this, for it is not a question of righteousness alone but of righteousness molded by kindness. And the question we must answer is: Taking into account the obvious historical development, is there any difference when we come to first principles?

Conclusions

It is easy, when engaging in a phenomenological description of the concrete ethos of the Old and the New Testaments, to lose oneself in distinctions. One finds enormous differences not only between but within the two Testaments. Moreover, the differences continue in history, from the time of Jesus until today, and the future will show further changes. This, however, is simply a banal affirmation that, as society and its institutions change, specific imperatives must be modified. Our question about an essential difference between the Old and the New Testament cannot be investigated on this level but only on the level of the first and enduring principles of morality, those that operate above the sphere of social change. This question has no easy answer because, as well as concrete changes in morality, there are shifts in linguistic and conceptual usage with which one must reckon. Nonetheless, it may have become apparent that the superiority of the New Testament ethic of love vis-à-vis the ethic of the Old Testament cannot be verified. Nor, indeed, is there opposition between an ethic of righteousness and an ethic of love or between a particular and a universal ethic of love.

In fact, this might have been expected—if, for example, one takes the fact seriously that all men, without exception, have fallen into sin—as Paul does at the beginning of his Letter to the Romans, looking at things the other way round (which presumes a common moral awareness). This is not to say that the New Testament brings nothing new to the human scene in terms of morality. It simply affirms the improbability that the "new morality" varies from the substance of ethical norms.

Charisma

The Burden of the Prophets

We will now speak about the burden of the prophets and begin with Moses, whom the Old Testament stylizes as *the* prophet figure and who appears in the New Testament in the Transfiguration alongside the other great prophet, Elijah, accompanying our Lord in the cloud. Moses was also the first of the prophets to complain about the burden that was laid upon him. The scene is set in the Book of Numbers, chapter 11, and in the wilderness, after Israel left Sinai. The people who journeyed with Israel were stricken with hunger.

> The rabble who had joined the people were overcome by greed, and the sons of Israel themselves began to wail again. "Who will give us meat to eat?" they said. "Think of the fish we used to eat in Egypt, the cucumbers, melons, leeks, onions and garlic. Here we are wasting away, stripped of everything; there is nothing but manna for us to look at."...
>
> Moses heard the people wailing, every family at the door of its tent. The anger of Yahweh flared out, and Moses greatly worried over this. And he spoke to Yahweh:
>
> "Why do you treat your servant so badly? Why have I not found favor with you, so that you load on me the weight of all this nation? Was it I who conceived all this people, was it I who gave them birth, that you should say to me, 'Carry them in your bosom, like a nurse with a baby at the breast, to the land that I swore to give their fathers'? Where am I to find meat to give to all this people, when they come worrying me so tearfully and say, 'Give us meat to eat'? I am not

> able to carry this nation by myself alone; the weight is too much for me. If this is how you want to deal with me, I would rather you killed me. If only I had found favor in your eyes, and not lived to see such misery as this." [Nm 11:4-6, 10-15]

An "overwhelmed prophet," he delegates his oppression and even overwhelms his God, who replies:

> "Yahweh will give you meat to eat. You shall eat it not for one day only, or two, or five or ten or twenty, but for a full month, until you are sick of it and cannot bear the smell of it." [Nm 11:18-20]

But there is not just one answer. A second is attached to it, and it resumes the theme of "burden":

> Yahweh said to Moses, "Gather seventy of the elders of Israel, men you know to be people's elders and scribes. Bring them to the Tent of Meeting, and let them stand beside you there. I will come down to speak with you; and I will take some of the spirit which is on you and put it on them. So they will share with you the burden of this nation, and you will no longer have to carry it yourself." ... Then he gathered seventy of the elders of the people and brought them round the Tent. Yahweh came down in the cloud. He spoke with him, but took some of the spirit that was on him and put it on the seventy elders. When the spirit came on them they prophesied. [Nm 11:16f, 24f]

Suddenly, the mood changes. A different tone infuses the scene—almost ironic. The elders, the dignitaries, dance—and continue to dance. Prophets are not merely bearers of a burden, they are also dervishes; otherwise they would not be able to bear the burden. God inspires them to dance. Nor was Moses just a prophet; he held responsibility for government, which now he was to share with others. But to ensure success, the others had to acquire some share of the prophetic spirit; and thus we arrive at the heart of the problem of institution and charism.

The Church has always insisted that the Spirit is at work in the official ministry. She is right, and here she has documentation for this view. Saul, too, as soon as Samuel anointed him and before he recovered his she-asses, fell among the prophets and began to dance. Only the king who can dance possesses the Spirit as well. How many bishops dance, speak in tongues, are inspired? (That would be something! It was something even in those ancient days.) But worse was still to come, for only now does the narrative come to the point.

> Two men had stayed back in the camp; one was called Eldad and the other Medad. The spirit came down on them;... They began to prophesy in the camp. The young man ran to tell this to Moses. "Look," he said, "Eldad and Medad are prophesying in the camp." Then said Joshua the son of Nun, who had served Moses from his youth, "My Lord Moses, stop them." Moses answered him, "Are you jealous on my account? If only the whole people of Yahweh were prophets, and Yahweh gave his Spirit to them all!" Then Moses went back to the camp, the elders with him. [Nm 11:26-30]

To some extent, he forced them to reflect on what was happening to them, for they were to learn from it. Those who held office had received gifts from the Spirit; they had learned to dance. But the Spirit did not bind himself to them; he leaped into the camp, where many anonymous folk were living in their tents, and here sought out his dancers. No one had nominated them or presented them for ordination; no one expected them to dance, least of all at this unappointed place. Immediately, the prophet of the establishment was worried. Joshua, the designated successor, sensed danger and protested. He asked that this prophesying be forbidden, but Moses refused to let him be led astray by such folly.

Charisma

Nevertheless, one has the impression that, throughout the whole of history, the official prophets have always wanted to do away as quickly as possible with such unordained, troublesome prophets in the midst of the camp.

The gentlest manner of liquidating them is to integrate them in the clergy—for example, by creation in the Jerusalem temple, after the exile, of a lower grade of Levites, called prophets, and the founding by St. Francis of an order that harmonized with canon law.

Often, harsher measures were taken. Thousands of years before the great prophets of Israel, in the royal city of Mari on the Euphrates, they would cut off the hair and the fringe of the garments of unordained prophets and place them in the royal palace, thus acquiring magical power over the persons of the owners, so that they could be proceeded against should they prove harmful to the perceived interests of the kingdom and its gods.

It was no different in Israel. When Ahab went to war and Micaiah warned him of approaching defeat and death, the king had a quick answer: "Put this man in prison and feed him on nothing but bread and water until I come back safe and sound." Here, too, we see the confidence of the true prophet, for Micaiah replied: "If you come back safe and sound, Yahweh has not spoken through me" (1 Kgs 22:28f).

Or is this saying meant as the opposite of confidence, as an indication of the prophet's need of the future as a test, which will give definitive proof of which spirit possesses him? This is the "burden of the prophets" in a third and most sever sense. It is not men and their distress that are the burden of the prophet, nor the unpredictability and inconvenience of free charism that are the burden of the official ministry; it is the unpredictability, the incomprehensibility, the ultimate uncertainty about God himself that are the real burden of being a prophet. This is the burden that is peculiar to prophecy.

But we go too fast. Let us look again, first of all, at the way in which the prophets were felt to be a burden by those in authority. Amos, the Judaean, appeared in the northern, neighboring state of Israel, calling men to repentance and threatening destruction. Spontaneously, throne and altar joined to oppose him. Rather, the correct order is "altar and throne," for

> Amaziah the priest of Bethel then sent word to Jeroboam, king of Israel, as follows. "Amos is plotting against you in the heart of the House of Israel; the country can no longer tolerate what he keeps saying. For this is what he says, 'Jeroboam is going to die by the sword, and Israel go into exile far from its country.'" [Am 7:10f]

The consent of the king having been given, the high priest summoned this foreign prophet, who had dared to mount the pulpit in church and say such things. Amaziah let the clink of the handcuffs be heard under his jacket and, playing the part of the friendly adviser, said to Amos:

> "Go away, seer; get back to the land of Judah, earn your bread there, do your prophesying there. We want no more prophesying in Bethel; this is the royal sanctuary, the national temple." [Am 7:12f]

Yes, the guardians of public order make heavy weather for prophets, who are a burden, for they are not accommodating. And yet Amos had been right; Israel went into exile. It would have been better not to have exiled the prophet from Israel.

Things become even more bizarre if throne and altar do not join forces, and if the Church opposes the prophets while the state protects them. This happened with Jeremiah, who describes such a situation in chapter 26 of his book, giving special attention to the different groups and personalities. Certainly it was no everyday commission that Jeremiah received. It struck at the heart of all the faithful for it had to do with the symbol of all symbols, the temple.

> At the beginning of the reign of Jehioakim, son of Josiah, king of Judah, this word was addressed to Jeremiah by Yahweh. "Yahweh says this: 'Stand in the court of the

> Temple of Yahweh. To all the people of the towns of Judah who come to worship in the temple of Yahweh you must speak all the words I have commanded you to tell them; do not omit one syllable. Perhaps they will listen and each turn from his evil way: if so, I shall relent and not bring the disaster on them which I intended for their misdeeds. Say to them, "Yahweh says this: 'If you will not listen to me by following my Law which I put before you, by paying attention to the words of my servants the prophets whom I send so persistently to you, without your ever listening to them, I will treat this Temple as I treated Shiloh, and make this city a curse for all the nations of the earth.'" [Jer 26:1-6]

Jeremiah did exactly as he had been instructed, and all who were in the temple heard him. We have a list of the three groups: "The priests and prophets and all the people heard Jeremiah say these words in the Temple of Yahweh" (Jer 26:7).

The priests—that is clear. The people—they were pilgrims. The prophets—they were the prophets attached to the temple. If you like, they were the domesticated prophets. They paid heed to their patrons, as we see:

> When Jeremiah had finished saying everything that Yahweh had ordered him to say to all the people, the priests and prophets seized hold of him and said, "You shall die. Why have you made this prophecy in the name of Yahweh, 'This Temple will be like Shiloh, and this city will be desolate, and uninhabited'?" And the people were all crowding round Jeremiah in the Temple of Yahweh. [Jer 26:8f]

They were, in fact, a lynching party, but proceedings in a capital offense required the presence of a high-ranking royal official. The palace was near the temple, and "hearing of this, the officials of Judah went up from the royal palace to the Temple of Yahweh and took their seats at the entry of the New Gate of the Temple of Yahweh." At the place, that is, where they presided over such processes.

Then comes the indictment:

> The priests and prophets then addressed the officials and all the people [now the whole people belong, to some extent, to the court and no longer represent the indictment]: "This man deserves to die, since he has prophesied against this city, as you have heard with your own ears." [Jer 26:10f]

This, obviously, is a very brief summary by the narrator of the speeches of accusation. He sums up the rest of the process in a similar way.

First we have the defense speech by the defendant:

> Jeremiah, however, replied to the people as follows, "Yahweh himself sent me to say all the things you have heard against this Temple and this city. So now amend your behavior and actions, listen to the voice of Yahweh your God: if you do, he will relent and not bring down on you the disaster he has pronounced against you. For myself, I am, as you see, in your hands. Do whatever you please or think right with me. But be sure of this, that if you put me to death, you will be bringing innocent blood on yourselves, on this city and on its citizens, since Yahweh has truly sent me to you to say all these words in your hearing." The officials and all the people then said to the priests and prophets [the verdict is then given by the royal representatives, along with the congregation of people], "This man does not deserve to die: he has spoken to us in the name of Yahweh our God." [Jer 26:12-16]

Only by way of postscript are we told what most likely had set the tone of the undoubtedly lengthy discussion and proceedings. It had been an argument from precedent:

> Some of the elders of the land had risen to address all the assembled people. "Micah of Moresheth," they said, "who prophesied in the days of Hezekiah, king of Judah, had this to say to all the people of Judah, 'Yahweh says this:
> > Zion will become ploughland,
> > Jerusalem a heap of rubble,
> > and the mountain of the Temple
> > a wooded height.'
> Did Hezekiah, king of Judah, and all of Judah put him to death for this? Did they not rather, fearing Yahweh, entreat his favor, to make him relent and not bring the disaster on them which he had pronounced against them? Are we now to burden our souls with such a crime?" [Jer 26:17-19]

This whole constellation of the officials against the "church" and for the prophet is well worth examination. Why should such a thing not recur in our own times? Perhaps we should be able to view it with understanding. Somehow or other, Moses and Aaron, *should* be able to embrace one another, in spite of the fact that Aaron ate the golden calf. Perhaps it is easier for the laity than for the clergy to submit to the incomprehensibility of God.

Life must be hardest for those who (perhaps in the bright morning of their lives) were once genuine prophets—who learned to dance, to penetrate to the heart of things, to speak and to act with effect—but whose hour has passed. Meanwhile their enrollment among the prophets became assured, as with an honorable "no" they failed to respond to what people expected of them. Even more common, they had no idea that the Spirit was no longer with them. Moreover, they lived by being members of the band of temple or court prophets. What a secret burden their being a prophet must have been for them, and what a burden they must be upon true prophets, if now they stand opposed to them. For is the true prophet ever utterly certain of being a prophet?

A curious chapter (28) in the Book of Jeremiah tells of the encounter between two prophets, Jeremiah and Hananiah, after a critical situation had arisen. Judah had rebelled against its political overlord, Babylon, and the rebellion had been put down. The city of Jerusalem had been temporarily spared, but the king and the leader class had been deported to Babylon. Mere puppets ruled the country now. In God's name, Jeremiah commented in the most concrete terms upon the situation, and all his oracles made the point that the people should make the best of things and not cherish false hopes. But otherwise he was alone in this view. The fact that the temple and the city of Jerusalem were still untouched, in spite of all that had happened, was made the religious starting point of fresh, fantastic, messianic hopes, and these hopes were encouraged by many prophets. For Jeremiah, this was a very severe test, which he could not dispose of at one blow, as the dispute with Hananiah shows.

> That same year, at the beginning of the reign of Zedekiah, king of Judah, . . . the prophet Hananiah, son of Azzur, a Gibeonite, spoke as follows to Jeremiah in the Temple of Yahweh in the presence of the priests and of all the people. "Yahweh, the God of Israel, says this, 'I have broken the yoke of the king of Babylon. In two years' time I will bring back all the vessels of the Temple of Yahweh which Nebuchadnezzar, king of Babylon, carried off from this place and took to Babylon. And I will also bring back Jeconiah, son of Jehoiakim, king of Judah, and all the exiles of Judah who have gone to Babylon—it is Yahweh who speaks. Yes, I am going to break the yoke of the king of Babylon.'" The prophet Jeremiah then replied to the prophet Hananiah in front of the priests and all of the people there in the Temple of Yahweh. "I hope so," the prophet Jeremiah said. "May Yahweh do so. May he fulfill the words that you have prophesied and bring the vessels of the Temple of Yahweh and all the exiles back to this place from Babylon. [Jer 28:1-6]

We have to picture the scene. Jeremiah had expressed his message in a way that could not be misunderstood. For weeks he had walked through the streets of Jerusalem with an ox yoke round his neck, explaining to all who would listen that this was how they should adapt themselves to the king of Babylon. He now stood, with this yoke around his neck, in the great temple square, crowded with people, and confronted the other prophet, who took up Jeremiah's theme.

Hananiah also spoke of the yoke of the king of Babylon, but said that Yahweh would break it. Jeremiah, clearly, was in no position to reply; indeed, he had his doubts. Prophets who herald calamity have a prejudice of authenticity on their side, but the prophet who preaches salvation—whether he is sent by Yahweh or not—will be recognized only when this salvation arrives. But this general and not very convincing argument was all that Jeremiah could present against Hananiah, and so, before all the people, Hananiah proceeded to the climax of his prophetic utterance. From Jeremiah's sign he manufactured his own.

> The prophet Hananiah then took the yoke off the neck of the prophet Jeremiah and broke it. In front of all the people Hananiah then said, "Yahweh says this, 'This is how, two years hence, I will break the yoke of Nebuchadrezzar, king of Babylon, and take it off the necks of all the nations.' " [Jer 28:10f]

What did Jeremiah, publicly repudiated and humiliated, do? "At this the prophet Jeremiah went away," is the terse comment, and he revealed nothing of what was in his head. Perhaps he was aware of nothing, except that it was good to be able to go on his way. He must have had experiences with his God that made it conceivable that God allows one prophet to say one thing and then the other to say the opposite, without bothering about the justice or injustice to the first. Jeremiah could not have been certain that Hananiah was a "pseudoprophet," a false prophet.

In this context, the Greek translation introduced this term; it does not occur in the original. Only later did Jeremiah realize that Hananiah had not delivered a genuine divine oracle, when he was given a new saying to deliver to Hananiah:

"Go to Hananiah and tell him this, 'Yahweh says this: You can break wooden yokes? I will make them iron yokes instead. For Yahweh Sabaoth, the God of Israel, says this: An iron yoke is what I now lay on the necks of all these nations to subject them to Nebuchadrezzar, king of Babylon.' "
[Jer 28:12-14]

Having received this new word from God, Jeremiah could act fearlessly, and he did. But the burden he had borne as a sign through the streets was by no means only a sign of the burden to be borne by his people under foreign rule, their deported brothers, living in political and economic hopelessness. We can also see this yoke as a sign for Jeremiah personally, of the burden that being a prophet is in itself. It is the burden of standing before a God who, in drawing a man close to himself, becomes increasingly distant and more incomprehensible.

No other prophet has left such bitter words on being a prophet and how it affected his relationship with his God. There are the so-called "Confessions of Jeremiah," scattered among oracles and narratives in no recognizable system. They comprise a subjective and almost foreign *corpus* within the otherwise objective and impersonal text of the book.

> Woe is me, my mother, for you have borne me
> to be a man of strife and of dissension for all the land.
> I neither lend nor borrow,
> yet all of them curse me.
> Truthfully, Yahweh, have I not done my best to serve you,
> interceded with you for my enemy
> in the time of his disaster, his distress?
> You know I have.
>
> Yahweh, remember me, take care of me....
> Realize that I suffer insult for your sake.
> When your words came, I devoured them:
> your word was my delight
> and the joy of my heart;

> for I was called by your name,
> Yahweh, God of Sabaoth.
> I never took pleasure in sitting in scoffers' company;
> with your hand on me I held myself aloof,
> since you had filled me with indignation.
> Why is my suffering continual,
> my wound incurable, refusing to be healed?
> Do you mean to be for me a deceptive stream
> with inconstant waters?
>
> [Jer 15:10-11, 15-18]

How this text mirrors the passage from joy to misery! Fist of all (as Gerhard von Rad described it), there is an almost instinctive relationship to God's word, a sensuous desire for God: "Your words came, I devoured them, your word was my delight and the joy of my heart." But familiarity with the word of God brought isolation from men.

The prophet is different; he is solitary, he is cursed, for he has no good news to give. His God sets him in opposition to others. Even more, he sets him against his own heart. Rejection by others is his despair.

The most dreadful denial comes in the last verse. Life is so bad that it seems as if God himself has withdrawn from Jeremiah, who loses even that security, which had upheld him hitherto, in spite of his bitter message. He experiences Yahweh as a dried-up stream. Like a *wadi* in the Negev, which sometimes runs with water, sometimes dries up completely—so has his God become for him. An unreliable river.

But there is something else too: it is just as impossible for him to live and *not* be Yahweh's prophet. "You have duped me Yahweh, and I have let myself be duped." (Jer. 20:7)

That was how it began; Yahweh was like a partner in a love affair. Then he acted with greater power: "You have overpowered me: you were the stronger." [Jer 20:7]

It is bliss to be overpowered by this God, even though

> I am a daily laughing stock,
> everybody's butt.

> Each time I speak the word, I have to howl
> and proclaim: "Violence and ruin!"
> The word of Yahweh has meant for me
> insult, derision, all day long.
>
> [Jer 20:7–8]

The extent to which this was spiritually distressing is shown by Jeremiah's thought to flee from being a prophet. But like the prophet Jonah, who wanted to flee across the Western Ocean from his commission, was foiled:

> I used to say, "I will not think about him,
> I will not speak in his name anymore."
> Then there seemed to be a fire burning in my heart,
> Imprisoned in my bones.
> The effort to restrain it wearied me,
> I could not bear it
>
> [Jer 20:7–9]

And so he remained a prophet. He gave himself up to his dark destiny, whose end is hidden from us because tradition trickles out. His burden was heavy; but in the moment he wanted to throw it down it became a burden he could not relinquish.

This is the burden of the prophets: the distress of men, for they have to intercede with God for men. Prophets, in turn, become a burden to men, for prophets are never asked to proclaim what men want, and they always run counter to our thoughts. For them, their ultimate burden is their special vocation—their God, indeed. This is the heaviest, yet the sweetest burden of the prophets.

Life is not made easier by the prophets. But is that a reason for wishing to be rid of them?